PK

VAN DER BYL

PK

VAN DER BYL

african statesman

Hannes Wessels

Also by Hannes Wessels:
Strange Tales from Africa

To the civil servants:
that remarkable breed of men and women who seved their country superbly and
selflessly and made Rhodesia one of the best-administered countries in the world.
Their earnest endeavours have been trashed by their successors but for those of
us who lived through those tumultuous times, we will never forget.

Published in 2010 by 30° South Publishers (Pty) Ltd.
3 Ajax Place, 120 Caroline Street, Brixton
Johannesburg 2092, South Africa
www.30degreessouth.co.za
info@30degreessouth.co.za

Front cover image courtesy of William Higham

Design and origination by 30° South Publishers (Pty) Ltd.

Printed and bound by Pinetown Printers, Durban

ISBN 978-1-920143-49-7

CONTENTS

FOREWORD

PK van der Byl first came to my attention prior to the break-up of the Federation during 1962, when the newly formed Rhodesian Front won a surprise electoral victory and came to power under Winston Field. PK was elected to represent Hartley in the Southern Rhodesian parliament.

At the time, Rhodesians had a somewhat jaundiced view of the British, or 'Poms' as we called them. We had been exposed to a surfeit of chinless wonders whose arrogance and superciliousness actually betrayed a lack of confidence in themselves, but filled the average Rhodesian with contempt. Having said that, I served with some wonderful British soldiers in the 22 SAS Regiment in Malaya and they were an entirely different kettle of fish.

My early impression of PK was therefore most unfavourable, because at first sight he appeared to have all the characteristics of a chinless Pom. I remember wondering how Ian Smith, a down-to-earth Rhodesian, had seen fit to accept him into his party.

Thereafter I saw little of him, but watched his progress with interest. I really only got to know him well when he became Minister of Defence and I was commanding the Selous Scouts. General Walls warned me that PK would want to involve himself with the Scouts but I was told that the *status quo* remained unchanged; I was to report to him alone on operational matters pertaining to the Scouts and he would report to the Prime Minister. From the tenor of this conversation I came under the impression that the General and PK did not get along very well.

Details of my subsequent meetings with PK are covered in this narrative, but I was soon highly impressed by him. Unlike many of the more pedestrian types in the military and political hierarchy, PK was focused and absolutely determined to do whatever it took to win the war. He was ready to go to any lengths to achieve this, including getting down to basics and involving himself in combat situations where people were killed and he was personally in the firing line. Vilified in the international press as an unrepentant racist, he was totally committed to the welfare of his black troops. On tactical issues, it must be said, some of his ideas bordered on the bizarre, but for every bad one there were ten good ones. This is undoubtedly why he was resented by some of the deadwood in the hierarchy of the armed forces who were too timid to think outside the box. He was fond of quoting Marshal Saxe who famously said: "It is not the high-ranking officers who win wars. It is the good ones!" But to me the greatest service he provided was the massive morale boost he gave to our servicemen and -women; all of them: the air force, the hard tough men of the Rhodesian Light Infantry, the SAS, the Selous Scouts, the African soldiers of the RAR, the Grey's Scouts and the men and women of the Rhodesia Regiment. Once they had recovered from the shock of his sartorial style, his accent and his disregard for holy cows, they took to him wholeheartedly. PK, unlike many of his colleagues, always saw the bigger picture and his eccentricity, sense of humour, and determination to win at all costs lifted the spirit of the entire country.

In the light of history there is little doubt in my mind that South African Prime Minister John Vorster, in his misguided effort to win favours from African leaders, scuppered Rhodesia's chance of survival, hastened the collapse of white rule in Africa and altered the course of continental history when he forced Ian Smith to dismiss PK van der Byl as Minister of Defence.

PK loved his adopted country and would gladly have given his life for it.

Lieutenant-Colonel Ron Reid-Daly CLM, DMM, MBE

ACKNOWLEDGEMENTS

I am greatly indebted to the van der Byl family for giving me the opportunity to write this book. Also to Justice Hilary Squires for his erudite recollections and the Marquess of Salisbury for sharing his memories and insight into the British political establishment. Thank you to Peter Petter-Bowyer for allowing me to use excerpts from his book, *Winds of Destruction*, and Al Venter for digging into his personal archives; to Lin Mehmel for her hospitality, support and encouragement; Peter Bieber, Captain Malcolm Napier, Archduke Otto von Hapsburg, Costa Pafitis, Richard Passaportis, Monica Germani, Peter Simmonds, Verity van der Riet and William van der Byl for their time in helping me research this narrative; Eddy Norris for his stellar efforts on my behalf in contacting people through his ever-expanding audience in his ORAFs newsletter, and to Lionel Dyck and David Heppenstall for their military memories; to Marge Bassett who did such a fine job of recording PK's political life through notes and records of press reports. Thanks to 'Rusty' Drysdale for allowing me to publish his poem, and to my old friend Nigel 'Sumph' Fleming who watched over me with an eagle eye, never slow to pounce on sloppy prose and intemperate opinion with wit, wisdom and lethal sarcasm.

Hannes Wessels
Darling, June 2010

INTRODUCTION

PK was an aesthete: cultured, confident, eccentric, elegant, and intelligent. Possessed of a deadly sense of humour, people were often unnerved by him, which led to many misjudging him. Since it was difficult to stereotype him, people often jumped to quick and erroneous conclusion. But, as his great friend Archduke Otto von Hapsburg once remarked, this uniqueness of style and countenance took great courage. He was his own man with his own mind and that manifested itself at first glance in every aspect of his personal presentation.

Bearing this in mind, it is not difficult to understand why he despised so many of his harshest critics. It was not what they said that troubled him so deeply, but the fact that they meekly followed a political fashion parade without the individuality of purpose to buck the trend in order to be their own masters. Much of the world labours under the misconception that the white man is a relatively new arrival on the African continent and following on from this believes there is good reason for questioning his right of tenure in lands perceived as belonging to blacks. The van der Byl family, their progenitors having arrived at the Cape over 350 years ago, are living proof of how bogus this view is, and their story is in a sense a vivid and colourful chronicle of the white man in Africa. Their story is instructive in that it belies the widely held belief among the white Africans' multitude of critics that their time on the continent has been characterized by unruly plunder, leading to the accumulation of undeserved wealth. Like so many of their compatriots, generations of van der Byls have confronted adversity in the shape of civil strife, political uncertainty, disease, pestilence and war. It is simply not fair to say that they sought, or received, anything resembling an easy ride to riches.

Out of this constellation of farmers, frontiersmen and fighters came Major Piet van der Byl and then his son, PK, about whom most of this book is about. Son was much like father; they both came off the land but hankered for the thrill of political and military combat for which they were confident they were well equipped. Like his father PK was not in politics because he had to be, but because he enjoyed the cut and thrust of debate and, more importantly, because he believed in a cause—a cause for which he showed he was quite prepared to die. This is why he disliked hypocrites and opportunists and loathed the people who tried to score cheap political points on the back of his country's tragic travails. He well knew that post-UDI Rhodesia was the easiest political bandwagon in the world to ride which is why it attracted the pious attentions of an army of journalists and politicians who needed a safe platform from which to build their careers. For them, attacking white Rhodesians was certain to draw universal applause, leaving only the shrillness of the invective to argue over.

This book tries to capture the mood of the times with particular emphasis on the story of Rhodesia and the eventual destruction of that country. It is within this context that PK, his life, times and thoughts are so illuminating, because he epitomized much of who Rhodesians were and what they stood for. And like his countrymen he was vilified, but in the process of defying the world Rhodesia produced no representative to match PK in articulating his country's case with such style and erudition. Add this to his steely self-confidence, bordering on contempt for those who disagreed with him in his defence of one of the world's most despised countries and one is left with a hugely combustible state of affairs from which, much to the dismay of his enemies, he did not flinch.

Sadly, the modern world is no less fraught with the troubles that flow when people of different racial and ethnic backgrounds enter into a communion of groups with uncommon values and it is this problem that poses a massive threat to the present peace that pervades much of the developed world. PK and the people he served grappled with this same problem in Rhodesia and their proposed remedies were adjudged unacceptable to the international community. But subsequent events now force any person of objective mind to call into question that verdict. Rhodesia will go down as a pinprick in history, but issues of massive contemporary import arose and were confronted within the context of what became known as the 'Rhodesia Problem'. Revisiting this rich and violent patch of history and looking again at the problem through the eyes of PK and his colleagues may be more illuminating than many would like to admit.

In this age of virtual anarchy in Africa, where countless countries have been ravaged and destroyed by avarice and corruption on the most colossal scale, his conduct as a public figure was exemplary and at a level that can scarcely be contemplated in the culture of contemporary African political behaviour. The record shows he was never touched by serious scandal or financial impropriety; that he was cut from the old cloth that believed it was a privilege to serve and he did so selflessly with a generosity of spirit and purpose that seems to be largely lost to the world today.

If PK van der Byl erred, it was in his naïve belief that reason, common sense and morality would surely prevail as the country's critics inevitably concluded that the facts could not sustain the charge that Rhodesia was a humanitarian hellhole and a threat to the peace of the world. Alas, he was wrong. The world he left behind at the end of World War II had radically altered itself and with the collapse of the British Empire came the morphed mindset that insisted white rule was simply not right, no matter how benevolent or competent. This madness was almost too much for him to comprehend and would frustrate him to the end of his days.

The moral of this rather sad story is that politicians seldom really care about other countries and peoples despite their noisy protestations. So much of what is said is meretricious nonsense designed to disguise real motives and confuse an often ignorant electorate. And this is the nub of the Zimbabwean tragedy that continues to this day; virtually none of the international actors, either in Africa or abroad, has ever been sincere about considering the needs and wishes of the true majority. If they had, the outcome would have been very different. The terrible truth is the only people who did sincerely care were the whites who led Rhodesia, and in this endeavour PK was a towering figure. He rests atop a hillock overlooking the family home. He loved history and in return his affection is being rewarded, because history now shows he was right about Rhodesia and the rest of the world was wrong.

Rhodesia: the early days

In 1505, more than 150 years before van Riebeeck landed at the Cape, Antonio Fernandez, a Portuguese *degredado* (convicted criminal) was sent into the east African wilderness in search of gold and local knowledge in return for a pardon. Travelling from Sofala, south of present-day Beira, he walked to the Odzi River and up to the Zambezi, keeping meticulous records along the way.

He survived and returned to Portugal but Gonzalo da Silveira, the Jesuit priest who followed him, came to a miserable end. No sooner had he converted the local royal establishment ruling the then Kingdom of Monomotapa (in what is today northeastern Zimbabwe) to Christianity than Arab Moslems, fearing Christian inroads, caused foment among the new converts. In 1561 the priest was strangled before being thrown to the crocodiles that infested the Musengezi River. He would be the first missionary in the territory to 'save' the African who would later kill him, but certainly not the last.

By this time, the Kingdom of Monomotapa was already in decline but a punitive mission was led by Francisco Barreto, the newly appointed Portuguese governor. Leaving Lisbon with three ships and 1,000 men he arrived in Africa in 1569 having suffered casualties at sea but worse was to come. Men in armour quickly succumbed to the tropical heat and, with the malarial scourge, his ranks were soon ravaged.

Although victories were recorded in engagements with regional tribes, the force was rendered impotent by the conditions and Barreto himself died at Sena on the Zambezi in 1571. From this point on, the Portuguese confined themselves largely to the eastern littoral and left the hinterland to its own devices. The next notable intrusion would come as a result of ructions in the southeast of the continent that triggered the arrival of Mzilikazi.

Born in 1792, son of Matshobana in the Zulu kingdom of Shaka, Mzilikazi rose to command the venerated Khumalo clan. Rising to prominence as a feared warlord, he fell out with Shaka and fled north. Roaming south of the Limpopo for some 20 years, he met and befriended Robert Moffat in the Marico Valley before Boer pressure drove him north into what is now Matabeleland, in 1838. Leading some of his people north to the Zambezi, a surrogate chief known as Nkulumane was named as his replacement in his absence. Incensed, Mzilikazi slaughtered the pretender and his supporters before unleashing his warriors on the local tribes[1] which were plundered and subjugated. He died in 1868 and was succeeded by Lobengula.

Then came the white man.

Cecil John Rhodes was born in Bishop's Stortford in Hertfordshire on 5 July 1853. One of eleven children born to the local vicar, he was educated at the village grammar school before sailing for Africa in 1870 with £2,000 given to him by an aunt. Arriving in Natal, he joined his brother Herbert on a cotton farm before moving to Kimberley in 1871. Proving a shrewd operator he quickly amassed a small fortune before returning to England and Oxford, where he gained a BA. Maintaining his links to South Africa, he was elected to the Cape parliament before graduating and quickly immersed himself in the politics of the day on his return. Determined to further British interests he struck a blow for Empire when he successfully brought Bechuanaland (now Botswana) into the British realm to the dismay of acquisitive Boer 'freebooters'.

In 1887, with the discovery of gold on the Witwatersrand, Rhodes formed Goldfields of South Africa and soon thereafter took control of the Kimberley diamonds, simultaneously becoming the dominant figure in the world diamond trade. But money and power were only incidental to Rhodes's grand design, which was no less than bringing Africa under British control. To this end, Rhodes arrived in London in April 1888, brandishing the Rudd Concession which he had wheedled out of Lobengula through his emissaries. His immediate goal was to convince Prime Minister Salisbury that it was in Britain's interest to give his expansionist plans a royal stamp of approval by granting a charter. But he was frustrated by the timidity

---

[1] These tribes would become known collectively as, alternately, the Shona, the Mashona or the vaShona.

of a British government that was reluctant to share his expansionist zeal. Undaunted, he decided to take matters into his own hands, with his own resources and his own men. A key ally was Lord Nathaniel Rothschild, one of the richest and most influential men in Britain. He liked Rhodes, believed he was a sensible investment and particularly liked his grand plan which would, in the full course of events, bring the coveted goldfields of the Witwatersrand under the British flag. In Rhodes's favour was Salisbury's wish to extend British hegemony as long as his government's political and financial exposure was limited.

Having secured the money and the support of the British government, Rhodes switched his attention to finding the right men. Over lunch at the Kimberley Club in the diamond capital of South Africa, he explained his thoughts to Frank Johnson, the man he asked to lead his occupying force. The two agreed most recruits would be from a military background, but Rhodes wanted more: tough and resolute they should be, but also gentlemen in the classical sense of the time and possessed of the eclectic array of skills required to build a country.[2] It has been suggested that the same qualities he would later mandate for those applying for his scholarships were applied to the selection of the chosen few who would be deployed in the extension of Empire. As a result, top Cape families were invited to contribute their sons, and doctors, lawyers, chemists and farmers filled the ranks of this elite body of men who rode north and colonized the country that came later to bear its founder's name.

In a harbinger of what was to come, on the day the column camped on the Shashi River, the first activity engaged in had nothing to do with conquest … it was a game of rugby.

Then they crossed into the territory that would become Rhodesia and into a dangerous new land. Lives would later be lost in battle, to disease, wild animals and other natural calamities, but the tide of history was swiftly turning and for better or worse, the white man had arrived. On 13 September 1890, some 200 men stood to attention as the Union Jack was

---

[2] A more cynical rationale suggested is that Rhodes wanted well-to-do families involved so there would be a stronger response in the event the men got themselves into trouble.

raised at a place they called Fort Salisbury. The claim had been staked. This unsettled the Portuguese to the east. Their cocky new neighbours were limbering up to block their own expansionist plan being plotted in Lisbon which would have absorbed the vast hinterland between the colonies of Angola and Mozambique, thereby establishing a Lusitanian empire of massive proportion in Africa.

The arrival of Rhodes's pioneers interdicted this. Unsurprisingly, it was not long before the Portuguese problem escalated into fighting, and following several skirmishes on the eastern frontier, a bold young captain by the name of Patrick Forbes decided to take matters into his own hands. With pluck, daring and less than a dozen troopers, he invaded Mozambique and attacked the Portuguese garrison in Vila de Manica. Determined to seize the port of Beira for the Crown, his plan was thwarted by British Prime Minister Salisbury who wasted no time in ordering Forbes to desist and return immediately to British territory. Unbeknown to Forbes, the attack was a breach of a non-aggression pact between Portugal and Britain that had not been violated in several hundred years.

The following year, a boundary convention was signed with the Portuguese and Dr. Leander Starr Jameson became administrator of the territory. Under his authority a telegraph to Salisbury was installed, construction of the rail link to Beira commenced and Dominican nuns opened the first school in Salisbury.

But peace reigned only briefly. A mere three years after the occupation, Matabele chieftains, frustrated by suppressed inaction, decided to return to their old plundering ways and attacked Shona villages in the vicinity of Fort Victoria (now Masvingo). This type of lawlessness was unacceptable to the colonizers and Rhodes's pioneers were ordered into action. The violence was suppressed but at some cost to the new arrivals and in a famous battle on the Shangani River on 4 December 1893, Captain Allan Wilson and all his men perished at the hands of a Matabele impi. Three years later, in March 1896, the Matabele Rebellion broke out, followed by an uprising in Mashonaland some months later.

Ultimately, the native rebellions were suppressed with a mixture of force and diplomacy on the part of Rhodes but the violence had taken its toll on the new arrivals of which over ten per cent, mostly women and children, had been killed. Farms and mines had been badly damaged along with infrastructure; however, tales of heroism boosted morale and the survivors quickly displayed renewed determination to recover and resume nation-building.

With conquest, the white interlopers had put an end to the endemic tribal genocide and quickly insisted upon changing the mindset that killing another human being was a right of might. Frontiersmen in the classic sense, the pioneers were essentially magnanimous in victory and, unlike their counterparts in North America and Australia, refrained from further attacks on the natives who now fell under their authority.

Subjugation to the rule of white law was anathema to the black people but they were forced to live with it on pain of punishment. Ironically, the Zezuru people (one of the several tribes making up the Mashona), who would probably have been wiped out by the Matabele in the course of time, were saved by white intervention. Had this not happened, a Zezuru child by the name of Robert Gabriel Mugabe might never have been born. His journey into the living world was made safe by the white man he would grow to revile and ultimately destroy.

In 1899, a legislative council was established for what was now known as Southern Rhodesia, while the railway reached Salisbury from the coastal port of Beira. But progress did not come without adversity and rinderpest and foot and mouth disease took a heavy toll on livestock, added to which a series of crippling droughts devastated farmers, throwing the nascent agricultural economy into turmoil. In spite of all the obstacles, a spirit of enterprise and endurance prevailed and most of the problems were tackled and eventually overcome. Against this backdrop, a parsimonious British government merely looked on, offering little more than moral support.

With still much to do, Cecil Rhodes died on 26 March 1902 at his cottage in the Cape near Muizenberg. He was buried at his own request in the Matopos Hills outside Bulawayo. Many of his former Matabele adversaries came to pay their respects. That year also saw the Boer War come to a merciful end—not only for the South Africans but also for the Rhodesians whose economic challenges had escalated as a result of the conflict. Financially hamstrung by the fact that the territory was under a charter vested in the British South Africa Company, the settlers' call for greater control of their destiny became more strident. This was tempered by fear of being discarded and absorbed in to the South African Union; an option considered unpalatable by most.

With the 25-year validity of the charter set to expire in October 1914, an election for the Legislative Council took place in March of that year. Most of the candidates called for greater local control but in the final analysis it turned out that the majority had greater confidence in the directors of the Charter Company than they did in the Colonial Office. As subsequent events would prove, this was a prescient decision, however it was very clear the majority supported the idea of self-government, thus the dispute was limited to timing and method.

The 'Spirit of Rhodesia' was summed up by an anonymous writer when the country was divided over whether or not to forsake self-rule and become part of the Union of South Africa:

> We have experienced a Native War, a Native Rebellion, the Boer War, The Great War, the Rinderpest, and East Coast Fever, drought and floods, adversity and prosperity. From these the Spirit of Rhodesia has been compounded; and everyone who has been touched by the magic wand of the spirit of Rhodesia is a 'Rhodesian'. Our people have come from the four corners of the earth, mostly British but no matter what nationality they were; if they were of the fit the country took them unto herself and gave herself unto them and they became Rhodesians. That is what we mean when we say 'Rhodesia for the Rhodesians'.[3]

With the outbreak of World War I attentions shifted to matters more pressing and the life of the Legislative Council was extended to 1920, during which

---

[3] A. P. DiPerna: *A Right to be Proud*. Books of Rhodesia, 1978

period political activity all but ceased. The year saw a contentious election but Responsible Government candidates all but swept the board in the final tally. A watershed had been reached; the Charter Company no longer wished to retain control and the Imperial Government did not want the financial responsibility.

Whatever happened next, the Charter Company had presided over the establishment of a Western outpost in which the rule of law had taken hold and the foundations for future development had been laid. Rail lines connected all the major centres, intertribal warfare had been stopped, health services established, schools built, while mining and agriculture provided the economic muscle.

On 1 October 1923, just over a month before PK van der Byl was born, there was some relief among the settlers in Southern Rhodesia when London conferred 'self government' on Salisbury after the white voters chose home rule over union with South Africa. This signal event was largely thanks to the efforts of Colonial Secretary Winston Churchill, a champion of Empire who had noted the ability of white Rhodesians, and wanted to let them loose on that part of the 'Dark Continent'. Across the globe, he was at that time facing down nascent stirrings of nationalism in India where Mohandas Gandhi, an English-educated barrister, was rallying the populace to the *Swaraj* cause, designed to rid the country of the British Raj. In 1915, Gandhi had arrived back in India from living in South Africa, an angry man. Frank Welsh, in *A History of South Africa*, says, "Racial prejudice, rather than a disinterested struggle for equality, was very much at the bottom of the Indian case. Quite as much as any white, Gandhi and his followers resented the 'mixing of the Kaffirs with the Indians'."

With this problem burgeoning, the refreshing news that reached Churchill's ears was of determined colonials in southern Africa imbued with the same spirit of Empire as he.

He wasted no time in garnering support for their cause, well aware that Rhodesia had rapidly become, to all intents and purposes, independent, that the Europeans (the whites) there were quite capable of mastering their own destiny and that London had only a bit part to play in the colony's affairs, apart from retaining a veto over certain legislation which had never been exercised.

With self-government, the British South Africa Company turned over administrative control of the country to the settler representatives under the Southern Rhodesia Constitution Letters Patent. Of interest, this included a demand by the Imperial Government for payment to it of the sum of £2,000,000 by not later than 1 January the following year. In return, the new government would obtain "all the unalienated lands in Southern Rhodesia other than the Native Reserves ... [and] all the rights and interests of the Crown in the alienated lands in Southern Rhodesia and the quit rents payable by the Company in respect of the lands appropriated for its commercial purposes".

The fact that any consideration at all was payable irked the settlers who well knew the British taxpayer had contributed nothing to the development of the country, but such was the determination of the Rhodesians to be done with London and allowed to get on with the job of nation-building they paid it anyway. British parsimony may yet come back to haunt them. The land the settlers purchased from them in good faith was subsequently confiscated by the government of Robert Mugabe on the grounds that it was 'stolen'. If this be the case, the original sale was fraudulently misrepresented and the British government may be expected to compensate the dispossessed.

Probably the first signal of what was to come was received with some foreboding when the Duke of Devonshire, the new Colonial Secretary (succeeding Winston Churchill) announced the Doctrine of Paramountcy which made it clear that in future, the interests of the Africans would be considered before those of the settlers. This sentiment quickly washed through the white communities and sent representatives scuttling to a series of conferences at the Victoria Falls to thrash out a formula for future development. However, despite the doubts, a feat of nation-building arguably unmatched anywhere was underway, of which Rhodes would have been proud. The people he had selected and facilitated had taken a primitive land by the scruff of the neck and transformed it into an orderly polity with a diverse and dynamic economy capable of generating real wealth, thereby lifting the living standards of all its inhabitants.

As an indicator, population growth among the black people would prove spectacular; from an estimated 300,000 at the point of occupation to six million by the middle of the next century.

A maturing form of white nationalism took place as the first generation was born in the new country; pioneers became folk heroes, sport moulded communities and an incipient colonial brotherhood blossomed, introducing a culture of loyalty, honesty and trust which saw businesses built on a handshake. Unfettered by excessive rules and regulations, it was a 'can do' culture that was perfect for the performers and testing for the talkers.

Between the World Wars the country's economy grew steadily but malaria killed hundreds of settlers and the global depression of the 1930s ended the hopes of many aspiring businessmen. The added challenge of distance to the sea made it costly to transport export goods to the ports.

An innovative and functional solution to the country's communication woes was the introduction of tarred strip roads. Unsightly, they nonetheless worked and distances became less daunting, leading to growth in all economic sectors. During this period agriculture gained a firm foothold, while more and more of the country was electrified. Forbidding tracts of land in the Lowveld were brought under the plough and the irrigation pipe and out came sugar, citrus, cotton and wheat in copious quantities. Intelligence and toil transformed a wilderness into a bountiful producer.

On the political front, the country was so well governed it drew little attention from the Commonwealth Office and Rhodesian representatives participated and contributed usefully in Commonwealth and international fora. It seemed clear then, that of all the British possessions in Africa, the most obvious candidate for independence would be Rhodesia but none of the players had any idea that in years to come the values upon which they premised their conduct would be spurned and scorned by the very political establishment to which they paid homage.

CHAPTER ONE
The family

The Cape is the place of the snoek and the cod
Where the Cloetes speak to the van der Byls
And the van der Byls speak only to God

The van der Byl saga starts right at the beginning with the Myburghs, the maternal progenitors who arrived at the Cape with Jan van Riebeeck in 1652 aboard three ships: *Drommedaris*, *Reijger* and *Goede Hoop*. Their mission: to establish on the barren lands of the Cape Flats a victualling station for the vessels of the Dutch East India Company operating from its headquarters in Amsterdam. Most of the new arrivals were from the lower rungs of Dutch society, as few Hollanders of the time joined the army or navy except out of lack of alternative employment. Holland was the world's greatest trading nation and the Dutch East India Company was possibly the world's first multinational corporation.

The new arrivals battled against conditions and circumstance. The crops produced meagre results and the Khoikhoi, from whom meat was expected to be acquired, had disappeared almost without trace into the mountains. The bands of San (Bushmen) who remained lived lightly off nature's pickings and had little to offer. As a result, the first fleet that arrived needing refreshment, far from being provided, had to provide the providers.

Van Riebeeck hated the Cape and the local inhabitants; "… dull, stupid, lazy, stinking people",[4] he wrote. He yearned to return to the Dutch Indies where his future would be better served but his calls went unheeded.

---

[4] Frank Welsh: *A History of South Africa*. Harper Collins, 1998

Despite low morale and in the face of constant pilfering by the natives, the gardens began to produce and a limited supply of meat was slowly but surely secured.

However, with labour a constant problem and company policy forbidding the use of force against the Khoikhoi—whom van Riebeeck had been instructed to treat with "great gentleness"—a decision was made to import slaves. In 1657, the first shipment arrived from Angola but most of the farming burghers were too poor to afford them. At this point there were 144 people on the station. Just when the wheels of progress seemed to be turning smoothly, bloody violence erupted in 1659 following ructions over cattle theft and a burgher was killed. The first of what would be many conflicts between the white interlopers and the natives of the 'Dark Continent' had begun.

With dissension increasing, over 40 discontented settlers stowed away and returned to Holland with negative reports of van Riebeeck's management of the Cape station. As a result he was fired in 1660 but continued to command until his replacement, Zacharias Wagenaar, arrived in April 1662 and van Riebeeck left the following month. Although out of favour with his principals, he was happy to board ship and sail away but for better or worse the white man had arrived in Africa and was there to stay.

Against this background, Gerrit van der Byl was born in Overschie near Rotterdam in 1640. He married Sophia van Tempel in Holland in 1660 and probably arrived in the Cape in late 1668, bringing with them their only child, a six-year-old son named Pieter. The voyage was not without risks but most pressing was the threat of being becalmed. A passage that lasted over four months due to lack of wind would bring scurvy and inevitably death to at least some of the passengers and crew.

In his diary Governor Simon van der Stel describes the tribulations at sea:

> Add to this the bad outfit of the sailors and especially of
> the soldiers, many of the latter being deserters and afflicted
> of army diseases. They ... become dirty and wet from bad

weather and rain. Having no change they are obliged to turn in with their wet clothes; this causes a close stinking atmosphere to the great injury of general health. One infects the other and many, without asking whether their bodies can bear it, go to sleep in the open air during the night. Then there is the unvaried consumption of salt meat and pork, and especially of grey and white peas which are the daily pot-food, and in length of time become musty in the hold, while the beer likewise becomes sour ...[5]

Described by company officials as a "fine, suitable and well conducted man", Gerrit soon made his mark at the Cape and was appointed a Messenger of the Court in July 1669. Five years later he was made a deacon in the local church and acquired a 30-acre property below Devil's Peak, somewhere near present-day Mowbray which he named Varietas. In 1677, Gerrit became a member of the Burgher Council and two years later, the same year Simon van der Stel took over as commander of the Cape, he was appointed its chairman. For reasons unclear he left the settlement the following year and, along with his friend Henning Hüsing, relocated to Stellenbosch becoming the first commercial farmers in the area. He acquired a 110-acre property on the north bank of the Eerste River which he named Vredenburg[6] (Castle of Peace). The property was located near some lay land owned by Adam Tas, which would become famously known as Libertas.

In 1682, Gerrit, along with Messrs. Hüsing, Grimpe and Elberts, was one of the first four members of the newly constituted Heemraad (Council) and in 1686 he was elected its first elder. As magistrates they were authorized to preside over civil actions to the value of £2 1s. 8d. Their municipal duties included tax collection from farmers levied against the number of sheep and cattle in their possession and collection of death

---

[5] M. Whiting Spilhaus: *The First South Africans.* Juta & Company

[6] The farm was later taken over by Cecil Rhodes as part of his venture into fruit farming.

duties. In 1685, the office of Landdrost (similar to the office of Sheriff in England) was established by the Commissioner.

In 1688, the year that Gerrit's son, Pieter van der Byl, married Anna Bosch in Cape Town, 180 French Huguenots arrived, fleeing religious persecution in their homeland. While their numbers were a welcome boost, van der Stel had no intention of allowing them to interfere with Dutch predominance and most were settled in the area that now comprises Franschhoek and Paarl. While initially marginalized, these people—stout and resourceful by nature—eventually played a pivotal role in Afrikaner development out of all proportion to their numbers. Their womenfolk did much to alleviate the critical shortage of bridal stock that had seen many of the settlers turn to slaves and half-castes for wives.

In 1694, Pieter was made a church deacon in the Stellenbosch congregation and four years later became a local councillor. In 1698, Gerrit van der Byl died and Pieter inherited Vredenburg and Varietas, firmly establishing himself among the ranks of the local landed gentry.

In 1704, his son Gerrit was born and in the same year he acquired another farm to be known later as Klavervlei near today's Riebeek Kasteel. At the same time a strong strain of resistance to abuse of power was about to show itself in the van der Byl genes.

Widespread dissatisfaction with the way Simon van der Stel and a handful of top company officials were amassing land and wealth had started to boil over. When officials saw fit to purloin farmers' wagons for furthering their own personal needs, a demonstration jointly led by Pieter took place in 1706 in front of the Stellenbosch Drostdy. Infuriated by this effrontery, van der Stel had the ringleaders, including Adam Tas, flung into the dungeons at The Castle in Cape Town. Weeks later on 4 April, Pieter, Henning Hüsing, Jacobus van der Eeyden, Ferdinand Appel and Jan van Meerlust were deported to Holland to answer for their actions. They sailed away in one of 15 Dutch East Indiamen amid a barrage of cannon fire, accompanied by nine English ships.

However, as men of learning, on their arrival in Europe, they argued their case well and the Lords Seventeen[7] were persuaded that all was not well with the administration of the Cape. To the surprise of many they announced the recall of van der Stel and the dissident burghers were permitted to return to the Cape. Pieter arrived back on 11 July 1707 and wasted no time in involving himself in a dispute over interest owed him on money he had lent the Colony of Stellenbosch prior to his temporary exile.

The Treaty of Utrecht was signed in 1713. While bolstering Dutch security against French aggression, it was a mixed blessing for Holland which saw a contraction in her economy and her decline as a maritime power as Britain assumed supremacy. Recession impacted on the Cape and company officials showed a reluctance to sponsor further emigration to further develop their far-flung asset. The Cape was in the doldrums and a decision was taken to rely on slave labour in the main for whatever stimulation was required.

Pieter van der Byl, however, continued to prosper and bought another farm from Barend Lubbe near Vredenburg in 1716. Shortly before his death in 1723, he purchased another property near Riebeek Kasteel. He was survived by his second wife, Hester, who lived a further 20 years and continued to be active in the property market. He had fathered ten children, the oldest of which was Gerrit who is in a sense the father of all the South African van der Byls.

Gerrit, along with his brother Lambertus and sisters Rykie and Catharina, was confirmed in the Dutch Reformed Church of Stellenbosch on 28 October 1726. In the same year he bought his first farm—De Leeuwenhoek near Paarl—before inheriting Vredenburg following the death of his mother. By the early 1730s, there were 53 families in the Stellenbosch area who had at least one family member owning over 10,000 vines, with over 70 per cent of the farmers owning slaves. In 1745, Gerrit

---

[7] Effectively the Board of Directors of the Dutch East India Company

married Elizabeth Grove who bore him 12 children, five of whom failed to make it to adulthood. The oldest son to survive was Pieter Gerhard who was born at Vredenburg on 28 June 1753. Like his father and grandfather before him Gerrit went on to become a councillor, elder and deacon and set a martial precedent that would be followed by many van der Byls when he became a captain in the Stellenbosch Cavalry. At the time security was an ongoing concern with sporadic Khoikhoi raids on isolated farms. This mounted force was geared to deal with the threat but tobacco and brandy lured many of the offenders into the socio-economic mix which seemed to put a lid on the problem.

While slavery was a component of company policy, the directors were protective of the Khoikhoi and farmers accused of treating them poorly were severely punished if convicted. But social and economic pressure was intense and as a people the Khoikhoi inevitably lost their identity and morphed into what would become known as the Hottentots, while those of mixed race were referred to as Basters. More enterprising than the Hottentots they acquired some property and wealth and managed to establish a community and culture of their own. This independence of mind later saw this group leave the Cape under the leadership of Adam Kok who led his people on a long trek northward to what became known as Griqualand.

Despite economic setbacks, maritime traffic at the Cape increased and between 1726 and 1750, an average of 75 ships a year stopped at Table Bay.[8] With the help of slave labour the settlement was rapidly transforming into a colony supported by a growing community of subsistence farmers under an administration run by a governor and selected company officials, with security provided by the burghers who had undergone military training. Between 1703 and 1780 the area of occupation grew tenfold to include an area of 286,000 square kilometres.[9]

In 1752, Gerrit bought the farm Joostenberg near Muldersvlei and built on

---

[8] Hermann Giliomee: *The Afrikaners.* Tafelberg, 2003

[9] Ibid

it four years later. He died in 1767 and three years later, following a fire that destroyed her home, Elizabeth bought a dwelling on the Libertas. In 1773, she married Dietrich Bleumer, who had recently arrived from Germany, but the union ended in a bitter divorce four years later and Vredenburg had to be sold on public auction. The highest bidder was Bleumher himself and thus the ancestral home of the van der Byls was lost just one year short of a century after coming into the hands of the family.

At the age of 23, Pieter married Sophia Myburgh in Stellenbosch on 29 September 1776. Sophia would provide Pieter with ten children before dying in 1789, aged thirty-five. Pieter remarried Hester de Wet in Tulbagh in January 1792 and five years later bought the farm known as Welmoed between Spier and Meerlust where his first father-in-law, Philip Myburgh, lived. Like his father, Pieter was a cavalry captain and a member of the College of Heemraden.

With the Cape growing in stature as a trading town, farmers in the rural surrounds prospered and expanded with the number of vines increasing fourfold in the second half of the 18th century. Wheat production also surged. By the turn of the century the pastoral gentry had acquired sufficient wealth to indulge themselves and many of today's Cape country mansions are a product of this period. In 1781, the Cape's richest man, Martin Melck, died.

While the gentry tried to marry within their familial ranks, the shortage of women made this all but impossible and a blurring of class divisions occurred, which saw the commercial pie more evenly spread as the rich elite absorbed women from the middle class.

With Holland in a political bind following the war of the Armed Neutrality which ended in 1784, economic decline followed. The cost of the presence at the Cape was telling on the Dutch East India Company when a British fleet under the command of Sir James Craig arrived in False Bay in June 1795. Fighting followed, with the burghers showing themselves to be far hardier fighters than the Dutch regulars but defiance could not last in the face of British power and the colony was surrendered to the Crown on 16 September of that year.

Three years later, on 4 October 1798, Pieter Voltelyn van der Byl was born at Welmoed in a colony that was now part of another empire but in terms of day-to-day life and administration the changes were minimal. While Craig held sway, Dutch officials continued their work almost unfettered and little changed. In the districts, however, there was the whiff of rebellion as independent-minded burghers resisted submission to British rule and made strenuous demands for their own republic, but early opposition fizzled out. Between 1799 and 1802, Roger Curtis, a young naval lieutenant, visited the Cape and wrote a rather scathing report:

> The Dutch colonists are in general tall and robust in stature and inclined to corpulency. An unvaried regularity prevails throughout their lives and the history of a day is that of the whole period of their existence. They rise early, breakfast at eight, dine at twelve and sup at nine. In the country they are still earlier in the meals. Immediately after they rise they drink coffee; and between meals fortify their stomachs with a 'soapie', a glass of strong spirits. After dinner they smoke a couple of pipes and then retire to enjoy a nap for two or three hours during the heat of the day. The pipe fills up all the intermediate intervals. Their cookery is gross and dishes fat and greasy.
>
> The course of life followed by the ladies, with the exception of the pipe and the soapie is much the same. The *ufrow* or mistress of the family when not employed in household affairs, sits supinely in a large chair in the hall, watching the slaves, or takes the air in sauntering or lounging on the *stoep*. It is not to be wondered that these sedentary habits generally occasion great corpulency; and they account for the magnitude of some of the ladies up the country. The ruling passion of the Dutchman is avarice. Of literature they know nothing, and they are seldom seen with a book.[10]

---

[10] Frank Welsh: *A History of South Africa.* Harper Collins, 1998

In 1802, British parsimony and Horatio Nelson's view that the Cape was of no great strategic value led to a change of heart in London and the Cape was ceded back to Holland in the Treaty of Amiens in March of that year.

The following year Jacob de Mist arrived to take over as Governor-General, determined to abolish slavery. However, economic realities dampened his zeal and the practice continued unabated. In 1806, in the course of war with France, British troops recaptured Cape Town and in 1811 war broke out with the Xhosa tribes in the Eastern Cape following the murder of Landdrost Stockenstrom who had become a pivotal figure on the eastern frontier.

A mixed force of Boers, regulars and the newly formed Cape Regiment was raised, led by new Commissioner, Colonel John Grahame. He found it "detestable work, forced to hunt them like wild beasts", but this did not curb his ruthlessness in ordering that "every man Kaffir ... if possible the Chief should be destroyed".[11] The war would continue for another 50 years. In 1814 the Cape was formally ceded back to Britain for a consideration of £20 million, henceforth becoming a permanent part of the Empire.

Pieter van der Byl inherited the eastern half of Welmoed, the other half going to his brother. He married Johanna van Breda on 7 November 1818. A capable man, he bred horses, helped found the town of Napier and was a member of the Cape Legislative Council. Considered of sufficient importance, he entertained the Prince of Orange and Prince Alfred at Welmoed. He died at Tygerberg on 5 July 1849.

This was a time of social fluidity at the Cape, unlike the rest of southern Africa where racial and class distinctions were more rigidly drawn.

By the 1820s, 'free blacks' formed at least one quarter of the population and 16 per cent of marriages were of a mixed nature. But this was also a time when the Afrikaners started to emerge as a people with a separate identity. No longer did they consider themselves Dutchmen—they had become Afrikaners.[12]

---

[11] Idem

[12] Hermann Giliomee: *The Afrikaners*. Tafelberg, 2003

Johannes Albertus van der Byl was also born at Welmoed on 10 June 1825 and took over Fairfield in 1853, where he later farmed most of his life. The house he moved into was not the original which had burned down and was rebuilt in 1832. As a young man he took some of his inheritance and went to London to study where he met John Brand who would later become president of the Orange Free State. Inheriting large tracts of land he returned to South Africa with sheep from Rambouillet, cattle from the King George Essex stud and thoroughbred horses. He married Hester Anna Myburgh at the age of 25 and was asked to serve in the Legislative Council.

Their son, Pieter Voltelyn, was born at Cloetesdal on 13 September 1851. As a young boy, out riding with his brother Bertie the two were shaken by the sound of guns at sea. Alighting on a horse cart they sped to toward the sound of the guns to discover a ship aground and in considerable distress. With the arrival of their father they built fires to signal a point of relief and assisted the passengers and crew on land. It proved to be a troop ship carrying a Guards Brigade to reinforce the British forces, then engaged in what became known as the Zulu War. Over 1,400 crew and troops were landed in need of food and shelter which was provided by the van der Byls. When Lloyds of London arrived to settle the damages claim, Piet and Bertie, adamant they were only doing what was right and dutiful, refused to be reimbursed. Word of this reached the ear of Queen Victoria who sent an engraved silver cup as a gift of thanks.

At an early age young Pieter was sent to public school in England, returning to South Africa only when he was eighteen. During the voyage he recalled the vessel was becalmed, in the doldrums for over a week. His abiding memory was an empty crate flung overboard that bumped against the side of the ship for the duration. Also aboard was a wistful young adventurer by the name of Freddy Selous who was making his maiden trip to the continent where he would achieve universal fame. The two became firm friends and Selous would visit the family on all his future visits to the Cape.

Meanwhile, a burgeoning sense of Afrikaner national pride came very visibly to the fore in January 1852 when, at the Sand River Convention, the British agreed under some pressure to the independence of the Transvaal. Thus the first of the Boer republics was born, to be followed two years later by the British withdrawal from the area north of the Orange River, ushering in what would become known as the Orange Free State.

In 1873, Johannes van der Byl contracted dysentery while big-game shooting and, on a coastal voyage home with no medical assistance, his condition worsened with the onset of blood poisoning. He died at Elsenberg the same year and was buried in Wynberg.

The Afrikaner desire for self-rule suffered a reverse in early 1877 when the British government, desperate to bring the recalcitrant Boers back under Imperial control, breached the convention and annexed the Transvaal. However, Zululand was the immediate imperial prize as the British fomented war with the Zulus. War indeed broke out as the British invaded Zululand. Almost immediately a British column was comprehensively destroyed at Isandhlwana on 22 January 1879. Revenge followed in August following the dramatic events at Rorke's Drift when General Garnet Wolesely defeated the Zulus at Ulundi and captured their monarch, King Cetswayo.

The following year Paul Kruger boldly reclaimed the sovereignty of the Transvaal. At the same, time a precocious entrepreneur from England by the name of Cecil John Rhodes founded a company called De Beers and the seed for a number of conflicts was sown.

Pieter van der Byl married Adelaide Taylor, a woman of Scottish descent on 28 February 1881. Three years earlier his mother Hester Anna became the owner of Groote Schuur and Pieter was soon a landowner of some significance, farming some 45,000 acres in the Bredasdorp area. He is remembered by his son as a "man of character … trusted by everyone for his word was his bond. Non-Europeans, who had never seen him before, would hand him considerable sums of money to hold for them. No receipt was asked for or given." Adelaide was also a product of a fine English education and schooled in the classics. She would play a leading role in the early education of her children.

The day after their wedding the Boers dramatically defeated the British at the battles of Majuba and Laing's Nek and at the Treaty of Pretoria which followed self-government was handed back to the Boers under British suzerainty. Not to be outplayed by the British, Germany under Bismarck formally colonized what would be known as German South West Africa in 1884. Later the same year, at the Berlin Conference on the future of Africa, the 14 nations represented agreed to a vigorous campaign aimed at the elimination of slavery. Two years later the city of Johannesburg was founded following the discovery of gold on the Witwatersrand and Cecil Rhodes established Consolidated Gold Fields as a means of expanding his already sizable fortune.

CHAPTER TWO
Major Piet

Pieter Voltelyn, who would become known, liked and respected as 'Major Piet', was born in Caledon on 21 February 1889, the same year that Rhodesia, the country that would endear itself to his son became a work in progress.

Four years later his grandmother, Anna van der Byl, then 64, having rented Groote Schuur house and estate to Cecil Rhodes received a letter from him in England asking to buy the house. Rhodes, who had led a peripatetic existence, had fallen in love with the place and had decided that he wanted to spend the rest of his days there. When Mrs. van der Byl responded with a figure of £10,000 Rhodes replied, "Fancy price!" The immediate response was, "Fancy house!" Rhodes, probably realizing he had little negotiating room, promptly concluded the deal.

And so it was, with Cecil Rhodes ensconced as Prime Minister of the Cape Colony, young Piet began the process of growing up. His earliest memories of life at Fairfield revolve around the ablutions:

> At home on the farm, Saturday was also hot-bath night for the children and with coal unknown and firewood scarce we were allowed only two buckets of hot water each. At Fairfield the bath was a large tin affair in the nursery at the end of the house connected to the kitchen by an 80-feet-long passage and we took it in turns to bathe. One advantage of being the last was that, although the water was rather less clean and more soapy, it contained, by that time six buckets of hot water.
>
> Part of the children's duty was to dry up the floors, and, at the end of our ablutions we were in the habit of lifting the large

bath, containing some ten gallons, onto a foot stool to facilitate the process. I was about three at the time and doing my share of the mopping when the bath fell off the foot stool sending a wave of water toward me. In horror, mindful of the biblical story of the Flood I tore down the long passage for the safety of the kitchen! Looking over my shoulder to see what lead I had, I was overtaken by the deluge about halfway. I tripped and the water passed over me.[13]

He recalls an early life where Fairfield house, like most of the homesteads in the area, was open to travellers and passersby who needed shelter. Because horses could do no more than ten hours a day in harness, sundown was invariably a time for strangers to arrive seeking assistance which was freely given. His father insisted upon four rules:

1. Never to eat anything in front of his coloured playmates without sharing.
2. To doff his hat to whomsoever showed him that courtesy, even if it be a native tramp.
3. Never to appear afraid to take some action or offer leadership when in front of the labourers or their children in a time of crisis.
4. To run home as fast as possible in the event he saw a snake.

Aged seven and in his first year of school at Feldhausen in Claremont, young Piet was thrust into a dilemma as to how best to follow his father's commands when summoned by some coloured children to address a crisis that regrettably involved a snake. Despite the nature of the threat he moved decisively, mindful that being the son of the 'master' he had to lead and for the moment felt compelled to ignore the 'run from the snake' rule. He then elected to follow the third rule and attacked the reptile with a stick, killing it to the delight of his audience. It was soon thereafter that he began

---

[13] Piet van der Byl: *From Playgrounds to Battlefields*. Howard Timmins, 1971

learning to shoot and aged nine his father let him loose after francolin and guinea-fowl with gun dogs to shoot over. It was the beginning of a lifelong love affair with the gun and the dog.

While the Western Cape was tranquil, ever bigger discoveries of gold were being made up north on the Witwatersrand and British concerns about this wealth slipping from their grasp had much to do with the ill-starred Jameson Raid which was initiated in Rhodesia in December 1895.

The assault was botched and ended in ignominious defeat for the attackers. The following month the political reverberation resulted in the resignation of Cecil Rhodes as Prime Minister of the Cape and tensions between English- and Afrikaans-speaking South Africans were significantly heightened. President Kruger in the Transvaal, who had grown to like Rhodes, expressed his great disappointment at the deception visited upon him by the Prime Minister of the Cape and the territory lurched closer to conflict.

Aged eight, Piet remembers the trip to Cape Town to visit his grandmother which started at 3.30 in the morning in a two-wheeled cart drawn by four horses with luggage strapped to the back. First stop was at Caledon some five hours away at a speed of little over six miles per hour where horses were rested before boarding a mail cart and moving on to Houwhoek. There the group spent the night before the morning journey to Sir Lowry's Pass and on to the station and the train to Cape Town. While staying with his grandmother at Klein Westerford he was rushed to see Groote Schuur burning down. He recalls the great sadness felt by his grandmother who was so terribly fond of Rhodes who, he recalls, felt an equally strong affection for her.

Aged ten, Piet was in the saddle armed with a Lee Enfield .303 in pursuit of baboons, accompanied by his coloured *agterryer* (lit. after-rider). The young hunter was quickly impressed with the defensive and tactical skills exhibited by these animals and increasingly frustrated by their consistent vigilance which saw him ride home repeatedly empty-handed. Only after a feint and deception, followed by an excellent shot over long range did he record his first kill but valuable lessons had been learned that would stand him in good stead in the tests of time that lay ahead. As fate would have it, not far from his hunting grounds, his country was edging closer to war as Alfred Milner snapped at Paul Kruger's heels.

While championing the cause of the *Uitlanders*, the so-called foreigners, as the *casus belli,* the real reason for Milner's belligerence was lying deep under the Transvaal soil; the gold of what had become known as the Witwatersrand.

Their eyes firmly set on the prize, the 'big men' of the financial world, like Nathaniel Rothschild and Alfred Beit, quietly but firmly insisted that Cape Governor Alfred Milner demand that British troops be dispatched to South Africa. The money-men suggested it was all that would be required to force Kruger and the Boers to capitulate. To increase the pressure, Rothschild would later threaten to dump his British government treasury bills. This may well have caused a run on the British pound and the collapse of the government. Unable to compromise further Kruger rebuffed additional demands and war followed in October 1899.

Boer commandos promptly invaded the Cape and Natal with skill and astonishing aggression. 'Black Week' ensued and in December a large British force under General Sir Redvers Buller was defeated at Colenso in Natal; the Boers had seized the upper hand.

But amidst the storm of war the quiet life in the country continued for the van der Byls. In the same year that fighting broke out, the family played host to now-famous Frederick Selous who came to Fairfield in pursuit of more prosaic prey: a bontebok specimen for the South Kensington Museum in London.

To facilitate this, Piet's father wrote to the Attorney General seeking permission but was turned down as the species was 'Royal Game' and out of season. However, this did not deter Selous who was by this time unused to being regulated, so, on receipt of news that the magistrate in Bredasdorp was absent, an illegal hunting party, including young Piet, set off in search of their quarry.

After studying a herd for some time Selous eventually loosed off a shot which caused consternation and some embarrassment as the resulting casualty turned out to be a female. Piet remembers both Selous and his father being in a "terrible state". However, a further search produced a dead male, indicating that the bullet had passed through one and killed another. Both animals were rapidly removed back to Fairfield but further embarrassment followed when no less a personage than the Archbishop of Cape Town arrived while Selous was in the process of skinning and butchering the poached antelope.

School at Diocesan College Preparatory School began in the same year. With the Boer War raging Piet reveals a martial culture developed at the school which gave rise to military-style games that included severe punishment for 'defaulters' and young Piet— by his own account, "a sickly and unattractive specimen"—did not have a happy time of it.

In 1901, anti–British sentiment was further fuelled by news of Field Marshal Herbert Kitchener's concentration camps which eventually came to house over 120,000 inmates, of whom over 27,000 died. And in the following year the war moved decisively south as the Cape erupted in bitter fighting, with British forces reacting to a determined Boer assault led by General Jan Smuts.

While Smuts moved south, Piet was with his father at the nearby farm Duinefonieff, some five hours by horse and cart from Fairfield. They were going about their business when a man on horseback, dispatched by the magistrate at Bredasdorp, arrived with alarming news. Word was that Smuts had broken the British line, had Table Mountain in sight and was expected to swing through Caledon and Bredasdorp.

This was troubling information. Piet's father and grandfather had been born British subjects and had been in the employ of successive British governments. Their loyalty to the Crown was well known. The authorities warned that Smuts might well visit Fairfield and burn it to the ground to teach them a lesson for collaborating with the enemy.

Father and son immediately prepared the transport and set off at speed. Of great concern to the former was a new consignment of whisky recently received at Fairfield which he was determined would not pass Smuts's lips.

"I can't let that damn fellow get the whisky," he exclaimed as they hurried home but alas the road was blocked by a flooding Slangrivier which brought them to a halt and forced a fast redistribution of luggage and precious shotguns, two of which were then slung around young Piet's shoulders.

Braced for a dunking, with whips cracking the two forged forth, pinning all their hopes on the fortitude and muscle power of the steeds which performed splendidly. However, midway across water coursed over the seats, forcing the two to their feet, but despite the setback motion was not lost and it was with relief they made land on the far side.

After giving the horses a brief rest the journey was rejoined. Fairfield was reached on a dark and damp night but all was quiet and so it remained. Only later did the family discover the rains had also inconvenienced Smuts who had been forced to abort his plans and divert to Oudtshoorn, where he linked up with his forces and continued the fight from there.

In May 1902, with the spectre of protracted guerrilla war looming ever larger as the hard-line Generals de Wet and de la Rey continued to urge resistance, the Treaty of Vereeniging was finally signed, bringing the conflict to a merciful end.

While peace returned, Piet was not thriving. Having missed school frequently due to illness, he did not excel academically or in sports and thus passed most of his schooldays unhappily. Spurned by most of the pupils, he was offered little succour by the masters.

A rare high for him during this period was a conversation he overheard between two masters. The one ventured that van der Byl is "a feeble young wet", to which the other replied: "Yes, quite. But you must admit he will never lie to you."

This incident made a mark on the young man and left him with a lifelong predilection to try and find something good to say about everyone no matter how desultory their performance.

Developing glandular fever aged 15 he was sent home from school. "I was backward and stupid and at the bottom of my class," he writes in wonderfully self-deprecating style, "possibly the reason I became a politician and ended up a Minister."[14]

Anxious to make a fresh start in a different area of academia, young Piet was pleased at the news that his father had entered him for Pembroke College, Cambridge. However, prior to this he had to be prepared by a private tutor in the village of Ortonwaterville near Peterborough. Aged 18, Piet found digs in Trumpington Street and began college. Asked what sport he would like to participate in and, knowing he had an unimpressive record in this department, he sought something different and plumbed for rowing, despite Pembroke being a poor performer in this field of athletic endeavour. Determined to make his mark he took the challenge seriously, forsook many of the more pleasurable pursuits available to students, practised hard, excelled and became the first Pembroke man in 29 years to win a Blue at Cambridge for the sport.

Piet wrote fondly of his six years in England:

> Britain was the most wonderful empire in existence … The people as a whole lived and behaved graciously and with modesty in an unostentatious way … Flamboyance or talk about themselves, relations or possessions was just not done. Everything was played to unwritten rules or conventions and if you broke them you were 'out'. Simplicity, tolerance and good manners to all were the yardstick of behaviour. Along with the privileges, they were prepared to carry the full responsibilities that went with them, and also to give leadership.
>
> The working class, particularly in the countryside had the same type of quiet dignity and self respect. If they touched their cap to the Lord of the Manor it was not from servility but from civility.

---

[14] Piet van der Byl: *From Playgrounds to Battlefields*. Howard Timmins, 1971

Arriving back at Fairfield with a Master's degree in agriculture soon after the Cape Colony, Natal, Orange Free State and the Transvaal united to form the Union of South Africa, Piet was put to work fencing the property with a gang of coloured labourers.

Life on the range was hard physical toil which required him to sleep out in the veld for several weeks at a time. Occasional relief came with his father's visits bearing news and food but his life was soon destined to change when, in 1911, a letter arrived from General Methuen, officer commanding the British garrison in South Africa. The general, needing a young man with local knowledge, invited Piet to join his staff on manoeuvres in the Caledon district the next day.[15] He impressed immediately and it was not long before he was summoned, along with his father, to the office of General Smuts who was then Minister of Defence in the government led by Louis Botha.

Invited by the general to join the army on a permanent basis, he reported for duty at the Staff College, Bloemfontein some months later. Completing the course six months later, he was appointed staff captain in the Eastern Cape, headquartered in Port Elizabeth, before a transfer to Oudtshoorn. When a miners' strike on the Witwatersrand took the government by surprise, Smuts reacted aggressively while busying himself with reorganizing the Defence Department. Piet, now based in Pretoria, was made a junior general staff officer.

While Piet was moving steadily up the ranks, on 28 June 1914, Gavrilo Princip gunned down Archduke Franz Ferdinand in Sarajevo, an event that shook the world. The next month Piet found himself on manoeuvres with the 10th Hussars, The Royals and a brigade of artillery. Ironically, Kaiser Wilhelm II was the Colonel in Chief of the Royals and despite war looming, the regiment held a special parade in his honour. Barely weeks later Britain declared war on Germany and shortly thereafter General

---

[15] This letter was only received timeously because Piet's father decided to wait for the mail before the two left for Cape Town. Letter in hand Piet decided to accept Methuen's offer and this twist of fate shaped the rest of Piet's life. As a result of this he met Methuen and this is how he became known to Smuts.

Botha, his country bitterly divided over the issue, took South Africa into hostilities as an ally of the British. This did not sit well with a sizable constituency and in October an Afrikaner force under Boer Generals de Wet, Kemp, Beyers and Maritz went into a state of armed rebellion against the government of Louis Botha. For Piet van der Byl and his ilk, serving officers loyal to the government of the day, this was a sad and difficult period as the rebel leaders were liked and respected by the people they were now in conflict with.

Ultimately, Botha and his troops stood firm and the uprising was quashed. But not wishing to compound the damage done to national morale, the vanquished were in the main shown lenience by the authorities; a notable exception was made of Captain 'Jopie' Fourie. Because he had not resigned his commission before changing sides, he was court-martialled, convicted of treason and sentenced to death by firing squad. An appeal for clemency was rebuffed and the death warrant duly signed by General Smuts. Fourie was an associate of Piet's who liked and respected him, and was deeply troubled by Smuts' decision in this instance.

With civil hostilities over, General Botha turned his attention to defeating the Germans in German South West Africa and Piet prepared to face a foreign foe. On 20 December 1914, Piet, as part of Botha's Northern Force under the command of General Skinner, sailed from Cape Town and arrived outside Walvis Bay four days later. Fearing mines and expecting determined resistance, they were surprised to execute the landings without a shot being fired and the town was easily occupied. Days later Swakopmund was captured and skirmishes followed but resistance was light. However, despite South African successes it was not until the end of April the following year that Botha's men really showed their mettle and by the first part of May the capital, Windhoek, had been taken, along with much of the colony.

Headquartered at Karibib, Piet, along with his fellow staff officers, busied himself with preparation for the northern advance on the German positions. At this time, news arrived of the sinking of the passenger liner

Lusitania, which outraged the Allies and propelled America into the war. Emotions were simultaneously inflamed in South Africa where German-owned businesses were looted and burned.

Looking for a way to end the war in South West Africa, an armistice was declared and arrangements were made for the German Army Commander Franke and Governor Seitz to meet Botha at Giftkuppe, the midway point between Karibib and the German HQ at Omararu. Piet van der Byl was dispatched on a motorbike to liaise with the Germans on the final details of the meeting. In the course of this journey he narrowly missed a nasty encounter with a German patrol. Although flying a white flag, it was in tatters, having been lacerated by thorns so the Germans were not immediately aware he travelled under a flag of truce. He was apprehended but explained the problem. Eventually convinced of his bona fides, he was allowed on his way.

The meeting that followed was characterized by bluster and threats from the Germans who wanted a permanent ceasefire while the outcome of the war would be determined in Europe. Botha would have none of it, so hostilities recommenced.

Six weeks after the failed peace talks, Botha continued his advance in bold and determined style. "The pace was so hectic," recalls Piet, "that I have but a hazy recollection of the events."

Heading for Otavifontein but wanting to deny the Germans an opportunity to know his force levels, Botha preferred to move at night; he was too fast for the Germans. Ever the brilliant tactician he invariably avoided direct confrontation, moving fast enough to encircle and trap his foe and cause their defeat. Thus it was Piet entered Omararu for the second time, but on this occasion without a white flag.

However, Botha was in a hurry and in no mood for celebration. Early the next day he ordered his men back into the field on course for Kalkfeld and a large German stronghold which was again outflanked by Botha's commandos moving swiftly at night into positions around the German cantonment. With Kalkfeld neutralized, Botha carried on at a furious pace; so much so that at various points during the advance Piet found himself asleep in the saddle but no time was allowed for dallying. The Germans were staggered when the major objective at Otavifontein was reached nine days later. With Manie Botha leading 1,200 men in the vanguard, the former Boer commander, in what Piet describes as "a masterpiece of courage and decision", captured the vital water reservoir, which unnerved the enemy and threw the Germans into retreat. While General Botha pondered his next objective—the heavily defended German garrison at Khorab—a request was received from the German High Command requesting an armistice but again the talks failed and fighting resumed. Botha's well-organized advance continued and, after two more attempts at a permanent ceasefire had failed, Botha sent an ultimatum warning both Franke and Seitz of the direst consequences if they did not capitulate.

Around midnight Piet was woken in his billet near Otavi to receive word that a German officer was approaching aboard a railcar. Dressing quickly he was immediately dispatched by General Collyer to meet the emissary. Arriving at the siding, the two saluted and Piet raced back to his lines with a sealed envelope, which he handed to Collyer. It contained a letter from the German governor offering to surrender. The war for German South West Africa was over.

Botha's campaign was a military masterstroke. Outgunned and outnumbered, leading an army of mostly raw conscripts, the general had taken less than six months to overwhelm the enemy and acquire possession of a territory half as large again as the then German Empire. Writing in 1971, Piet remarks ruefully: "Let the black statesmen at the United Nations remember this when they glibly talk of wiping us off the face of the earth."

He goes on to write of Botha: "He was blessed with Solomon's gift; an understanding heart and an intensely sympathetic and understanding man. His personal charm, which so quickly won men's hearts, derived its main strength from the kindly attitude which he adopted to those who served him."

But for Piet, while one campaign had been won, there was a new German challenge to be overcome across the continent. Unfortunately for him, the conditions would be harsher and the foe far wilier. Preparing for the campaign, he was sent to Rust en Vrede[16] in St. James to collect documents, codes and ciphers from General Smith-Dorrien. Then he travelled to Pretoria to discover he would be staff captain to General Smuts; that his next theatre of war would be German East Africa and leading the enemy would be the redoubtable General von Lettow-Vorbeck. In a war that both sides were convinced would be short, a titanic struggle awaited.

Arriving in Mombasa on 19 February 1916, Piet and fellow staff officers travelled to Nairobi before the journey south toward German-held Moshi, in the foothills of magnificent Mount Kilimanjaro in Tanganyika.

It would not be long before Piet saw his first action at the two hills known as Latema and Reata near Salaita, a vital strategic location from where South African troops had earlier been forced to retire. On 11 March 1916, two South African infantry battalions attacked with bayonets fixed and hard fighting at close quarters continued through the night.

Dawn broke to see opposing forces in disarray in thick bush, leaving commanders on both sides at a loss as to who held the upper hand. Only when the day brightened was a small contingent of Rhodesians, led by a Lieutenant-Colonel Freeth, discovered atop one of the features. Piet was promptly rushed into action, gathering troops to reinforce Freeth's precarious position and the Allied contingent managed to hold on to their hard-fought gains. With Latema and Reata in hand, Smuts took Salaita and moved his army closer to Moshi but under very difficult circumstances.

Adding to Allied woes, bees became a constant scourge, causing men and horses to succumb to stings while Germans and their loyal askari harassed them as the clouds blackened, signalling the imminent arrival of rain. Struggling to maintain momentum the downpours came early and were intense, bringing Piet and his soldiers to a sodden halt.

With movement curtailed it was not long before the men's rations were

---

[16] A palatial, beachfront home that was being built by Sir Herbert Baker for Cecil Rhodes. Struggling to breathe Rhodes had wanted to spend more time by the sea when he died.

cut and morale dropped. At this point Denys Reitz[17] who had served with Smuts in the Boer War, joined his staff and a close friendship between Piet and Denys began.

It was also in the course of these traumatic events that another legendary figure, in the form of Hannes 'Jungle Man' Pretorius, became known to Piet. Having moved north and settled in German East Africa after the Boer War, Pretorius had run afoul of the authorities and bore a grudge. Now with war raging and having a unique knowledge of the lie of the land, he posed a threat to the Germans. Evading arrest he fled to Mozambique before finding his way to South Africa, where he offered to assist Smuts.

Returning to Tanganyika he moved behind German lines with his askari, causing mayhem; he was a pivotal figure in the sinking of the *Konigsberg* which had harried the Royal Navy from its lair in the Rufiji delta. He let Piet know that in his numerous encounters with the enemy he took all possible measures to avoid killing black German askari but did all he could to kill white Germans.

One of the British staff officers serving with Smuts from his HQ at Moshi, and who became known to Piet, was Richard Meinertzhagen who would also write his way into East African warlore. Brilliant, witty and ruthless he impressed and Smuts and became his premier intelligence officer.

While liking and respecting the South African commander, his view of the man was measured: "He is a bad tactician and strategist and an indifferent general but in many ways a remarkable soldier," Meinertzhagen wrote.[18]

In the field, of growing concern to Smuts was the condition of his troops and he was determined to get into the mix to see for himself. To do this he travelled to Kondoa Irangie with Piet, who remembers:

---

[17] Reitz would later write *Commando*, a classic of the Boer War and go on to serve as South African High Commissioner in London.

[18] Piet van der Byl: *From Playgrounds to Battlefields*. Howard Timmins, 1971

I was shocked at the appearance of van Deventer's[19] men. Some friends of mine … I did not even recognize. All had that dirty grey look caused by malaria, dysentery and sheer malnutrition. Many were almost in rags. Their boots were worn out and they seldom wore dry clothes. As to the horses and mules, large numbers were unshod and disease was killing them fast. Other mules were lost owing to a stampede when attacked by lions.

In May, with the ground finally hardening, Smuts and his staff moved south out of Moshi, battling through jungle perfect for ambushes and crossed the Pangani River. But to add to the general's woes, word filtered through that a German freighter had broken the British blockade and offloaded a wide array of supplies. Smuts's hope that von Lettow's campaign was about to run out of steam was simultaneously dashed.

Needing to know how well the new weapons and ammunition were distributed, Piet was sent to garner information under a flag of truce. Ostensibly wishing to talk to the German commander about ensuring an uninterrupted quinine supply for Allied PoWs, Piet found himself face to face with von Brandis, the Chief of Staff. Softening the mood with a letter from Smuts and gifts of whisky and tobacco, the two belligerents chatted amiably. Listening carefully Piet was left in no doubt that the Germans were thoroughly irritated by the continuing problems caused them by his friend 'Jungle Man' Pretorius and von Brandis told him the reward for his head had been increased.

Finally spying a serial number and date on a rifle held by an attendant askari, Piet made a mental note. Bidding farewell, he made it back to his camp with the rifle details. The information passed, the experts concluded that the resupply had indeed reached the enemy in the north. There was now no doubt in anyone's minds that the war was far from over. The terrain that had so suited the South Africans in South West Africa was not available to them in the east and the lack of mobility, along with disease and

---

[19] General van Deventer, Smuts's divisional commander.

logistical challenges, was wearing Smuts and his soldiers down. Toward the end of 1916, Piet, along with General Smuts, reached Morogoro on the main railway line connecting Dar es Salaam to Kigoma on Lake Tanganyika and here they set up an advanced headquarters. Early in the New Year, Frederick Courtenay Selous visited and they were able to catch up on all that happened since his visit to Fairfield. He left after lunch and two days later, having been hit by machine-gun fire while in command of a group of scouts prowling the enemy lines, he died.

Soon after this incident Piet was posted to Dar es Salaam as General Staff Representative. He was deeply upset by the condition of the wounded who appeared to be getting very little quality medical care under the supervision of unsympathetic British officers. Lacking the rank to rattle too many cages, he worked in concert with the Senior Medical Officer to improve the lot of the infirm. At the end of January he was joined by Smuts and shipped to Lourenço Marques en route to Pretoria. In his wake German East Africa was still not a place of conquest; von Lettow was unbeaten and unbowed. Pleased to be back in the Cape, Piet was spending time with his parents at Fairfield when news arrived of significant setbacks suffered by the British on the Western Front. Refused permission to offer his services overseas, Piet offered to pay his own way but still the authorities demurred. Threatening to resign his South African commission and travel abroad as a private citizen if he was not allowed back into the fray, he was eventually granted his request.

Braving the submarine menace, Piet sailed from Cape Town aboard the *Kenilworth Castle*, escorted by the cruiser HMS *Kent* and made harbour in Sierra Leone five days later. However, much to his dismay, a collision with a destroyer which accidentally detonated some depth charges it was carrying, saw the liner evacuated and Piet arrived in England with a pair of pyjamas, a forage cap, a pair of slippers and a one-pound note.

Setting off from the docks for the shops to re-equip himself, he was blocked by a major in the Military Police wearing Brigade of Guards insignia who wanted him to explain why he was wearing military headdress with pyjamas. He found Piet in an angry mood: "Here I have come 6,000 miles to fight for your blasted country," he barked, "in a ship wrecked by your damn navy and the moment I put my head out of doors I am stopped by a trench-dodger, who as a member of one of the finest regiments in the world, should be in France, not Plymouth!"[20]

Finally, refreshed and properly dressed, Piet reported to General Smuts at the Savoy in London and took up staff duties. Here he was pleased to be told that the general had secured him a commission as a second lieutenant in the Brigade of Guards but was subsequently desperately disappointed on hearing he had failed the medical examination and would not be accepted. Struggling for a slot, Piet was pleased to be accepted by the Royal Air Force and ordered to report to the flying school at Upavon. Here he was happy to find the commanding officer was a Rhodesian by the name of 'Zulu' Lloyd who had served under Piet as a private soldier in South West Africa.

Although missing an active role Piet recalls his association with the flyers with affection:

> ... a very happy period, free of all responsibility, among a magnificent crowd of gallant youngsters. The fighter pilot in those days was to the RAF what the Guardsman was to the infantry ... Independent-minded, casual in dress, often untidy in appearance he was deliberately allergic to the discipline of the barrack square type. He had to be a lone hunter, equipped by nature with the cold courage of those who go after big game on their two flat feet and alone. The slightest error of judgement or loss of nerve ... and nothing could save him. If his luck was out the end was lonely.[21]

Piet was still at Upavon when news of the Armistice came through early in the morning of 11 November 1918. But back in German East Africa, Piet's old adversary, von Lettow-Vorbeck, refused to believe Germany had lost, declined to surrender and made ready to move his troops to Portuguese

---

[20] Ibid

[21] Ibid

East Africa to continue the fight. However, finally convinced all was lost for the Fatherland he signed surrender terms on 25 November at Abercorn in Northern Rhodesia.

By the end of the war roughly 3,000 German soldiers leading their askari had propelled a war that demanded the deployment of over 150,000 Allied troops along with over a million support personnel, and cost the Allied exchequers as much as, if not more than, the Boer War. The death toll among African soldiers from Kenya exceeded 45,000 and among British imperial units the toll was over 100,000, equalling the number of British soldiers killed on the Somme. The true figure may even have been double that.

One Lieutenant Lewis, having experienced the slaughter of every single man in his half-battalion on the Western Front, wrote an illuminating letter to his mother from East Africa. "I would rather be in France than here," it read.[22] One of the great guerrilla campaigns in history had finally ended.

Shortly after the end of hostilities Piet was commanded to Buckingham Palace to receive the Military Cross from the King as recognition of his services in the East African campaign. Posted to an RAF squadron in France he struggled with his health as a recurrent fever, probably contracted in East Africa, sent his temperature soaring to alarming heights, but thanks to the ministrations of a dedicated Irish doctor he recovered and was ordered to report to St. André-aux-Bois as adjutant to one of the RAF wings. This was an enjoyable time but by this stage Piet was anxious to return to South Africa and after a brief sojourn in Cologne he successfully applied to be demobilized and returned to London.

Always with an eye for the bespoke, he spent some time in Bond Street and Saville Row recharging his wardrobe, before discovering his return home would be delayed some months while a medical board assessed his health in order to determine his war pension. During this time Piet was invited to tea at Stanley Baldwin's (later to become British Prime Minister) when a "very beautiful young woman" arrived. That night, while dining

---

[22] Edward Paice: *Tip and Run*. Phoenix, 2007

at St. James, Piet was introduced to her. Her name was Joy Astley-Jones and Piet was struck by her; however, too impatient to dally any longer in England he renounced any claims with regard to his medical condition, paid a nostalgic visit to Cambridge and raced at Ascot before finally securing a berth on a crowded ship home.

It was on board ship that Piet van der Byl last met General Botha when he visited him in his cabin. His parting words displayed an astonishing prescience the rest of the world would pay a catastrophic price for ignoring.

"General Smuts and I are very worried about the peace negotiations," said Botha, referring to the deliberations at Versailles. "Britain is fair and reasonable but the French want to be harsh on Germany. I fear, if they get their way, it will lead to serious troubles in the next 20 years or so, unless we can get President Wilson to see our point of view." As it turned out, President Wilson did not see their view, took a hard line on Germany and the course was set for an even greater tragedy.

Piet arrived back in South Africa early in 1919 and pondered a future as a farmer, a prospect which he found agreeable. Meanwhile, in the grand confines of the Palace of Versailles, the Paris Peace Conference was under way and an exacting price was being paid by the vanquished. German South West Africa, where Piet had begun his war, was assigned to South Africa under a League of Nations mandate, sowing the seeds for another level of conflict in years to come. His second theatre, German East Africa, was seized and became a British colony.

Enjoying the peace, it was a surprised Piet who then chanced upon none other than Field Marshal Douglas Haig at the Kenilworth races, fresh from his command on the Western Front. The two only exchanged pleasantries but serendipity struck the following day on Muizenberg Beach when they again chanced upon one another.

This meeting led to a longer conversation. Here, Haig explained that he and his wife were guests of Sir Abe Bailey at Rust en Vrede and invited Piet and his father to call on them. The offer was accepted and during the course of the visit Haig announced he needed an aide-de-camp to accompany him on his three-month tour of South Africa. He offered the post to Piet who happily accepted and so a new and important friendship was born.

Late in 1921, Piet heard of the break-up of the Astley-Jones marriage and was spurred into action. He wasted no time in telling his parents he was taking himself off to London in the New Year and left for England. After a lunch there he took Joy for a stroll. Passing a confectionary shop he asked, rather presumptuously, if a certain cake in the window would suffice at a wedding. She said it would and Piet's proposal of marriage was accepted. The union was formalized at Marylebone Church on 21 January. Soon thereafter the couple returned to South Africa and Fairfield to live the farming life but it was not long before Jan Smuts, then Prime Minister, and Piet were back in touch.

This led to a meeting in February 1922, when Piet, Joy and the general lunched at the Civil Service Club. That afternoon, clearly perplexed, the general walked alone to the train station before boarding a special rail car bound for Johannesburg.

There industrial unrest, partly inspired by communist agitators had spilled into the streets. The old war horse was in no mood for compromise. Artillery was ordered into action on the streets, aircraft bombed the industrial suburb of Fordsburg and police were ordered to shoot at will. Two days later the insurrection was quelled but critics protested the heavy-handedness of the reaction.

At this time, Sir William Hoy, general manager of South African Railways, was in the process of talking Smuts into committing to the electrification of the rail system. Smuts, possessed of an acumen that easily understood issues of this nature, was quickly convinced that this was a priority and immediately mentioned seeking the services of Piet's cousin Hendrik.

The son of Pieter Gerhard van der Byl, Hendrik was born in Pretoria in 1887 and educated at Franschhoek and Victoria College, Stellenbosch. Regarded as one of the most brilliant physicists the college had ever produced, he graduated aged 21, and then left for Germany to continue his studies where his brilliance landed him a research post in the United States with American Telephone and Telegraph. There fame was soon earned with his treatise on 'The Thermionic Vacuum Tube' which led to the construction of the valve that made long-range telephony practical and changed the world.

His impact back in South Africa was huge and it was not long before his colleagues were looking on in wide-eyed disbelief as he spelled out his plans. Insisting that South Africa's future lay in cheap power and steel, he exhorted his flummoxed compatriots to "Think big … plan for the future and think in millions."

When word of van der Byl's vision reached him, an alarmed General Smuts sent for him to seek clarification on the amounts of money he was talking of raising. Hendrik was forthright. "General," he explained, "for every £10,000,000 you spend now you will save £100,000,000 for South Africa in 30 years' time."

Smuts, to his great credit, understood and agreed. With that he took his country by the hand and ushered it into the industrial age. Eskom was the first of his dreams to become a reality, Iscor the second.

CHAPTER THREE
PK is born

PK was born into a privileged world in Cape Town on 11 November 1923, a fateful precursory date for both Rhodesia and its mortal enemy the Soviet Union.[23] Interestingly, one of the people who came to pay their respects to mother and father and see the baby was the last slave born on Fairfield. A reminder of a painful past, he had had a good life in the employ of the family and bore no grudges.

PK's birth was not unusual. Up to that time over 1,500 white children had been born on the estate. His infancy was a world of nannies, governesses and doting servants in a rambling home situated on one of the largest tracts of privately owned land in the Cape. This was Africa's version of the landed gentry.

"Growing up on Fairfield was quite a lonely affair," recalled PK's younger brother William. "It was very remote. We did not mix much with the other [mainly Afrikaner] families in the area. I'm still not exactly sure why, but we didn't, so PK and I really had to amuse ourselves. We were encouraged to play outdoors as much as possible—once I remember clearly being chucked out by our German governess and made to play in the middle of a howling gale."

While wanting for nothing the boys were drilled in horsemanship and hunting by father 'Major Piet' who later recalled in his book *Top Hat to Veldskoen*:

> When he [PK] was a very small boy I used to take him for hours on the pommel of my horse sitting on a cushion. As

---

23 1923 was the year the USSR came into being.

we returned up the last 200 yards of the lawn I would let old 'Greywing' gallop full out and PK at the top of his voice would sing 'gallopy, gallopy, gallopy here comes the Galloping Major … hey, hey here comes the Galloping Major'.

Later when PK was riding his horse beside me, the brute bolted. I drew back hoping he would run himself out and the rider gain control. But when a barbed wire fence came into view, with the horse still going full out, I realized action was necessary to avert a bad smash. So I galloped up beside him and taking the boy by the arm, told him to get his feet out of the stirrups and pulled him off his saddle, meaning to drop him gently on the ground. Bending down I nearly had him landed when my horse, seeing this strange thing at his side, shied badly and I fell off. There we sat on our bottoms while the horses ran home, breathing alarm and despondence as to our fate, till we arrived back on foot.[24]

In the early days of PK's childhood his grandfather dispensed with £800 of the family's money in a real estate venture trying to buy 50 per cent of the seaside resort, Hermanus. Seeing an investment bonanza, he sent his manager with cash but forgot to follow up with the man. Weeks later, he learned the manager had acted alone and spent the money elsewhere. A fortune set to be made had vanished.

While Major Piet always had one eye on the political arena, Fairfield under his guidance was progressive. It became the first farm in the area to convert, amidst great fanfare, to tractor power in the 1920s. By the time PK's grandfather died in 1925, Major Piet was earning £700 a year and while life seemed set fair he narrowly escaped death himself. A viral infection acquired during the East Africa campaign recurred during a boat cruise to Madeira. Fighting a raging temperature, weeping sores and a face so swollen he could not see, he slipped into near-death delirium.

---

[24] Pieter van der Byl: *Top Hat to Veldskoen*. Howard Timmins, 1973

Ominously, the only antiseptic lotion available on board was that used for cleaning butcher blocks. He says he fought hard to survive because

> I was my father's sole executor and heirs had to be paid out, assets had yet to be realized and I was then the sole manager on the farm. I made up my mind I must live. I sent for the doctor and told him I alone could cheat death and asked him to leave me alone. I had a vague idea of how my body was fighting the blood poisoning ... and it all depended on which side could muster the most reinforcements. I remembered an axiom that Clausewitz [the German military tactician] had taught; if your enemy starts to waver or break, discard caution and use all your reserves. I imagined my leucocyte army having got the enemy on the run; tearing into them. I came around some time later. My temperature had dropped and I felt the crisis was past. Though I did not have another attack I was still desperately ill with my eyes still swollen shut and the stench of pus running down my face nearly making me sick.

The following year, during a walk on the farm PK and his father were attacked by an irate high-stepping cock ostrich. Armed only with a metal-tipped walking stick Piet fought the bird off, inflicting a neck wound as it prepared to stomach-rake him. It staggered back and Piet grabbed it by the neck, forcing it to the ground. While trying to strangle the bird it staggered to its feet and fled.

A feature of life at Fairfield was Joy's garden about which she was passionate. Wanting only the best flora, many of the plants were imported from Kew gardens. Strangely she banned all things orange and allowed red only if it was a rose.

She frequently said, "There should always be an element of intrigue in a garden. Separate intimate areas with hedges, high shrubs or banks of tall flowers. When you round a corner or through an arch it should bring an element of surprise and pleasure. Always have a bench or two so you can sit and enjoy it all." Interestingly Joy's other passion was what she termed "dirt-shopping". PK's colleague, Lin Mehmel, remembers:

> It translated into antique shops at the lower end of the market where "these shopkeepers don't always recognize what is good and what isn't". She had a whole ritual of not showing too much interest then she would pounce. She never had to bargain; she had a repertoire of expressions and invariably left with a bargain price. Joy got rid of most of the Cape furniture at Fairfield preferring English pieces. She turned it into a little British enclave.

PK first met British royalty at an early age when Edward, Prince of Wales (later King Edward VIII) decided to abandon the royal train at Worcester and motor to Fairfield by car with his detective and chauffeur. Although Piet knew the Prince was coming, he was obliged to keep the details secret until the last moment. When finally he broke the news to the domestic staff there was pandemonium.

Two-year-old PK greeted the future king resplendent in white smock and hat, whereupon a royal red rose was pinned to his chest. The van der Byls kept close links with the royal family through their friendship with Princess Alice, whose husband later became Governor-General of South Africa.

On 12 September 1928 Major Piet was elected to parliament on a South African Party ticket. He would remain in the assembly for 37 years. Soon thereafter the Great Depression struck and PK went to Western Province Junior School after a short spell at a nearby Anglican school.

By the early 1930s world recession had hit South Africa hard; businesses were folding, unemployment was high and agriculture and mining had failed. In neighbouring Rhodesia identical problems occurred when the tobacco and mineral markets collapsed. There, high unemployment forced many middle-class whites to join work camps and road gangs at a few shillings a day. Thanks to them over 600 miles of strip roads were laid which played a huge role in opening up the new country. It is of interest to note that at this time, Salisbury's Manica Road was the only tarred street and a few others had pavements. Africans, recently from the bush, loitered in loincloths carrying spears and clubs. Their women did a brisk trade in live chickens borne in hocks on their heads while native policemen encouraged adult females to cover their breasts. To African females, only recently exposed to Western mores, this was a mystifying request. It was also at this time, 1932, that the Nazis were establishing themselves in Germany and Antonio Salazar came to power in Portugal. This unimposing intellectual would have a profound impact on African history and emerge as the last of the great European imperialists. Unlike other European leaders, the monastic Salazar would remain steadfast that Portugal must keep its empire at all costs. Unrepentant to the end, he insisted Europeans were essential to the well-being of the African people and would prove a loyal friend to both PK and Ian Smith in the years ahead.

"When one looks at the depredations that followed decolonization in Portugal's African territories one is forced to conclude he was right," says Lin Mehmel. "Chaos and carnage followed. Sadly Salazar's death, while there were other contributing factors, would mark a prelude to the events that would lead to the destruction of Rhodesia."

As it turned out PK's first visit to Southern Rhodesia was as a teenager on an elephant-hunting trip in 1935. During his stay he and his father marvelled at the newly commissioned Victoria Falls high-suspension bridge; at that stage the longest in the world. A love affair with Rhodesia and big game hunting was born. Little did he know it but PK would return to the bridge 40 years later for endgame political talks on Rhodesia's future.

School days were bleak, remembered brother William:

> We both ended up at Bishops.[25] PK was no bookworm, hated
> school, most of the masters and hated sport. School was not a

---

[25] Diocesan College in Rondebosch, Cape Town

happy place for him at all. The only sport he liked and excelled at was shooting which he enjoyed all his life and became very good at. Fairfield, from a farming point of view also held little appeal for PK throughout his life. Fairfield was home to many coloured families but 'Big Joseph' stood out. Handsome with very blue eyes, I have to say he looked like a van der Byl. I'm of the view that something funny went on there … I think my grandfather might have been up to tricks. World War II was an interesting time because during this period we had Italian PoWs working on the farm. One was a mechanic, another worked in the kitchen. We had to look after them and were happy to do so. They enjoyed it funnily enough and so did we. It was a very useful arrangement. Most of them were Florentines and very capable people.

At this time Danie Hoffman was Dad's secretary in Bredasdorp; an absolutely wonderful bloke whose son Gesparus worked on the farm for a while. Gesparus was incredibly strong and used to be hauled out of school to go and sort out fights.

On one occasion, PK was about 12, when a big fight broke out and one of the intervening policemen emerged with a broken jaw and another one with a broken arm. Gesparus hit the brawler once and knocked him out. This individual then went to jail and upon release went to work for Gesparus and remained in his employ for the rest of his life.

Hilary Squires,[26] although junior to PK at Bishops recalls, "PK's parents attended chapel at school on occasions. With both his father and grandfather having been politically involved it was not surprising PK would take a keen interest in politics. His parents caused quite a stir when they arrived. His

---

[26] Squires would later serve as Minister of Defence of Rhodesia before moving back to South Africa after independence. There he would serve as a judge and attract huge national attention in the politically charged trial of Schabir Shaik, whom he would convict and jail on charges relating to then South African Deputy President Jacob Zuma.

mother looked the archetypal snob with a self-estimation only slightly lower than the archangel."

Ever the contrarian, in a land where rugby is religion, PK remained unimpressed with the sport: "It seems one of the more distasteful facts about rugby is having to shove one's delicate head between two rather unattractive backsides and push. To add to this discomfort is the knowledge that something similar is happening behind one. It's just not very understandable that one puts ones head between a man's legs, bearing in mind that quite often one does not even know his name. I must confess I had a singularly undistinguishable school career both on and off the sports field."

"PK was not built for the more popular South African games [like cricket and rugby]," remembers a friend:

> Being tall, possibly overgrown and somewhat gangly he did not fit the mould. That said he more than made up for his sporting inabilities with classic conversational remarks about those whom we came across and somehow seemed able to express one's own views that had remained unvoiced. He had impeccable manners and when it was felt necessary, the ability to charm the horns off a cow. Being a wartime evacuee it became clear his interest in me was concerned with wartime Britain and in particular politics and our way of life in England. I shortly discovered that while his roots were Afrikaner his family had a knowledge and interest in much that was dear to me. At Bishops we were both members of the Cadet Force. The annual camp took place on the heights above Simon's Town. We boasted an excellent drum and wind instrument band so that a ceremonial march-past was quite an event.

For PK, welcome breaks from boarding school came in the form of weekend visits to the Mount Nelson where Major Piet and Joy stayed while parliament was in session. Joy was always happy to take him shopping and regularly indulged him with ice cream and long-playing records. The cinema was another treat. A friend remembers going with PK in the family car, pockets bulging with chocolate, which Joy insisted "was good for you".

It was while visiting his parents at the Mount Nelson in January 1939 that PK met the first love of his life. Also staying at the hotel was the Bjorn family, recently arrived after a four-day flying boat trip from Cairo. PK's eyes rested on their daughter Maureen, whom he promptly asked for a game of table tennis and a lifelong friendship was born. In a letter to Casimir van der Byl following PK's death, Maureen recounts being introduced to beer shandy by PK and of his subsequent visits to her parents' Claremont home where "we had tea, meals, played croquet and romped with the dog Laddie". PK was soon inventing stories of dentist appointments to better pursue his new amour.

Love of the outdoors was already an abiding passion and PK was 15 when he shot his first buffalo, following this with a lion downed the next day. First to receive word and a photograph of his trophies was Maureen Bjorn.

The hunt took place in Northern Rhodesia on the magnificent estate of an English eccentric with an interesting history, by the name of Stewart Gore-Brown. In 1911, as a young British officer, Gore-Brown was appointed to the Anglo-Belgian Boundary Commission to define the border between Northern Rhodesia and the Belgian Congo.

He fell in love with the surrounding countryside and determined to return when his work was finished. He was back in 1914 and set off on foot from Ndola on the Copperbelt with 30 porters looking for a piece of land to buy. He recounts:

> We suddenly came upon what I thought was the most beautiful lake I had ever seen. I was surrounded by hilly country, and along its shores were groves of rare trees, of a kind sacred to Africans. Friendly folk inhabited the one big village on the lakeshore and there were a dozen herds of different wild game.

The surrounding land seemed to be reasonably fertile judging by the crops that were ripening there. I knew at once that I had found what I was looking for.

He soon purchased 10,000 acres of land near the lake for two shillings an acre and called it Shiwa Ng'andu.

The First World War necessitated a return to England but six years later he returned as a retired lieutenant-colonel and set about building the estate with an army building manual, single-minded determination and indomitable energy. Using local materials and recruiting and training builders, carpenters and blacksmiths, he built cottages for his workers, a school, chapel, hospital, post office, workshops and later an airstrip. The elaborate manor house overlooking the lake was finished in 1932. Fittings and finery had to be shipped from England and hauled by ox wagon to the farm. Throughout, his wife Lorna took an active interest in the local culture and environment, encouraging research and carrying out anthropological studies. This unusual individual became part of local legend and his story must surely have had an impact on the young van der Byl.[27]

While PK's upbringing was certainly one of considerable wealth and privilege and included legions of staff and servants, parental care was taken to keep the children's feet on the ground.

From the outset both brothers learned that power and privilege counted for nothing without matching standards and that authority had to be evenhanded. Race and class were major factors but they were made to understand abuse of power was unacceptable. This was family tradition and a reason why coloured families lived peaceably on Fairfield for generations.

Life skills learned on Fairfield undoubtedly shaped PK's 'soft' approach to African politics which later so incensed South African Prime Minister John Vorster and ultimately led to his sacking as Rhodesia's Defence

---

[27] Later, Gore-Brown took an active interest in politics. Unlike many of his white compatriots he was supportive of the concept of black majority rule and assisted Zambia's Kenneth Kaunda in his political ascendancy.

Minister. What PK actually said to Vorster that day is unknown, but what is known that he took exception to the South African premier's lecture to him on black-white relations. PK knew Vorster and Foreign Minister Pik Botha were urban Afrikaners from white enclaves who had had virtually no interaction with black people. As far as PK was concerned they were unable to fathom, empathize or communicate with blacks and this rendered their judgement on racial matters fundamentally flawed. With considerable justification he felt Rhodesia's blacks were happier and better governed than their counterparts in South Africa and resented being patronized by the South African Prime Minister.

The powerful Vorster, who couldn't have liked PK's imperious bearing, was definitely unhappy when later learning of PK's remarks that the "Rhodesian government knew more about handling 'munts'[28] than Vorster did". The wrathful South African premier held Ian Smith's feet to the fire until he fired van der Byl.

---

[28] Derived from the Shona word *munhu*. It is widely recognized as a pejorative word but this belies its genesis.

CHAPTER FOUR
War

On 3 September 1939, when PK was nearly 16, Britain declared war on Germany. "Britain's declaration of war split the South African government," recalls Hilary Squires:

> Smuts wanted war and Hertzog wanted the country to remain neutral. PK's dad was a ruling-party MP and he came to Bishops to take PK to watch the momentous debate that would ultimately take South Africa to war. This was an unheard of privilege for a schoolboy. Smuts carried the day with a slender majority but needed support from the minor parties. The Governor-General Patrick Duncan did not want to dissolve parliament and call an early election and asked Smuts to form a new government. So the rump of the United Party carried on and Herzog took his people into opposition.

South Africa voted 80 to 67 to enter the war on 4 September and was one of the first Commonwealth countries to declare for Britain.

In Rhodesia, such was the enthusiasm to join up that limits on volunteers were imposed to save the colony from economic collapse. In years to come, neither PK nor Ian Smith could embarrass British Labour politicians with details of Rhodesia's proud war record despite the fact that many of them, for one reason or another, had not served in the armed forces. By May 1940, Neville Chamberlain had resigned, leaving Churchill to head a coalition British government steeling itself to resist Hiltler's advances.

Champing at the bit while watching from afar, a young PK matriculated in 1940 and entered Pretoria University. Reading arts brought neither satisfaction nor result and he found little common cause with his fellow Afrikaner students. He was regarded with suspicion and hostility as an Afrikaner with an English accent *and* as the son of a pro-British cabinet minister. As it turned out, many Afrikaners, given the choice, would indeed have sided with Germany. Coming from a long line of soldiers it is probably safe to say PK never doubted his military destiny.

Realizing that South Africa had to maximize industrial capacity and product delivery in times of war Smuts called for the help of his old friend Hendrik van der Byl. At the time. Hendrik was at the top of his game and well on his way to a fortune when he received word that he was needed at home by no lesser a personage than General Smuts, who asked him to accept an appointment as Director-General of War Supplies. The position assured him of little more than endless hours of hard work in an alien environment and in a role that was unfamiliar to him but he accepted immediately. Running his eyes over the proffered contract he pointed to a blank space.

"What's this?" he asked.

"The space where you are to fill in what your salary requirements are, doctor," the emissary replied, adding, "I am instructed to tell you you may name your own figure."

Taking the document, Hendrik wrote £0.00 and handed it back.

For six years Hendrik performed his task with exacting success. His powers were vast, exceeding those of any cabinet minister, making him an unchallenged technocrat presiding over all aspects of South African industry. Throughout these demanding years he never drew a salary.

In early 1941, Fairfield welcomed more royals in the shape of King George II of Greece, his family and entourage. Crete had fallen to the Germans and the family had fled to South Africa. Following their arrival, General Smuts appointed Major Piet Minister in Attendance to the King and was immediately instructed to accompany Smuts by special train to the Cape to bring the royals ashore. Soon thereafter the family and courtiers were brought to Fairfield. Also in the group were Crown Prince and Princess Paul and Fredrika (later to ascend to the Greek throne), HRH Princess Katherina, Princess Aspasia, Princess Alexandria (later to marry King Peter of Yugoslavia), Colonel Levidis, comptroller of the Household and Mrs. Joyce Britten-Jones, a friend of the King.

William remembers: "We saw a lot of the Greek Royal family. I believe Smuts had a thing for Princess Frederika. She was a member of the Kaiser's family, a real tiger.

I am convinced one of the reasons Smuts lost the '48 election was because he was madly in love with her. Smuts's advisor Louis Esselen tried to focus him but failed. His mind was in Greece and that was that. She was King Paul's wife; he was besotted."

But Major Piet in his memoirs disputes this. "She was a one-man woman deeply in love with her husband. Determined, strong-minded, courageous and ambitious, she was determined that her son should occupy the throne of Greece."

"Esselen was very shrewd," says William, "famous for capturing Churchill during the Boer War. He ran the South African Secret Service during World War II. He was Smuts's closest adviser but Smuts ignored his advice and lost the election. Smuts was not a good politician. He was aloof, above it all and not a good judge of people. Too cold-blooded a man for my liking."

Again Major Piet disagreed with his son: "Smuts was not a conceited man but like all men he had a bit of vanity; and it was pleasing to his ego to be flattered by a beautiful, clever Royal Lady; that's all there is to it."

"Joy van der Byl got on exceedingly well with Smuts," says Lin Mehmel, "and I think there was a great deal of mutual respect."

At the end of 1942, PK was finally called for basic military training with the South African Armoured Corps camped at Kaffirskraal near Pretoria. Much to his chagrin he found himself sharing a Boer War bell tent with 14 other men. Here he completed basic infantry, gunnery and wireless training with driving instruction on the South African-designed Marmon Herrington armoured car. This was a vehicle designed for reconnaissance but was later used in offensive roles in North Africa. Powered by a big Ford V8 engine, PK attracted opprobrium for grinding the gears but finally mastered the vehicle. He excelled at shooting, receiving a sniper's badge worn on the battle dress sleeve.

From Kaffirskraal he was posted to the Natal Mounted Rifles. This he says was ironic: "I had never been to Natal, nor was I mounted, nor did I have a rifle."

William remembers:

On completion of basic training PK went to the Natal Mounted Rifles where he was a simple trooper. While here, Mother received a frantic telegram from him requiring money most urgently. She sent it on condition he didn't buy a motorbike. What she didn't know was he had been cleaned out playing poker. This was not to be the last time either. He loved the game but was actually not very good at it.

Eddy Feldman, who played a lot with PK many years later at the Salisbury Club, told me that PK was a consistent loser. He also played after the war in a Cambridge school that included members of the Royal Family. I joined them once. Quite a high-flying bunch and I won, but later discovered the cheque PK's pal gave me was extravagantly postdated.

An old comrade recalls: "PK ran foul of a sergeant named Clarke in the Natal Mounted Rifles because he could never fold his blankets correctly. As this was a daily routine, the rest of us had to help him out. This was typical of South African males who reputedly could do little more than pour a drink in a kitchen. Like old naval officers who could never find an engine room."

Shortly after the death of General Dan Pienaar in December 1942[29] and with the war escalating, South African forces had to sign the 'New Oath' which extended their remit from 'defence of the Union' to fighting anywhere in the world. As an enticement to sign, many of the troops were shipped back to South Africa where under General Everard Poole a new division was formed calling itself the 6th South African Armoured Division. A former comrade remembers:

> By this time, the North Africa campaign was all but finished. PK and I, as part of the Natal Mounted Rifles, assembled on Clarewood Race Course in Durban and were shipped off to North Africa with the 6th. Our mothers arrived to see us off and waved to us from the quayside while a lady sang patriotic songs.
>
> Our ship was the French liner, *Isle de France*, reckoned to be too fast for submarines. Just as well because over 10,000 men sailed on her to Port Said that day.
>
> Catering only worked if the men were divided into two shifts; some slept during the day and the others at night. PK and I slept comfortably on airbeds provided by our mums in the glassed-off *jardin d'hiver* [winter garden]. This was no bad thing until we reached the Red Sea area when it became baking hot and unusable during the day. PK was much occupied with cards throughout the voyage.
>
> On arrival at Kataba we again camped in tents and began the

---

[29] One of South Africa's most charismatic and popular military commanders, he commanded the 1st South African Infantry Brigade during the East African campaign fighting in the battles of El Wak, The Juba, Combolcia, and Amba Alagi. From 1941 to 1942 during the North Africa campaign, Pienaar fought in the battles of Sidi Rezeghh and Gazala. At Gazala, he was promoted to command the 1st South African Division which he led in the battle of Gazala, the retreat to Egypt, the defence of El Alamein and the final battle of El Alamein. He was twice awarded the DSO and mentioned in dispatches twice for his service in North Africa. He was killed in an air crash at Kisumu in northern Kenya on his way back to South Africa on 19 December 1942.

conversion of an infantry division into an armoured one. We were instructed in the driving of the Sherman and Mk III light tank.

The latter were known as Stuarts and powered with diesel and radial engines. The Shermans were petrol-powered and fitted with twin .303 Brownings and a 75mm gun. This could fire smoke, HE [high-explosive] or AP [armour-piercing] shells. The Stuarts mostly had their turrets removed which made their cross-country performance better and were often used to carry a section of infantry.

So the Natal Mounted Rifles became a regiment capable of reconnaissance in force and based around the make-up of four armoured squadrons each, with four troops comprising two Shermans and two Stuarts each. PK and I were in 'C' Squadron under Major Jackie Haupt.

While in Kataba we were once paraded in front of PK's father and Field Marshal Smuts. Although only a trooper at the time, PK was presented to the dignitaries along with the divisional officers. He had by now decided to be an officer in the British Army and seized his opportunity when Smuts spoke to him: "Well, PK my boy, here you are."

To which PK replied, "Yes, Field Marshal."

"Well, are you doing a more important job here than your father is doing in the South?" quipped Smuts.

As he had spent much of the last few months digging latrines, PK replied with commendable restraint, "Yes, Field Marshal, but I haven't had the same opportunities he had serving with you in the last war."

Friends in high places or not, PK was duly summoned ten days later by his CO and told to report to a British base. From there he was sent on WOSB [War Officers Selection Board] and then to the Hussars.

William recalls: "The Old Man wanted him in a top regiment there because he knew he would make the right connections. They were equipped with Sherman tanks. One of his more startling efforts there was when some bloody fool inside the tank accidentally let loose with a sidearm, sending a bullet ricocheting around the inside. PK was then seen strutting around outside the tank relating his near miss while warning other tank commanders to be 'bloody careful' with their pistols so they did not suffer the same fate."

PK later recalled his thoughts regarding Smuts many years later in an interview with journalist and writer Phillippa Berlyn: "One's impression is basically one of remoteness, but then again that was mixed up with the fact that one only knew him and about him as a remote figure of fantastic power and consequence. And to say that one knew him closely would be quite absurd … until of course one had got a good deal older."

It was soon after the Germans surrendered at Stalingrad in early 1943 and events were turning irrevocably against Hitler that PK was finally commissioned into the British Army.

"The 7th Hussars was a life-changing experience," says William, "from a small-town boy he was suddenly in the company of cavalry officers from very grand families … a pretty odd bunch, terribly 'ha-ha', but bloody fine soldiers. Their uniform—blue patrols—was extremely smart. The culture shock was incredible and it had a tumultuous impact upon him but he made the changes and got on with them. It was after this period that he came back to South Africa with this highly unusual, almost unique accent that everyone will always associate with him."

His first brush with real operational soldiering came when he entered the Italian theatre in mid-1944 shortly after the battle of Monte Cassino.

Princess Charlotte of Liechtenstein, or Lotti, PK's widow, recalls: "He told me how amused he was to find a leaflet from the Germans saying, 'When we bomb you must duck, when you bomb we duck. When the Americans bomb everyone must duck!' He was then involved in some minor battles but in the process of clearing out a house he was very distressed to discover the German soldiers were not men but boys and some of them had been killed. He did not like that at all."

PK recalled another Keystone Cops incident:

We were ordered to rendezvous with a Canadian section at this particular point. We arrived there and as usual the Canadians were late. There was no sign of them at all so I stopped in a grove of trees and told my driver to switch the engine off. It was all very quiet and peaceful and I was minding my own business on the turret when I turned around and to my great surprise I saw two rather filthy-looking Germans appearing out of the barn behind us. I immediately reached for my pistol in order to engage the enemy but discovered to my great disappointment it had been purloined, I suspect by one of our dreadful South Americans, most of whom were terrible thieves. My predicament worsened when one of these plucky little Germans crept closer and hoisted a tube of some sort which he proceeded to aim it me. I had never seen a weapon like this and concluded his intentions were malignant, so I shouted to my driver to crank the turret around, which he proceeded to do, but this manoeuvre was thwarted by a tree which blocked the revolution. He changed direction but the same problem arose on the other side so our main gun was rendered useless in this particular situation. I then shouted to the machine gunner to man his guns and put down fire immediately but alas he, an Argentinian, was resting and unable to respond, so I leapt inside and kicked him very hard. He leapt into action but opened fire on our own people rather than the Germans so I had to kick him again. With that the German fired his bazooka and there was a huge blast but thankfully the projectile landed short of us and exploded without doing us any serious harm. Later we had crossed over the River Po and got mixed up with General Freyburg's New Zealand Corps who were rushing as hard as they could to get to Trieste. We turned off at Mestrě before going down the Causeway into Venice. I was the lead troop that day so I suppose it can be said I captured it. We camped for three days at Piazza Roma; from there we went into Carinthia as part of the occupation of Austria. I was subsequently appointed Intelligence Officer to the regiment and finally second-in-command of the Headquarters Squadron.

"Afterwards his battalion moved north to Venice," says Lotti, "and for some strange reason he was the first officer into the Grande Plaza there. I believe he was very obvious because he always travelled with a bath on the back of his tank. PK was always fastidious about personal hygiene and always well equipped for comfort. From there he moved into Austria, ironically to Carinthia near where I was later born. The people on whose estate he stayed during this time became great friends of his many years later."

"The war was the best part of my life," remembered PK. "Italy was a marvellous country and a splendid one to conquer. As a young officer one found oneself leading men who could be numbered among the finest British soldiers. And I must say life was very agreeable. There were no shortages and we lived in the finest hotels when not engaged in the fighting. The campaign was a good one. We were not involved in many major battles and had a relatively easy time. We didn't have an enormous number of casualties. One was fortunate to escape anything oneself, and largely it was a matter of great excitement advancing up Italy."

"Down the line, being in the Hussars was of great benefit to PK," maintains Lotti. "Membership meant he spent quite a lot of time at the Guards and Cavalry Club and came to know most of the top people in the British military establishment. It was these associations that helped him understand the British way of thinking and thus he was better able to read them than many of his colleagues in government. People like Lord Carrington knew he knew what they were all about and were therefore wary of him. This is why he was unwelcome many years later at Lancaster

House. Carrington only wanted people there he knew he could fool. PK and Ian Smith were therefore not wanted."

While the Allies continued their advance into Europe and the Americans pounded Japanese positions on Iwo Jima, life carried on much as before in Africa and, in October 1944, Major Piet went hunting buffalo near the Zambezi in Barotseland, Northern Rhodesia with his friend Jack Ashwin. Having downed one animal from a herd of 1,500 they were surprised from behind by two bulls charging out of a riverine thicket. With no place to hide the two stood their ground, fired, and turned the charge. It was also reported their bearers manfully stood their ground.

Meanwhile, with the war all but over, PK was based near Naples enjoying the company of Maureen Bjorn. Together they visited the fishing village of Amalfi, south of Naples. On 30 April 1945, Hitler committed suicide and a week later Germany surrendered. PK recalled the day: "We were sitting in the officers' mess at Mestrě at the time. The Germans had been on the run for so long we were expecting the surrender when it came. When the news actually came through I was playing cards in the mess and consuming large amounts of alcohol."

On 6 August, a nuclear device exploded on the Japanese city of Hiroshima, followed a few days later by another on Nagasaki. Japan surrendered. On 14 August, the war was over. At the time, PK was attending a party in Rome where he met and fell for Paula Khuen-Lutzoew but this soon caused problems. Although the van der Byls were not devoutly religious, the fact that she was Catholic earned the disapproval of Major Piet. As it turned out fate would intervene because a letter from a rival suitor trumped one from PK requesting her hand in marriage. Later, Paula came with her husband to farm in Rhodesia and the two remained lifelong friends.

CHAPTER FIVE
To Rhodesia

Notwithstanding Churchill's heroic war leadership the British electorate voted for change and Labour's Clement Atlee replaced him in 1946. One of the first people to hear from Atlee was General Smuts. The British PM was battling to break a deadlock between the government and the Steel Federation. At a loss as to what to do, he turned to Smuts, who dispatched a skilled negotiator in the form of the formidable Hendrik van der Byl, who swiftly settled the matter with a blend of steely resolve and fair play.

But no sooner had this issue been dealt with than the British government was back again, seeking further assistance. Faced with a financial crisis the British Prime Minister appealed to Smuts to help raise £80 million in order to ward off devaluation. Major Piet, then a member of the cabinet remembers: "Our government knew then that it had to face a general election in less than a year and that the main reserve covering its balance of payments was less than £100 million in gold. We also knew that if we complied, the opposition would make political capital out of it, yet that did not deter us and the same morning we made the loan at an interest rate of five per cent. This act of kindness," he lamented, "would be forgotten in Britain's rush to toady to black Africa."

"Soon after the war ended, PK went from Italy to Cambridge and did a law degree in 18 months which he completed in June 1947," remembers William. "It had been reduced from three years for returning servicemen."

Records show he obtained a Third Class degree in his Part II Law exams. Always beautifully dressed and carefully coiffured, at Cambridge he acquired the sobriquet 'The Piccadilly Dutchman'. Soon thereafter he went to the United States and Harvard University Graduate School of Business Administration for another year of study but found this unrewarding. "In my view it was a mistake," he recalled. "If one is not trained to the American system it is not very easy. One finds everything done in a totally different way."

But William has a more cynical view. "I think he spent a lot of his Harvard days driving around the US having a good time and not doing an awful lot of work."

PK wrote on his return, after touring the southern United States: "The Great Plains country is very similar in both terrain and economy to our Northern Cape and the Transvaal; both are expansive cattle-raising lands, only where Texas has oil we have gold and diamonds. Houston is booming with oil just as Johannesburg is rich with gold mines. The spirit is much the same. However, it is difficult to give one's impressions of America. Every state is different. I think what struck me most was the cost of living, which is fantastic."

Referring to the defeat of the United Party and the assent to power of the National Party led by Dr. D.F. Malan he expressed the view that the new government would continue to align itself with the West and was dismissive of talk of South Africa leaving the Commonwealth. "There is no real enmity toward the British," he wrote. But his father Piet, now on the opposition benches, was already sinking his teeth into his political opponents on the subject of apartheid: "... the greatest political fraud that has ever been put out about the country," he said in an address to parliament.

Quizzed by a reporter on the possibility of entering politics, PK was equivocal: "Not until I become financially independent and can be an honest politician."

"These words may have sounded whimsical at the time but the fact is history has shown he meant it," says Lin Mehmel:

> While he was criticized for a multitude of reasons during his time in public life, dishonesty was never one of them. Bearing in mind this man was reviled by many in the political realm there can be no doubt he was watched carefully but he, like

the government he served, was never seriously accused of any sort of financial impropriety. And this is salient because when one looks at the tragedy that is post-colonial Africa one has to conclude that a potent factor in facilitating this descent into ruin has been endemic and gross dishonesty on the part of African leadership everywhere. This curse was never visited upon Rhodesia and prosperity coursed through the entire country.

As expected, the cessation of hostilities proved a boon to Rhodesia as ex-servicemen, offered incentives, returned home in droves to develop the country's agriculture, mining and industry, as no-nonsense men with broadened perspectives, peacetime challenges offered no terrors to most of these individuals. An added bonus was the large numbers of quality non-Rhodesians employed at wartime training facilities in the country who decided to stay and help develop the country.

In 1946, Godfrey Huggins's United Party won a narrow victory over Jacob Smit's Liberal Party, which, despite its name, was conservative and aligned with South Africa's National Party. The electorate was forgiving of Huggins, deeming strong competent governance less divisive than the alternative and it was said that Rhodesia's civil service under the UP was the best in the world.

The following year, on 15 August 1947, India became independent and the British Raj came to an end as the viceroy Lord Louis Mountbatten handed over the reins of power to Jawaharlal Nehru. Soon thereafter the new nation of Pakistan was born and the stage was set for another post-colonial conflict.

Although the decolonizing of the Empire held dark prospects for whites in Africa, PK's primary interest in India was not linked to political developments but to Jim Corbett's recorded exploits there in *Maneaters of Kumaon*. Fired by Corbett's derring-do, particularly his pursuit of tigers with only a handful of cartridges, PK's obsession nearly led to disaster.

"We went buffalo hunting," remembers William, "and PK, trying to be like Corbett, set off alone after a herd with just a few cartridges and got involved in what eventually sounded like a bloody war. He came staggering out looking distinctly worse for wear and never went anywhere lightly armed again in his life."

The following year, 1948, PK found himself employment. "He got a job with Irvine and Johnson Fisheries," says William. "He didn't like it much but there was no place for him at Fairfield and he and Dad would have fought. Dad was very fond of him, but they were strong personalities and would certainly have clashed."

PK also had a good relationship with his mother. "Joy adored PK," recalls Malcolm Napier. "He could do no wrong in her eyes."

"I think he was dead bored back in the Cape," says old friend Eve Leslie. "He loved the excitement of the army and South Africa looked terribly dull at that moment in time."

In the same year Ian Smith, a quiet 29-year-old ex-serviceman, won a seat in the opposition Liberal Party in Southern Rhodesia's parliament. A former fighter pilot turned farmer who did his homework, he quickly earned a reputation as a forthright and formidable debater.

Significantly, Rhodesia's rejection of Smuts's invitation to become part of the South African Union turned out to be a decisive factor in the 26 May election, which saw D.F. Malan's National Party sweep to power. Had the Rhodesians accepted Union and participated in this ballot there is every reason to believe the Nationalists would not have prevailed and the course of history dramatically altered. At the same time, Major Piet narrowly lost his Bredasdorp seat by 259 votes to the NP candidate, W.C. du Plessis, but found his way back into parliament by contesting the Green Point by-election in October of that year and won by default when his opponent failed to post the cash deposit.

As much as defeat at the polls shocked Smuts, the loss of his own Standerton seat was a massive personal humiliation. He had campaigned for the enfranchisement of coloureds but the electorate had rejected him.

This led directly to the hated apartheid, the polarization of the country and the outrage of the world.

Of further significance, on 22 June 1948, SS *Empire Windbrush* docked at Tilbury carrying 500 Caribbean immigrants in an otherwise unremarkable event. However, the next month the British government passed the Citizenship Act giving Commonwealth citizens the right to live in Britain. This opened Britain's doors to a flood of immigrants who were welcomed and generously accommodated, leading to a radical demographic transformation that would impact massively on the country. Many years later PK would irritate his English acquaintances when he expressed the view that "England was no longer a sensible place for a white person to reside in".

Ironically, given the reputation he would acquire later Ian Smith turned heads of hard-liners in parliament in 1950 when he made a speech condemning the customary African payment of *lobola* (bride price) which he termed a "deal in human flesh". Explaining to the members that he saw himself as a guardian of his less sophisticated countrymen, he called for the practice to be curbed, but conventional opinion was opposed to interference in African custom unless absolutely necessary.

As Smith's reputation in politics grew in Rhodesia, PK's fame grew in more hedonistic pursuits in exotic locations. Linking up in Angola with a Senor Martins, a friend of his father's and a provincial administrator, or *chefe de poste*, he went on a hunt in southern Angola. Here he shot the tallest elephant ever recorded and shared the tusks with his host. The animal now stands in the Natural History Museum in New York. On the trail, Martins produced two excellent Bushman trackers who so fascinated PK that he later facilitated their transfer to his farm in Selous. They were not happy in Rhodesia in such unfamiliar territory, though, so PK returned them to their homeland. Interestingly, says William, "They were not like the Kalahari Bushmen. Small, the same build, but very black rather than yellow skin."

"Like many things it was largely a matter of luck," recalled PK. "I was in the field and came across the spoor of two bulls. We tracked them and shot the one that looked the better. I did not attach much significance to it at the time but after the elephant was measured it proved to be two or three inches taller than the world record."

Back in South Africa, his feet were getting itchier. "After working for a year in Cape Town I saw an article in a paper about an Afrikaans farmer who had made R48,000 on his first tobacco crop up in Rhodesia. I immediately decided a new adventure was opening. I phoned my father immediately but he was on his way to England so I rushed to the airport to ask him to give me some assistance. I simply said I need R50,000. My father said he did not have time to hear what the reason was. He said, 'Give me the documents and I will sign.' And that was that; I was ready to go north."

"He decided to make the family fortune out of tobacco in Rhodesia," says William, "and immigrated in 1951. In a sense, he was too late because tobacco had bottomed out and I think he was overeager to succeed. He paid too much for a farm in Selous which he purchased from the Light family, who clearly saw him coming. Mama put some money into the venture too. I was an articled clerk then and the plan was I would get the dividend for tax purposes and disburse the proceeds to the rest of the family. After a couple of years I saw a balance sheet that did not look too good and asked a few leading questions which did not go down well at all and I was removed from the Board immediately. Patricia Pitt tried to keep him on the straight and narrow from an accounting point of view. PK's problem was he had no farming experience and simply did not know enough."

PK never disputed this:

> I lost a lot of money in my first year farming when most of my associates were making handsome profits. But I was terribly happy there. I had loved Rhodesia since I was a child. I got to know it on hunting trips with my father. He too was fascinated by it. There was not much for me to do in the Cape. I wanted to go into politics but the trend was against me in South Africa. I suddenly got a rush of blood to the crotch about the tobacco boom and decided I was going to go up there and make the family fortune in a place I liked and wanted to be in. I had never seen a tobacco plant. The first one I saw was the one I grew. Far from making a fortune, I lost £10,000 in my first year and never

really recovered. Then I drifted into crime and politics. There
was a tremendous emotional appeal then. The Rhodesian was
the last good white man left; we were the renaissance people.

In a sign of what was to come in Kenya and Africa, Jomo Kenyatta and
five other Kikuyu leaders were convicted of rebellion against British rule
on 8 April 1953, and imprisoned. It was the same day the Central Africa
Federation was formed to bring together Northern and Southern Rhodesia
and Nyasaland, which had enthusiastic support from none other than
Winston Churchill. Repeating his performance 30 years earlier in securing
home rule for Rhodesia, he was convinced the formation would be good for
Britain, consolidate the position of the colonials and benefit Africa. Pushed
to fruition by Godfrey Huggins, it would bring a relatively sophisticated
administrative, commercial and industrial infrastructure from the south
into fusion with the unrealized potential in the north, while introducing a
vast pool of labour to be drawn from Nyasaland.

Initially opposed by Ian Smith because he feared it opened the door for
meddling by the British, he later changed his mind, sensing the undoubted
economic possibilities. He was also persuaded by Huggins's argument that
such a polity, heavily influenced by white leadership in Salisbury, would
provide a more effective bulwark against the spread of Black Nationalism
that threatened to consume 'white civilization' in Africa. In deciding to
throw in his lot with Huggins, Smith resigned from the Liberals (then the
Rhodesia Party) and joined the ruling Federal Party, determined to be part
of building "one of the greatest countries in the world."[30]

But Smith's fears would indeed be realized. While theoretically the
'settlers' were given unlimited power, their legal status would only prevail
so long as the union remained intact. Smith and Huggins were always
uneasy with this codicil as it allowed Britain a dominant re-entry position.
History now tells us it was an economic success but British indecisiveness
and the rise of Black Nationalism doomed it to failure.

---

[30] Peter Joyce: *Anatomy of a Rebel*. Grahame Publishing, 1974

In April 1955, at Bandung, Indonesia, the country's President Sukarno rallied the "disadvantaged, post-colonial, developing" nations of the world at an Afro-Asian conference from which the Non-Aligned Movement developed, an initiative which had enormous significance for Africa. Also known as the 'Third World', it became a force on the world political stage, less by any significant achievement than by sheer force of numbers. In the words of Paul Johnson, "So now, the very fact of a colonial past and a non-white skin were seen as title deeds to international esteem. An ex-colonial state was seen as righteous by definition. A gathering of such states would be seen as a senate of wisdom."

Reading the situation quickly, Red China moved in and positioned itself with the poor 'coloured' world against the rich 'white' world. Months later, Mao initiated an entente with Nasser in Cairo and China began her African campaign, which would heavily influence events in post-colonial Africa.

Sukarno wasted no time in declaring the moral equivalent of war: "This is the first intercontinental conference of coloured peoples in the history of mankind. Sisters and brothers! How terrifically dynamic is our time … Nations and states have awoken from a sleep of centuries. We, the people of Asia and Africa … can mobilize what I have called the *moral violence of nations* in favour of peace."[31]

While he may have had grand plans for the world, he ignored his countrymen and by 1965, Sukarno had bankrupted his country. He was overthrown in a putsch in the early hours of 1 October of that year. Sadly, many attendees of the Bandung conference would ape his road to economic self-destruction.

Back in Salisbury, Huggins' Federal government soon felt the Bandung ripple when black intellectuals, fired by Kwame Nkrumah's announcement that his country's freedom "will be a fountain of inspiration from which other colonial African territories can draw when their time comes". More ominously for the whites, he went on to state that "independence for the

---

[31] Paul Johnson: *A History of the Modern World*. Weidenfeld & Nicolson, 1984

Gold Coast is meaningless unless it is linked up with the total liberation of the continent".[32] Days later, violence erupted in Northern Rhodesia and the governor declared a state of emergency when riots swept the Copperbelt. This was followed by further outbreaks throughout the continent, as newly emboldened black politicians took to the hustings and urged their followers to defy their colonial rulers.

In 1956, with much of Africa in turmoil, PK had his first taste of politics when elected by the Selous-Gadzema district to the Rhodesia Tobacco Association Council. Having failed to distinguish himself as a grower, he had nonetheless impressed neighbours with intellect, commitment and passion for the community. Captain Malcolm Napier remembers PK's early days in Selous:

> One of his earliest employees was Farnabeck. His [Farnabeck's] father was on the farm when PK bought it and so the son came with it. He was supposed to have been called 'van der Berg' after an Afrikaner farmer from the area but his parents spelled it wrong and ended up with 'Farnabeck'. He would remain close and intensely loyal to PK throughout his life in Rhodesia and then Zimbabwe.
>
> I remember many happy occasions with PK on the farm. He had great style and dinner was always an occasion. I can remember one time when the 'boss boy' was absent, PK had to look after and sleep up at the tobacco barns. Unfazed, he had a tractor and trailer bring the dinner table to the barn where he dined with jacket and tie as was normal and proper.

"PK was devoted to Farnabeck," remembers Lotti, "and Farnabeck was very loyal. Not even charging elephants caused him to leave PK's side. He was a very good all-rounder and did everything for PK, including crashing cars for him on occasion! A very 'busy' chap, PK helped him with

---

[32] Peter Joyce: *Anatomy of a Rebel*. Grahame Publishing, 1974

accommodation for his various wives. Many years later, around 1995, we received word Farnabeck had been caught in possession of stolen property belonging to PK. PK very quickly told the police to release him and let him have whatever it was he had taken."

The next year, 1957, PK was made a Director of the United Dominions Corporation (Rhodesia) and also became Deputy Chairman of the Selous Farmers' Association.

"At this time Evan Campbell, later Southern Rhodesia's High Commissioner in London, took an interest in PK and encouraged him to get more involved with the RTA [Rhodesia Tobacco Association]," recalls William.

"The RTA became a pretty political body and that was essentially the beginning of his career in politics. I was not surprised when he went political. The 'Old Man' encouraged him like hell and, make no bones about it, he was very good at it. He was *pa se kind* [daddy's boy], while I argued all the time with my father. Father was a very strong and influential figure. Funnily enough, my grandfather would not allow my father to go into politics so he had to wait until grandfather died before making his move, but dad pushed PK all the way. He was, without doubt, the major influence on PK's life."

As PK was embracing politics, a former Rhodesia Railways social worker by the name of Joshua Nkomo was flexing his muscles in the Southern Rhodesian African National Congress and attracting growing attention. Thanks partly to his efforts, township riots took place in the coal-mining town of Wankie and a serious strike on the mine was organized, resulting in troops being called in and the leaders arrested on suspicion of planning an uprising. At the same time, to the north, decolonization was gathering pace.

Kenyan academic Mukui Waruiru, who founded the African Conservative Forum, relates the events from an unusual perspective:

On 6 March 1957, Ghana became the first black African country to gain independence from European colonial rule

(Sudan gained its independence in 1956, but it regards itself as part of Arab Africa, rather than black Africa). The Prime Minister of Ghana, Kwame Nkrumah, had won an election in 1956, campaigning on a platform of attaining immediate independence from British colonial rule. Nkrumah had served as Prime Minister from 1951 to 1956, a period in which Ghana enjoyed internal self-government, under the supervision of the British colonial governor in the country. The governor had the power to veto decisions by Nkrumah that he felt were harmful to the interests of the colony. This was the period in which Ghana enjoyed the greatest levels of freedom and prosperity in its history.

Most of the black African nations that gained independence after Ghana followed its path by establishing one-party dictatorships. Observers soon began to describe the practice of democracy in Africa as 'one man, one vote, one time'. In many cases, the winning political party at the independence elections used its majority in the national parliament to pass legislation outlawing the existence of opposition political parties. This left the ruling party with a monopoly of power. This trend challenged the widely held notion that pure democracy leads to more freedom. If anything, in many countries, Africans enjoyed greater personal freedom and prosperity under colonial rule, than they do today under independent governments.

Having being slower to react than the Chinese, the Soviet Union started to take notice of Africa and watched the unravelling of colonialism with increasing interest. Concerned that China had stolen a march on them, they opened an 'Africa Department' and plotted areas for subversion. Concerned white southern African politicians noted Moscow's plans for southern Africa but, try as they might, never rallied meaningful Western support against the Russian Bear.

In September 1958, Hendrik Verwoerd, educated at Milton College in

Bulawayo, replaced Dr. J.G. Strydom as Prime Minister of South Africa. Although a resolute and formidable parliamentary foe, first across the parliamentary aisle to congratulate him was Major Piet van der Byl. Years later the Major would hit the headlines for referring to Verwoerd as "a paranoiac", a comment which caused him to be ordered from the House of Assembly. The Major was in the throes of arguing strenuously to keep South Africa in the British Commonwealth and reject the republicanism favoured by the Afrikaner Nationalists but Verwoerd and his people were determined on an isolationist strategy, having largely distanced themselves from their traditional allies. In Verwoerd's view, looking at how Britain was behaving in Africa, the Commonwealth had so compromised itself it was already dead and he wanted no further part of it. In a sense, South Africa's international pariah status dates from this time. Despite almost universal antipathy Ian Smith held a contrary view of Verwoerd:

> He was in politics because he thought he knew what was best for South Africa. He was utterly incorruptible, lived very simply and what few know is he had his fair share of run-ins with big white business because he wanted to protect the black people from the white entrepreneurs whom Verwoerd knew would outsmart them. He wanted to uplift the black community but insisted it was better this was done in a segregated country. We in Rhodesia did not agree with this hard-line approach.

Meanwhile the Federation tottered amidst mounting internal dissent feeding directly off London's unwillingness for confrontation with the Southern Rhodesian leadership. Then, without consultation, Conservative Prime Minister Harold Macmillan suddenly announced a policy change for Nyasaland and Northern Rhodesia, embracing black majority rule. After its recent humiliation in the Middle East over Suez, the British 'Imperium' was in retreat.

From Westminster, leading the rearguard fight to save the Empire from collapse, was the 'Rhodesia Lobby' that included luminaries of the British aristocracy like Lords Salisbury, Robins, Hinchingbrooke and Captain Charles Waterhouse. Imperialists of the old school, they held considerable clout and remained convinced the white man had a long-term role to play. They tried valiantly, but ultimately unsuccessfully, to buttress Federal Prime Minister Welensky in his efforts to maintain white domination and keep the Federation intact.

While London and Salisbury feuded, PK was quietly enjoying the hospitality of the gentry, grouse shooting with Sir Malcolm Barclay-Harvey in Deeside on the Scottish moors. At the same time, his father outraged liberals in a speech in Johannesburg warning that "if given power in South Africa, Africans would install a Shaka Zulu-like dictatorship with all its horrors".[33] It was inevitable, he insisted, as Africans were only recently emerging from barbarism.

White fears were further heightened when, on 3 February 1960, Harold Macmillan, following on his 'Winds of Change' tour in Ghana, addressed the South African parliament in Cape Town and drove the same point home again. Imperialism, he told them in unequivocal terms, was dead and the days of white rule in Africa were numbered.

He was right.

---

[33] *Rand Daily Mail*, 4 September 1959

CHAPTER SIX
Chaos

Months later the streets of Leopoldville, Congo ran red as hundreds were killed in savage anti-white riots. The white south looked on at the spectacle with a mixture of dread and despair at the muted international reaction.

"The Congo was horrible," remembers Lin Mehmel. "The nuns and other white women were flown out thanks to, among others, the Rhodesians. Normally crisp, clean habits arrived blood-soaked and shredded. Once-covered heads appeared stripped and exposed. Haunted, horrified eyes told of the dreadful drama they had just lived through."

The fact that different standards were set to apply was illustrated when South African police repulsed a 20,000 strong mob attack on their post at Sharpeville, killing 56 people. Unlike the silence that followed the Congo killings, world outrage resulted. The anniversary of Sharpeville remains a hallowed date in South Africa's struggle and is recognized universally as a symbol of black resistance.

Despite the certainty of political turmoil, chaos and misery, the Congo was granted independence from Belgium on 30 June 1960. Far from seeking an orderly and peaceful transition, an unstable former postal worker named Patrice Lumumba took control of the new government and used the independence ceremony to launch a vitriolic attack on whites.

Within a week the army mutinied and the country tumbled into anarchy. Belgians were shot in the streets and hundreds of women were raped in an orgy of violence. UN Secretary-General Dag Hammarskjöld at his New York Headquarters refused to act. Brussels sent in troops ten days later to restore order, whereupon Hammarskjöld took the Belgian government to the Security Council and denounced their soldiers as a threat to peace and order. By the time it was over, hundreds were dead and 44,000 Europeans were forced to flee with what they could carry. In Katanga Province the moderate Moise Tshombe tried to establish a stable alternative government but was thwarted by Hammarskjöld who side-stepped the UN Charter and raced in 'non-aligned' troops to halt the secession and return Katanga to Lumumba's bloody clutches. The UN politely considered the Congo conflict an 'internal matter'.

Having orchestrated a genocide, Lumumba finally fell into the hands of troops controlled by Army Commander General Mobutu and was murdered. This prompted Hammarskjöld to describe his demise as "a revolting crime against the principles for which this organization stands".[34]

Furious about Lumumba's death ,the Secretary-General personally went to Katanga to oversee the deployment of UN troops and was killed when his aircraft hit a tree near Ndola, Northern Rhodesia in September 1961. Few in Africa mourned his passing while the Congo sank into disorder from which, half a century later, it has never recovered.

By now, seeing a colossal power vacuum mushrooming, the communist superpowers were aggressively recruiting and courting African nationalists while offering almost unconditional support to 'liberation movements' throughout the continent. Into their clutches fell a growing number of young Rhodesian blacks attracted by the promise of a new life in the Marxist motherlands, along with the exciting prospect of forging a new political dispensation in their homeland.

In October 1960, the Monckton Commission released a report suggesting the component territories of the Federation of Rhodesia and Nyasaland be allowed to secede as a prelude to gaining independence under governments elected through a universal franchise. It was the death knell of the Federation and a calamity for white Rhodesians.

At the same time, with political tensions growing, PK began his ascent to national politics through the RTA (Rhodesia Tobacco Association), which appointed him a representative to the Native Labour Commission. He also

---

[34] Paul Johnson: *A History of the Moderrn World*. Weidenfeld & Nicolson, 1984

struck up an important friendship with future Prime Minister, Winston Field, then leader of the Dominion Party.

In November 1960, Major Piet was back in the South African headlines when he involved himself in a public row with mining magnate Harry Oppenheimer. Oppenheimer's Progressive Party was emerging as a champion of a universal franchise and Major Piet accused the mining magnate of a political *volte face*. He quoted from a speech delivered by Oppenheimer in 1957 where he was forthright on the question of suffrage: "... the bulk of the native population has neither the education ... culture ... experience to fit it to take a sensible part in democratic processes ... and even if those difficulties were overcome ... there remains a very great risk that if they get political power they will use it not for the benefit of multiracial South Africa but for the benefit of an exclusive black nationalism."[35]. One of South Africa's richest men and long a beneficiary of cheap apartheid labour, the point of political opportunism was strongly made by the Major, which was deeply embarrassing to the Oppenheimer family.

By February 1961, Rhodesia was administered under a new constitution in which provision was made for a revised electoral formula allowing for 50 'A' Roll seats and 15 'B' Roll seats, together with a Bill of Rights. Technically the franchise was non-racial, being based on qualifications and means, but in reality the majority of 'A' Roll voters would be white. It was argued this would soon change as blacks became economically emancipated. Merit, not race, would be the final arbiter.

Prime Minister Edgar Whitehead argued, naively as it turned out, that acceptance of this constitution would lead to independence. British Commonwealth Secretary Duncan Sandys, addressing the Commons, concurred: "Apart from a few entirely formal matters we have found it possible to provide safeguards which will enable us to do away with all the powers at present reserved for the British government ... they are trifling, of an entirely formal constitutional type."[36]

---

[35] *Cape Times*, 19 December 1961

[36] Peter Joyce: *Anatomy of a Rebel*. Grahame Publishing, 1974

By virtually a 2:1 majority Whitehead received his mandate. Added credibility came when prominent Black Nationalist Joshua Nkomo, then leader of the National Democratic Party (NDP) threw his support behind the document. But optimism was soon dashed when the Commons White Paper on the Rhodesian Constitution was published and it emerged that the envisaged constitution actually increased the power of the Crown. To the shock and dismay of Southern Rhodesians, the Queen's representative would in fact have veto power over all legislation. Not for the first or last time, the Rhodesians felt they had been duped. "This," said PK, "was indicative of the total unreliability and duplicity of the British government. What they were saying was that the Federation was indissoluble."

There was more disappointment when Joshua Nkomo returned from a trip to London with a radically changed outlook. The Foreign Office mandarins had had their way; he now called for the constitution to be binned and advocated violent insurrection to overthrow white rule. (Subsequent revelations indicate that the Foreign Office included in its ranks a significant number of people who may have been taking orders from Moscow.)

At this point, PK and most of the Southern Rhodesian political establishment realized the Federation was finished and the British government simply couldn't be trusted. It was time to change tack, accept the new reality and apply their collective minds to salvaging the best possible deal for Southern Rhodesia. British MP Sir John Page remembers:

> The moment I felt the greatest shame in the Conservative Party was the day after Roy Welensky came to speak to the Foreign and Commonwealth Affairs Committee. When he got up he got a standing ovation, we banged the desks and he must have gone and thought, 'I have won over the whole of the Conservative Party.' About the next day … he had the carpet pulled from under him by Harold Macmillan and none of us made a bloody squeak. I said to someone, 'Isn't it ghastly, what we are doing to Rhodesia. Do you think everybody in the

Smoking Room is worried?' He said, 'Oh no, Jack, no one's thinking about Rhodesia.' On that second evening I sat on the back benches waiting for a 12 o'clock division or something with Lionel Heald, who had been a member of the Monckton Commission—Sir Albert [Robinson] knew him well. He was an old friend of mine and he said, 'Walter Monckton and the Monckton Commission agree that, if any of the three parts of the Federation should be given independence, all three should be. That was the deal.' And he said, 'I feel very ashamed and horrified by the fact that it didn't happen.'"

Back in South Africa, Major Piet remained in the thick of things, becoming embroiled in a war of words with liberal politician Colin Eglin who had accused him of adopting the Nationalists' *swart gevaar* (black danger) tactics of playing on white fears. Piet angrily denied this but went on to defend white civilization: "Civilized men bring to justice and punish members of their group who do not behave as civilized beings. But Black Nationalism will condone any act as long as the offender stands for Black Nationalism. Has any state in black Africa shown any desire to protect the rights of their minorities?" he asked.[37]

In March 1961, PK was on hand as best man to his friend Sir Thomas Pilkington, brother of Sonia Rogers, who married Susan Adamson at St. Agnes church in Kloof. He and Tommy would remain lifelong friends who shared a love of the outdoors. Two months later, South Africa became a republic with the swearing-in of Charles Swart as State President.

On 1 May 1961, Tanganyika became Tanzania under Julius Nyerere and immediately charted a radical course adopting Leninism and a one-party state, and embracing laws suppressing all basic human rights. Nyerere insisted this was a necessary prerequisite to defeating poverty. Afrophile academics in the West lined up to endorse him.

As a policy template the Arusha Declaration was framed and used to justify

---

[37] *Cape Argus*, February 1961

Tanzania's totalitarianism. Nyerere went on to claim the country was "at war" with Portugal owing to its presence in neighbouring Mozambique. Insisting "nobody was allowed to live off the efforts of others", he encouraged the arrest of "capitalists", leading to a purge on mainly Asian traders. Adding to the woes of his people a forced collectivization under the banner of *Ujaama* was imposed, resulting in widespread poverty and despair. In Zanzibar, despite a supposedly entrenched Bill of Rights inherited from the British, it was not long before Arabs and Asians were put to the sword and detention without trial became widespread.

In Rhodesia, on 17 November, an event of considerable significance took place when millionaire farmer and cattle baron Douglas 'Boss' Lilford invited Ian Smith, PK and some 80 people of various persuasions to a meeting in Salisbury. Sensing that a new political direction was needed, Lilford was happy to help with ideas and cash. As a result a new party, the Rhodesia Reform Party, was formed at this meeting and at its first congress in December declared the party leadership's intention to protect Rhodesia from one-man-one-vote. The speakers were unequivocal in the belief it would be a disaster for the white man and ultimately for the country. When Richard Harper and his Dominion Party joined, it became the Rhodesian Front and in March 1962, elected Winston Field, an affable and respected farmer, as leader. PK was an enthusiastic founder member.

Meanwhile, attempts to accommodate Nkomo and his followers turned to confrontation when troops were sent into the townships to suppress the terror raging out of control. This had continued for over a year, causing misery and mayhem to the urbanized Africans. When his NDP party was banned, Nkomo joined Ndabaningi Sithole to form ZAPU (Zimbabwe African People's Union), which would become an enduring force in the conflict ahead.

Early in 1962, with Katangese secessionists triggering more bloody violence in the Congo, Major Piet told a gathering of United Party loyalists that no handover to black people could be countenanced: "Unlike the whites, Chinese, Indians, Japanese and other non-European races who have created civilizations or produced new advances in human progress and discoveries, the Bantu has never created or developed anything himself," he said. He went on to say, "I am not against the Bantu, nor am I trying to belittle or speak contumely of them. As a people I have the greatest regard and respect for them and disapprove strongly of the National Party's treatment of them ..."

Later he raised more eyebrows when he postulated his idea that "an African Einstein would not necessarily be 'civilized'." This, he said, was a lengthy process that would take "centuries of cultural growth ... otherwise the veneer is too thin to contain the ferment and turmoil of barbaric aeons that lie behind."[38] Abroad, his views were not shared by literary luminary Susan Sontag, who wrote, "... the white race is the cancer of human history".

In the summer of 1962, Roy Welensky dissolved the Federal parliament and called for an early election in April. This one failed to materialize so another was called for in December which Edgar Whitehead was expected to win. What he hadn't anticipated was the massive voter swing to the right, as the politics of reason and appeasement had gone up in the smoke of the township fires. The new RF party won a shock majority of 35 'A' Roll seats and one of the 'new kids on the block' was PK, who was comfortably elected to represent the Hartley constituency.

On hearing his son had joined the parliamentary ranks, Major Piet's first comment was "How dreadful", but went on to flummox his questioners saying he was "very proud indeed" that his son had, for five years, held the world record for the biggest elephant ever shot (12ft. 6.5in). Asked about the similarity between the Rhodesian Front and the Afrikaner Nationalists, Major Piet was dismissive: "There is no similarity ... except that the Rhodesian Front also does not believe that power should be handed over, lock, stock and barrel to the Africans." Writing for the *Daily News* Africa Service at the time, Andrew Drysdale described PK as "well over six foot ... conspicuous by his elegance, the carefully creased tropical suit, high-standing stiff collar, monogrammed shirt and a carnation buttonhole. Yet

---

[38] *Evening Post*, 16 February 1962

his appearance and manner belie a rugged outdoor life in which big-game fishing and hunting are his main recreations."

Rubbing salt into fresh wounds, white Rhodesians could have had little doubt international opinion was against them when US Secretary of State Adlai Stevenson expressed the view that all whites in Africa were "settlers" who did not belong there and should make way for indigenous blacks. This remark immediately triggered the ire of Major Piet who, in a written rebuttal, reminded Stevenson (who he referred to as "the unctuous American") that his (Major Piet's) forebears had been in Africa longer than Mr. Stevenson's had been in America. He went on to make the point that the African population had more than doubled under white rule, while the aboriginal population of the US had declined dramatically. Stevenson offered no response but there was support in some United States conservative circles. William F. Buckley wrote in *Up From Liberalism*:

> We see in the revolt of the masses in Africa the mischief of the white man's abstractions: for the West has, by its doctrinaire approval of democracy, deprived itself of the moral base from which to talk back to the apologists of rampant nationalism. Democracy, to be successful, must be practised by politically mature people among whom there is a consensus on the meaning of life within their society … If the majority wills what is socially atavistic, then to thwart the majority may be the indicated, though concededly the undemocratic, course. It is more important for a community, wherever situated geographically, to affirm and live by civilized standards than to labour at the job of swelling the voting lists.

Buckley was comparing colonial Africa to the US's southern states prior to their Civil Rights legislation to make his point: "Does the vote really make one free? I do not believe it necessarily does … Being able to vote is no more to have realized freedom than being able to read is to have realized wisdom. Reasonable limitations upon the vote are not recommended exclusively by tyrants or oligarchs (was Jefferson either?). The problem of the South is not how to get the vote for the Negro, but how to train the Negro—and a great many whites—to cast a thoughtful vote."

But Buckley distanced himself from southern segregationists who opposed the black vote on genetic grounds. "There are no scientific grounds for assuming congenital Negro disabilities. The problem is not biological, but cultural and educational."

On 9 October 1962, Uganda became independent under Milton Obote. Following the pattern of Africa's hard men, Obote soon tired of the constitutional limitations on his power. A particular political nuisance was the Bugandan leader King Mutesa, whom he wished to be rid of. To help with this problem he recruited Idi Amin, a former British Army boxing champion given to violence. Mutesa survived an attack but fled into exile in the United Kingdom. Days after Mutesa's departure, President Kwame Nkrumah, Black Africa's founding father, fell from power in a military coup.

To the fury of many on the left, at the time PK was fond of quoting an article from the *Cape Argus* of 10 November 1962, which reinforced his view that Africa would be lost without white leadership. The Northern Rhodesian director of elections, Nalumino Mundia, had stated in a speech that, "This is the last deal we make with the white man. If he refuses to [support us] he forfeits his birthright and that of his offspring. Whites and Asians in Northern Rhodesia cannot be trusted."

Despite the uncertain future of Crown subjects, then British Minister of State, R.A.B. Butler, despite earlier assurances to the contrary, approved the secession of Nyasaland and Northern Rhodesia late in 1962. The fate of Southern Rhodesia was ignored and the colony left in limbo.

Later that year PK returned to Fairfield to spend time with his parents. In an article in *The Argus* on 22 December, a staff reporter commended father and son on the "enormous amount of work both had done on Fairfield to preserve the indigenous fauna", adding that both men "have introduced new birds and animals to the district and both have hunted big game".

By this time, PK owned three farms, having 300 acres under tobacco on his Selous farm. This made him one of the biggest, if not necessarily most successful, growers in the country. Known as the Selous Tobacco Estate, his manager was Nick Prilieux. While PK's farming credentials remained open to question, his father remained a champion farmer receiving record prices for 362 bales of wool sold in Cape Town. Experts said the 'Fairfield clip' was the finest and largest to be offered for sale. In November, Major Piet was offered the chairmanship of Old Mutual but turned it down insisting that his parliamentary constituents would suffer.

In January 1963 Winston Field took the office of Prime Minister without ever having made a speech in the chamber. The apparent beneficiary of an 'anyone but Whitehead' vote, his charm, courteousness and common decency still could not save him. The party hard-liners were not impressed with his release of detainees and the inviting of Joshua Nkomo back into mainstream politics. Men like Smith, Harper and PK van der Byl were equally unhappy with his accommodating stance on Britain.

In an interview at the time with the *Daily News,* Field, rather naively as it would turn out, was adamant that Black Nationalism would burn itself out:

> While I want to see the African improve his lot, I do not believe in handing over complete political power to them; not now nor in the foreseeable future. This does not imply that I am against the 14 African MPs in the Southern Rhodesia House … [But on Black Nationalism] I am absolutely against it. It is something that has been hurling itself against us but I have the fundamental belief that there has never been a force in human history that has been able to retain its power and momentum forever. I am quite certain that this will happen to African Nationalism. Some of the heat will be turned off us here just as has happened in South Africa. From every point of view we must resist pan-African nationalism. It is whipped up and used as a tool. The rewards to those running it are very great indeed, but it has nothing to offer the people as a whole.

White Rhodesians were again outraged when an under-prepared Nyasaland was handed independence on 1 February 1963. Hastings Banda, a 67-year-old British-trained doctor, returned home to lead it to self-rule. Two years later he declared Malawi a republic, a one-party state and himself president for life. Although a prototype African dictator, he was pro-West and maintained close links with white Africa, earning disapproval among his peers. He finally relinquished power in 1993 at 97 and died four years later, leaving Malawi impoverished.

In June 1963, Field attended a Federation dissolution conference, believing Butler's assurances that participation virtually guaranteed independence. Some in his party wanted to boycott the meeting, believing the British to be temporizing but Field wished to be there to ensure legal formalities were followed. The doubters were vindicated when Butler later denied giving any of the assurances Field insisted he had received.

In August Ndabaningi Sithole, disillusioned with Nkomo's leadership, formed his ZANU (Zimbabwe African National Union) party, which would grow into a terrifying liberation army. Soon internecine fighting broke out in the townships as rival parties fought bloody turf wars.

"I was chairman of the parliamentary caucus on foreign affairs at the time," recalls PK, "and I called the committee together to express my concern that the incumbent Conservative government in Britain might soon be replaced by a Labour one which would be less sympathetic to us in Rhodesia. I suggested we meet the British and accept everything they asked of us, short of an immediate handover to black rule, and in about 18 months' time, go to Victoria Falls, tear it up and drop it down the Devil's Cataract. My listeners were shocked. We were all simple God-fearing colonials and this idea of mine was considered so outrageous my colleagues began to wonder if there was in fact a place for me in the Rhodesian Front, which they insisted be based on honesty and upright behaviour. The sort of chicanery I was advocating was anathema. A few months later I was in London and my Conservative friends, people like Julian Amery, Patrick Wall, Airey Neave and Lord Salisbury, were of exactly the same view as me. My view was that the British do this sort of thing all the time, so why not us?"

Later, an entertaining parliamentary exchange at PK's expense had Mr. J.R. Nicholson, UFP for Salisbury City, implying dilettantism: "If he will give me the name and address of a good tailor," said Nicholson, "I, for my part, will give him the name and address of a good economist."

Also in 1963, PK announced his engagement to Sonia Pilkington, which was later cancelled. Subsequent events were to bring another woman across his path who would play a big role in his life.

December 1963 was an eventful month: on the 12th, Kenya attained its independence, President Kennedy was assassinated on the 22nd and on the 31st the Federation of Rhodesia and Nyasaland was dissolved.

Following the break-up of the Federation, Marge Bassett, who had been employed for ten years in the Southern Rhodesian and Federal Civil Services, was shunted along the wide corridor in Milton Building, from the defunct Federal Ministry of Home Affairs to the (now Rhodesian) Department of Information.

Meanwhile, South Africa was also experiencing problems with British politicians when Labour MPs called for a boycott of South Africa over the proposed 90-day detention legislation designed to deal primarily with black militants. Major Piet asked why these same English politicians failed to censure Nkrumah over Ghana's indefinite detention policy, but no reply was forthcoming.

Elsewhere in Africa, bizarre governance became the norm. Julius Nyerere survived a coup early in 1964 thanks to British military intervention by Royal Marines, who found him hiding under a table. Back on his feet, he resumed the persecution of his people while his vilified ex-colonial masters looked on. But as far as the 'white south' was concerned, he was, as ever, quick to condemn Rhodesia's and South Africa's record on human rights and democracy.

In February 1964, with violence growing, Winston Field finally banned political meetings and detained several nationalist leaders, but confidence in his leadership had evaporated and on 9 April the RF caucus asked for his resignation.

The stage was set for Ian Smith.

CHAPTER SEVEN
Smith takes control

Marge Bassett remembers:

In March 1964, Mr. van der Byl was promoted by Mr. Winston Field to the front bench and appointed Parliamentary Secretary for Information to Mr. Clifford Dupont, then Minister of Law and Order.

On joining the Department of Information, he was given the vacant office next to mine and I was informed that I should carry out the necessary secretarial duties for him until such time as a 'proper' secretary could be officially appointed. (As a married woman with a child under the age of ten, I was not considered eligible for the position since it involved a considerable amount of overtime during evening parliamentary sessions.)

The post was duly advertised in a Public Services Board circular but no completely suitable applicant responded. This happened several times and the months went by. The post was still vacant when 'Minister' was taken ill at his house in Bath Road, Avondale. On one of my visits to receive his instructions on various outstanding urgent matters, he suddenly asked, "You enjoy your work, don't you?" When I replied that I loved it, he said, "Well then, let's not waste any more time. Let's get the Board to appoint you officially to the position!"

I was thrilled. It was the beginning of a long and terribly enjoyable association. He was wonderful to work for—demanding but appreciative. Never petty, he could always see the big picture. I respected him enormously and was always impressed with his command of the language when dictating from a few rough notes. He was basically a man who thrived in the open air; he was, after all, a farmer and a hunter who enjoyed interacting with people, but found being tied to a desk, dealing with papers, irksome.

"Marge was a legend in her own right," says Lin Mehmel. "The perfect minister's secretary: formally correct, always the immaculate introduction when ushering someone in to see 'Minister'. Incredibly efficient; I have no doubt without her PK would have been lost. She had a fantastic memory and was always there for PK when it came to remembering names and details."

On 13 April, the course of Rhodesian history changed when Ian Smith became Prime Minister charged with securing independence, restoring order to the townships and steadying jittery white morale. He quickly jailed Joshua Nkomo, whom he had identified as a primary source of trouble, in Gonakudzingwa, a detention camp in the remote southeast of the country. "It was a horrible place," reported Nkomo later. "The lions were just outside so we were always frightened of being eaten."

With excitement running high, many expected Smith to declare independence immediately and fearing this eventuality, British troops were placed on alert in Aden.

Instead he addressed the nation in measured terms: "No one in the British government, including Harold Wilson the Prime Minister, disputes the fact that Rhodesia is better governed and better prepared for independence than any other in Africa, but they insist on a transfer to black majority rule. This we fear will lead to the destruction of our country and all we have worked so hard to build.

Bear in mind that a report published by none other than the United Nations certifies that we in Rhodesia provide education for more of our people than any other country in Latin America and Africa. It is also a matter of fact that the black population of this country has increased tenfold in three generations."[39] Both Smith and PK would make these points repeatedly in the years ahead, but their entreaties would be generally ignored.

Typically cautious, Smith said he would proceed carefully but hinted the prospects for early settlement were gloomy. He insisted the 1961 constitution must be the basis for any final settlement, and not London's preference for immediate black rule. To gauge the country's mood he embarked on a countywide tour and found the majority happy to let him lead.

On a visit to South Africa shortly thereafter the press confronted PK about militant black nationalist arrests which had upset the English-speaking press. Irritated, he waved them away saying, "There had been no more arrests [in Rhodesia] than on an average night in Soho", and walked off.

"PK was like a chameleon with the television press in particular," remembers Lin Mehmel. "He would often change tack to suit the occasion and confuse many journalists. He could appear to be expounding lengthily on any given subject and at the end of it you would realize he had told you nothing. He would keep his cards close to his chest."

---

[39] It is interesting to note an excerpt from a review by John Robertson, a highly regarded Zimbabwean economist, of a book by Gideon Gono, the present governor of the Zimbabwe Reserve Bank who is generally considered one of the leading architects of the country's economic destruction. "Gono claims: 'The country perspired under the gruelling yoke of colonialism for close to one full century. Before attaining political independence in 1980, the country went through a bloody armed struggle, as the impoverished indigenous population resisted, and fought and won over colonial forces.' From this, he goes on to describe the many reasons why colonial distortions called for the adoption of unconventional measures. However, it is the carefully overlooked distortions that have emerged since independence in 1980 that are very much more in need of attention. Today, the population is more impoverished than it ever was during the colonial era, and as for the 'gruelling yoke', all the evidence suggests that the colonial authorities were never as harsh on the population as ZANU-PF is today. The colonial era created the most diversified economy and the best education and health services of any country in Africa. The result was one of the most developed of all the Third World's countries. As for the 'bloody armed struggle', this was sponsored and funded by the USSR and Communist China for their own ends. One day, an accurate history will show that indigenous people opposed the incursions in numbers that greatly exceeded the total of the so-called 'colonial whites'. It is perhaps for this reason that ZANU-PF has recently passed legislation prohibiting any possibility that any other political party might obtain support from abroad, the way its supporters did."

In return for support in Field's expulsion, Smith, recognizing a loyal lieutenant, appointed PK Deputy Minister for Information. As an early recruit to the 'information cause', PK recruited the controversial anti-communist Ivor Benson. There was a meeting of minds and together they expounded on the relationship between the Communists and the liberation movements.

PK quickly identified the BBC as Rhodesia's main enemy in the international media and suggested press restrictions might be necessary.

His relationship with the local media was no less fraught. He demanded responsibility of the editorial staff because "Rhodesia," in his view, "was in the frontline of the African struggle". Later that year South Africa was absorbed in the trial of Nelson Mandela that ended with his conviction and imprisonment after admitting acts of sabotage. He would remain in prison for 27 years.

In June 1964, PK spoke to the South African press on a visit to Fairfield. He insisted Rhodesians were loyal to the Queen despite the fact they "had precious little to show for it". He suggested Rhodesia had effectively taken the heat off South Africa because it was seen "as an easier nut to crack but they will find we are not".

In late June, Joy visited PK in Rhodesia. Talking to the *Rhodesia Herald*, describing herself as a "Victorian", she lamented the passing of time: "It may be a very interesting time in which to live but I think I would rather have lived in a more peaceful one."

"Joy was not everyone's cup of tea," recalls Lin Mehmel, "but I thoroughly enjoyed her company. She could mix the meanest martini which she would always offer before lunch and she always travelled with her own 'Noilly' and selected gin. She had no sense of humour and PK played on this. Knowing she hated trophy heads he would festoon his dining room with all these wild beasts prior to her arrival. This irritated her no end and he loved it."

Addressing the legislature in August 1964 with his father, Major Piet, in the audience, PK defended his stand against the BBC: "To suggest that the BBC, forming opinion in the minds of the people of England, has been an influence for good in any way, when you consider the criminality of large areas of London; when you consider the 'Mods and Rockers' and all those other things; when you consider the total moral underminings which have been taking place in England, much to all our distress, in the last 15 to 20 years, the Honourable Member can hardly bring that up as an argument in favour of the freedom of broadcasting."

Supporting his son, Major Piet said it was wrong for commentators to compare RF policies to those of the Afrikaner Nationalists, but assured Rhodesians, "The basic characteristics of our peoples [South Africans and Rhodesians] are very much alike. We are blood brothers." He also paid tribute to his son's oratory skills: "He is a better speaker than me; he speaks without notes."

In September 1964, with political violence spreading in the townships, Smith finally flew to London for talks with Alec Douglas-Home. His mission had the support of tribal chiefs but Home needed broader approval from the Rhodesian population. Despite this, Smith appeared upbeat on the BBC. He announced his agreement to provide evidence of majority support for the 1961 constitution and a modified franchise. UDI (Unilateral Declaration of Independence) was put on hold and spirits at home and abroad lifted.

On 16 October, Labour won the general election and Smith faced a new and wily opponent in Harold Wilson. Wilson said he desired an amicable settlement but majority rule was non-negotiable. Smith turned to his electorate and urged them to brace themselves. Wilson further warned Rhodesian whites to expect sanctions, abandonment, citizenship-stripping, non-recognition and expulsion from the Commonwealth should UDI be declared. The Rhodesian premier took it as serious provocation when Wilson wrote to a prominent black nationalist assuring him Britain remained implacably opposed to independence under white rule.

In late September, PK had a stormy parliamentary exchange with A.E. Abrahamson (RP), who called PK's adviser Ivor Benson "a Moseleyite with all that implies in its connections with Nazism", accusing Benson of "wandering around the Congo with a rifle shooting people". Responding,

PK accused Abrahamson of currying favour with black people to protect his business interests in what was soon to become Zambia. He went on to offer Abrahamson a deal: "If he is prepared to stop telling fabrications about members of my staff I will stop telling the truth about him."[40] The opposition responded by calling for PK's annual salary of £2,250 to be reduced by half. Roger Nicholson, the RP MP for Salisbury City, called him an "iceberg", adding that "more than half of what he does is concealed".

On 11 October 1964, the *Sunday Mail*'s 'Ajax' column offered the following on PK: "The parliamentary Secretary for Information hides beneath a somewhat supercilious expression of personal warmth and charm which he only reveals when he is sure of himself or among friends. It is a pity that a man so gracious on social occasions seems to believe in his public capacity that good manners are bad politics."

On 15 October, PK flew to Lisbon to meet his Portuguese counterpart before spending two weeks in London, Madrid and Paris. In France he met cabinet colleague George Rudland and Jean-François Poncet of the French-Africa Department, along with members of the French National Assembly. Ever the provocateur, PK spoke to Gavin Young of *The Scotsman*, claiming American researchers had proved a difference in the brain size between Africans and Europeans. He also agonized about Africa's population growth, calling Africans "indefatigable breeders" likely to double Rhodesia's population every 20 years. In a later *Citizen* interview he claimed the majority of British people were horrified by Harold Wilson's ultimatum on black majority rule.

Stormy political weather appeared across the Zambezi on 24 October 1964, when Northern Rhodesia became Zambia under former schoolteacher Kenneth Kaunda. Establishing his credentials, he soon sent the army to the Northern Province to crush a suspected uprising among Lumpa Church members. Thought to be colluding with residual white leaders, 1,500 people were killed and thousands chased into neighbouring Congo. The church, led by Alice Lenshina, was banned and a State of

---

[40] *The Chronicle*, 4 September 1964

Emergency declared. Rhodesians looked on in horror, blaming Whitehall for its credulous approach to African politics. In 1968 Kaunda banned all opposition and in 1972 declared a one-party state with himself virtual dictator. At independence he inherited an economy larger than South Korea's. When he left 27 years later, it was one per cent of the size.

By the end of the year, PK had tightened broadcasting rules, although the mainstream print media still refused to carry official government news. PK lamented the fact that "the editor of the *Rhodesia Herald* is strongly opposed to press control, yet he insists on exercising control over the Prime Minister's speeches". He explained his ministry's aim was "not merely to disseminate information from an interesting point of view but to win the propaganda battle". Propaganda he described as, "the propagation of the faith and belief in any particular ideology or thing". His department, he went on to explain, would also seek to "resuscitate the Europeans rights of survival".

A measure of calm had returned to the townships by year's end as a result of firmer police action, the proscription of ZANU and ZAPU and the banning of the inflammatory *Daily News* but few in the country believed their problems were over.

On 24 January 1965, Winston Churchill died and Ian Smith attended the funeral in London. Despite their growing antipathy he met Harold Wilson in what proved a cordial exchange but the Foreign Office knives were out. Smith was unaware he had been invited by the Queen to a luncheon of Commonwealth leaders at Buckingham Palace, as Wilson's people stealthily withheld the invitation. To their chagrin the Queen noticed the Rhodesian's absence and an aide was immediately sent to his hotel to set matters right. To the dismay of Wilson and his lieutenants, Smith joined the luncheon and was warmly welcomed by the monarch. Before leaving London, Smith reluctantly agreed to Wilson's request to have Commonwealth Secretary Arthur Bottomley visit the country to assess public opinion. Robert Salisbury remembers:

He came to see my grandfather after the funeral of Winston Churchill and they went for a long walk in the garden. He came inside after Ian Smith had left and said he had done his best to dissuade him but to no avail. He said, 'He's going to do it … he's going to declare independence unilaterally. I can't convince him otherwise.' Ian Smith was a straight and honourable man possessed of enormous conviction and strength of purpose but he was horribly in the wrong in my view. He should have left things as they were. PK then became friendly with my parents. Initially they did not take to him but then became very fond of him. Then later PK and Richard, my brother became very good friends.

At the end of February, Bottomley arrived in Rhodesia. He met the chiefs who told him they were the real leaders of the African people, that they supported the 1961 constitution and that he should ignore the radical nationalists. Although this seemed to be the majority view, Bottomley was shaken when he visited Nkomo at Gonakudzingwa and listened to him demand immediate power.

PK accompanied him on the trip and was reportedly displeased with Bottomley's accommodating stance. At a later meeting with farmers, one attendee likened Bottomley's visit to "talking to a brick wall". While no convert to the Rhodesian cause he nonetheless left with a changed view later reflected in London's softer line. Wilson told Smith he would not insist on power being transferred to those who have not served "a political apprenticeship", and affirmed his wish to oversee "a peaceful transition to majority rule".

In a letter to the *Cape Argus*, Major Piet van der Byl sniped at Bottomley's earlier remarks where he questioned the patriotism of Rhodesian cabinet ministers: "What right had this man Bottomley to question the patriotism of the Rhodesian cabinet ministers? While many of them were fighting for the Commonwealth he was sitting in the House of Commons on the first two syllables of his name."

Tackled by Clyde Sanger for banning the *African Daily News* and sacking anti-government broadcaster John Apelleby, PK denied there was censorship in the country "apart from religious books that show intolerance and pornography ... especially if it's dull".

The next day, when he and Ian Smith were glad-handing 1,500 rugby supporters at a Hartley 'braai and beer' function, Smith strongly hinted his junior minister was heading for the cabinet. Delivering part of his address in Afrikaans, PK delighted the Afrikaans press in South Africa, but drew heavy fire from the opposition's Roger Nicholson who insisted using the language of the south was unpatriotic.

On 31 March 1965, the Rhodesian parliament was dissolved.

By 7 May 1965, when Ian Smith decided to call early elections, PK had become a popular and able policy campaigner. He aggressively championed unilateral independence in the event of continued British recalcitrance and criticized big business for their caution on the issue. He warned of the distortions their financial power would have on the popular will and went so far as to compare the situation to Nazi Germany and Bolshevik Russia where industrial conglomerates and European financiers had underwritten revolutions. He insisted Rhodesia could not drift endlessly and was convinced sanctions would be a temporary problem.

"Do we remain Rhodesia by uniting and standing firm to save our country? Or do we become Zimbabwe and go the way of other countries to the north of us?"[41]

In the election that followed, the RF won all 50 white seats. Studying the wreckage the opposition had become, Smith's *bête noir*, the local press, lamented "the end of an era", adding: "The tradition of a liberal multiracial Rhodesia has been shattered. Uncompromising white supremacy, hitherto held at the Limpopo has advanced right up to the Zambezi. After the 1962 elections there may still have been a glimmer of hope for the liberals. Even that has been shattered. For the Rhodesia Party this is 'In Memoriam Week', with the electorate digging the grave and Mr. David Butler now

---

[41] Peter Joyce: *Anatomy of a Rebel.* Grahame Publishing, 1974

called upon to deliver the funeral oration." It was clear that Ian Smith, the 'simple farmer', had shrewdly judged the national mood and was in almost total control. Very much at his side now was the man from Fairfield, riding the same populist wave.

CHAPTER EIGHT
UDI

In mid-1965, in an alarming harbinger of what was to come, nine heavily armed ZAPU saboteurs were arrested in the southeast of the country on information supplied by local Africans. Under direction from Lusaka their arrival forewarned grim times for rural Rhodesia.

Following a visit to Salisbury in July by Secretary of State Cledwyn Hughes five near-impossible preconditions were tabled by London "before independence could be contemplated". It seemed to Rhodesians that Britain had been unduly influenced by trenchant criticism at the recent Commonwealth Conference where Rhodesia was prominent on the agenda and the government heavily criticized.

Edging toward isolation, Smith believed the country shared his survival strategy, which was to hunker down and tough it out. He reasoned the unsophisticated black population needed easing into governance and relentlessly argued the Rhodesians had been governing themselves since 1923. Why should they suddenly defer to Westminster, he asked. Hard as he tried, Smith could not get the British to understand that, unlike the essentially 'British' whites of Kenya, Rhodesians were Rhodesians first and British second. If Wilson and his men understood this, they found the sentiment offensive and rejected it.

On 12 September 1965, PK was guest of honour at Hartley's gold-centenary celebrations. Addressing over 300 people to mark the discovery of gold in the area, he lamented the passing of old values "which had been thrown to the wolves". He asked the audience to "remember the old hunters and prospectors who were prepared to face immense hardship in order to found the country. Motivated by the idea of spreading what was then the British Empire they brought with them values of justice and good governance". Controversially, he suggested Henry Hartley may have discovered the Victoria Falls before Livingstone, drawing instant applause. Urging all to embrace the pioneer spirit, PK foretold that the country stood "on the threshold of true and complete nationhood".

In September 1965, he flew to Europe for a six-week, seven-nation tour to put forward Rhodesia's case. At the same time, 40 Labour MPs called for the immediate use of force if the Rhodesian government declared UDI.

On 4 October, with tensions running high, Smith flew to London. He tried to put a positive face on his mission but most insiders knew it was doomed. On arrival it was made clear to him that all the great powers, the Commonwealth and even the Tory opposition, would not support UDI. The gauntlet was down but Smith remained defiant. "Nobody pushes me around," he said.

The discussions were protracted and inconclusive, leaving both leaders exasperated. Eventually Smith suggested maintenance of the status quo, which surprised Wilson but was also rejected. He again reminded Smith that transfer to black rule was the only objective of the British government. He also warned grimly that the military option was available to him. Smith recalled staring blankly into the eyes of the prime minister of the country he had so recently risked his life to defend:

On more than one occasion Wilson implored me to appreciate the wonders of being English. It was simply beyond his comprehension that we did not want to be English and fully integrated into their establishment. The fact that we actually preferred to be Rhodesians was seen as an outrageous affront. Sometimes, looking back, I think that, for the British political class, this attitude of ours was the biggest insult of them all. They worked on the assumption that everyone essentially lived with a craven desire to be English. That we did not have this compulsion caused them enormous anger and may have been the major cause of the bitter vindictiveness they would soon visit upon us.

When the talks deadlocked, Wilson furiously went public. In response Smith put his case so convincingly on British television that Downing Street ordered a subsequent interview with the Rhodesian premier on the BBC cancelled. Smith returned to Salisbury on 9 October, convinced he was out of options.

After his return, with tempers frayed, Wilson suggested a visit to Salisbury by Commonwealth leaders but this was rejected by Smith who knew the visitors had already made up their minds and that Wilson was simply playing for time. Gathering his thoughts he wrote to Wilson on 18 October, expressing serious doubts about Britain's sincerity in its pursuit of a settlement. With time running out, Wilson decided to visit to Salisbury himself on 25 October.

Summing up the mood at a meeting the following day, Smith made it clear that one group, the British, were playing with their "political lives", while the other, the Rhodesians, were playing with "their lives". Wilson listened but gave little away. He wanted to see for himself.

The next day he met a cross section of people from judges to black MPs and chiefs. Following his meeting with the chiefs, it was a visibly annoyed Smith who listened to Wilson express delight at the "colour" they brought to the proceedings, but rejected with a dollop of contempt their representative status. This was followed by drama when detainees Sithole and Nkomo were brought under guard to see Wilson. On learning they had not eaten that morning, he became furious and threatened to take the two leaders across the street for lunch, which embarrassed the custodial authorities into hurriedly providing food. Enjoying the moment the nationalists then loudly exhorted Wilson to use force immediately to bring about majority rule and install them in power.

They had strong support in this view from Michael Ramsay, Archbishop of Canterbury, who emerged as a vocal supporter of war against Smith. PK was outraged. "Certainly none of us in Rhodesia who 20 years ago fought with Britain against the common foe could ever have foreseen a time when the Primate of All England would publicly support the dispatch of our former comrades in arms to shoot down their kith and kin."

PK later explained that the Archbishop had demanded the RAF bomb Salisbury without delay. "At this time, the BBC asked me if I would go on television with the Archbishop and I said yes, but on one condition: that it is broadcast live because otherwise I knew they would tilt in favour of Ramsay. Needless to say he declined to appear."

Upping the ante, Wilson next insisted any agreement required not only total black support but also ratification by the majority of the British Labour Party. He further proposed the formation of a Royal Commission and Ian Smith was seen shaking his head in exasperation. The talks ended inconclusively. In another provocative gesture Wilson stopped off in Zambia and Ghana on his way home, showing solidarity with Kaunda and Nkrumah. Wilson genuinely believed sanctions would work within weeks should Smith's government act illegally. This was clearly as big a blunder as Smith's in believing they would be brief and ineffectual.

On 3 November, Wilson told the Commons that the gap between the two sides was unbridgeable and even if the majority of Rhodesians supported the settlement, he reserved the right to determine what would finally apply. This was the final straw for Smith, who declared a State of Emergency two days later.

PK flew home from Europe warning of the BBC's "total onslaught against Rhodesia", while criticizing their refusal to give Smith air time. On the evening of 10 November, British High Commissioner Skeen delivered a confusing and irrelevant verbal message to Smith. Smith and his cabinet later decided that on the morrow, 11 November, the declaration would be made. Much deliberation went into the wording of the document. It was eventually left to Messrs. Rudland, Ross, Williams and van der Byl, together with a calligrapher, to fashion the declaration. PK insisted on including the words: "To us has been given the privilege of being the first Western nation in two centuries to have the determination and fortitude to say—so far and no further." His paean to his adopted country would soon arouse strong emotions.

At around 9.00 a.m., Harold Wilson phoned Salisbury. He pleaded with Smith to act with restraint and resist those "with the bit between their teeth". Smith listened but was tired, distant and uncooperative. The fact remained: Wilson still insisted on a British veto no matter what.

At 10.00 a.m., Smith, his ministers and deputies gathered in the Phoenix Room in Milton Buildings to sign the declaration. The last time any such event had occurred was on 4 July 1776, in Philadelphia. PK would find himself with an indelible place in history and an enthusiastic signatory, but being a deputy minister, as a witness only.

The prominent Rhodesia historian Richard Wood says that the declaration had been planned for the day before. However, the rebel government, hoping for a last-minute concession from Britain, held back the formal announcement for 24 hours. The resulting coincidence between Armistice and UDI enabled the Rhodesian government to ambiguously claim that their act of rebellion was aimed, not so much at the Crown, but at Harold Wilson's Labour government. The fact that it was also his birthday was pleasing to PK.

Smith used his regular lunchtime newscast to break the news to the country's 225,000 whites and several million blacks. In words echoing the American 1776 declaration, he set out the case for independence, stressing the patience of Rhodesians in the face of Labour treachery.

Unsurprisingly, the broadcast was not well received elsewhere, and that included Pretoria where many had hoped that Rhodesia, as an alternative option, might even be absorbed into South Africa as a fifth province. "I asked PK if he had any regrets about UDI," recalls Lotti, "but he did not in a fundamental sense. He said they had to do something. It was just after the Congo debacle and the white Rhodesians were nervous. They had heard all about what had happened to the Belgians in the Congo and the stories were ghastly. Any suggestion of a transfer of power to the black majority might have triggered a mass emigration of skilled whites and this, he was certain, the country could not afford. He felt they had to do something to buy time."

Although viewed abroad as an aberrant act by a few reckless politicians, many Rhodesians, no matter their political persuasion, bought into UDI if only as the lesser of two evils. It was their home and their options appeared limited, if not non-existent.

So began an era of self-reliance, self-belief, industrial growth and unity in adversity. This new brashness of spirit was generally misinterpreted as a form of nonconformist frontier racism. "We honestly believed we were doing the right thing for our country," recalls Angus Graham, "and for all its people, white and black, and retaining a piece of the old Empire in the hands of people and a government that would always be loyal to the 'Old Country' as represented by HM The Queen, not to certain politicians who were known to have joined heartily in singing The Red Flag, people who in 35 years had reduced a great and justifiably proud Empire and nation to a third-rate power. Now we were trying to save one corner of it from the same fate. They hated us and called us traitors. So UDI it was to be."

On the subject, Mukui Waruiru writes:

> Ian Douglas Smith, the former Prime Minister of Rhodesia, can be rightly regarded as Africa's first classical liberal revolutionary. In 1965, he led a revolution for freedom, when he initiated the Unilateral Declaration of Independence (UDI) of Rhodesia from Britain. The UDI was intended to preserve Christianity, freedom, and civilization. For that courageous action, Smith became one of the most vilified men in history, and his country was subjected to comprehensive United Nations economic sanctions in 1966. He was falsely labelled a racist and white supremacist. But, unlike the architects of apartheid in neighbouring South Africa, he has never supported claims that blacks are inherently inferior. However, like Buckley, Smith recognized that the low levels of education and cultural development of most of the blacks made the establishment of a successful pure democracy a difficult undertaking.

Following Smith's declaration, Governor Humphrey Gibbs went through the motions of dismissing Smith and his cabinet, which was predictably ignored. Harold Wilson, addressing the Commons, spoke of the philosophical gulf between the two governments. Part of this was Labour 'class war': white Rhodesians were considered cocky, elitist, old establishment; everything they hated. He deemed the Rhodesian government illegal, recalled London's High Commissioner and announced a raft of punitive financial and economic measures, including a ban on Rhodesian agricultural produce. He also warned members of the Rhodesian security forces not to serve the illegal administration.

The dispute was soon referred to the UN Security Council by the British government, which escalated the crisis by increasing pressure, but frustrated future negotiations because Wilson henceforth needed to ratify everything through the UN.

Although UDI was universally condemned, Smith had unexpected support from the then Marquess of Salisbury[42] who applauded his honesty and reminded the world that Rhodesians had recently witnessed the gruesome events in the Congo. While not endorsing UDI, he urged empathy, but his appeal was ignored.

Swaggering into the fray, a hastily convened OAU (Organization of African Unity) conference resolved to topple the Rhodesian government by force, but was silent on how exactly it was likely to achieve this. Numerous UN member states endorsed this view and offered support.

Those abroad hoping for an early black uprising in Rhodesia were disappointed. PK reported "… there has not been a single incident. The Police Reserve has not been called out nor has the Territorial Army been mobilized." Later he would recount how "people who had been planning on leaving because of the uncertainty, decided [now that UDI had been declared] to stay. They were not prepared to hand over to the extravagant demands of the African Nationalists. Chaos reigned to the north but this was purposefully ignored by all our detractors who did not have to worry about the consequences of their actions."

Foreign reporters noted that despite the "unfolding international crises, only one police constable and a solitary African soldier guarded Smith's residence". Talking to the *Rand Daily Mail*, PK was in a

---

[42] The 6th Marquess of Salisbury

jocular mood, suggesting a new Rhodesian motto might be, "Dig in for victory with a Spartan diet of meat and *mielie pap* [maize meal]".

On 18 December, Smith confirmed that Gibbs's status as governor had been revoked, but made it clear "that one thing I will not be party to is doing anything that will embarrass this gentleman in the unfortunate situation he finds himself".

The British press, meanwhile, queried PK's membership of the Cavalry Club and what action might be taken against 'rebel' members. "None; it is a perfectly internal matter," advised the secretary.

"The Cavalry Club stayed loyal," says Lin Mehmel, "but there was concern during UDI about some of his friends from there. Many travelled to Rhodesia and some stayed and most were fiercely loyal to the British Government. We were worried that PK might be trapped in some way. They liked PK, not Rhodesia's stand … Weekends away with his ex-British army chums were always of concern to us. Tape recorders were hidden, with willing ladies forming part of the fun, so there was always the chance of him being compromised. The John Profumo affair was then a recent memory … Having said that, PK loved debate, discussion and controversy. He sometimes used his time with people not necessarily to convert them, but to bait and irritate them in cold calculated discussion."

On 19 December, the Security Council voted unanimously for harsh and comprehensive sanctions while hysterical OAU members threatened to sever diplomatic relations with London if the rebellion was not crushed immediately.

What happened next has only recently been released under the British 30-year rule releasing previously confidential state documentation to the public. Contained herein, source unknown, is the following information:

> Initial deployment was by No. 51 (Rifle) Squadron of the RAF Regiment to secure the airfield at Ndola, in November 1965. This was then established as a logistics 'air head', and joint force HQ. No. 29 with 16 Javelin all-weather fighters subsequently arrived, along with L/70 40mm Bofors guns

and Tigercat missiles.[43] The role of 29 Squadron was to protect Zambian airspace, and specifically the oil air bridge into the country. They frequently flew parallel flights along the Zambian border with RRAF Canberras on the other. It was not a happy venture: two gunners of 51 Squadron deserted to Rhodesia. They were subsequently recruited as trainee firemen on the railways. There were a number of disciplinary incidents involving army and RAF personnel in Zambia, these concerning their doubts about the potential of active service against 'their kith and kin'. In December 1965, a company group of the 1st Battalion, the Gloucestershire Regiment was airlifted to Bechuanaland to guard the BBC broadcasting station. This station commenced a propaganda campaign against the Salisbury regime. An old friend who was serving in the revamped 'C' Squadron at the time has stated that the unit did 'war game' operations to role-play the destruction of the transmitter and towers. This small garrison was reinforced by a logistical element that had war stocks of vehicles and ammunition, and necessary stores and spares for two infantry battalions brought from the British stores depots in Kenya. This commitment ceased in August 1967 on the creation of the nation of Botswana. All stores, vehicles (including Ferret scout cars) and equipment were handed over to the new Botswana Defence Force. An invasion of Rhodesia was at a very high level of planning in 1966. This was to involve the use of 3rd Division (the army's Strategic Reserve) as the main part of the invasion force. Using 16th Parachute Brigade, and 5th and 19th Airportable Infantry Brigades, and the Parachute Battalion Group from Bahrain. The Royal Navy was to provide a task force in the Beira Straits using the aircraft carriers HMS

---

[43] This deployment provided some embarrassment when the fighters were unable to vector on Ndola and 'enemy' Rhodesian air-traffic controllers assisted them in making a safe landing.

Eagle and *Centaur*, with Buccaneer strike aircraft and Sea Vixen fighters, with Scimitar aircraft supplying air-refuelling (both vessels air squadrons had been reinforced). HMS *Bulwark* and *Albion* (both commando carriers) were to deploy each a Royal Marine Commando and its support Wessex helicopter squadron (total of 28 aircraft) ashore at Mtwara in Tanzania. With the troops and their vehicles then being airlifted by RAF *Argosy* and *Beverley* transports to Livingstone in Zambia, the helicopters were then to self-deploy through Malawi and Zambia; the intention being to deploy the three parachute battalions and support units, four infantry battalions (19th Brigade, and the third 16th Brigade infantry battalion) and an armoured reconnaissance regiment (with Saladin armoured cars and Ferret scout cars) by air into Zambia using RAF VC-10, Belfast (both brand new), Comet and Britannia aircraft, also civil Britannia and Boeing 707 aircraft from BOAC and British Caledonia Airways. The USAF (32 x C-130 Hercules, eight Globemasters and eight military versions of the 707) and Royal Canadian Air Force (which was involved in the oil airlift) (with four C-130s and seven Canadian variants of the Britannia) would also give major support. RAF Victor bombers of Nos. 100 and 139 Squadrons, operating from Eastleigh in Kenya, were to bomb the RRAF bases of New Sarum and Thornhill runways, each having four aircraft carrying 35 x 1,000 pounder bombs. At the same time troops of 22 SAS Regiment were to seize the civil airports at Salisbury and Bulawayo by a coup de main; this followed by parachute insertion of a battalion group into both locations from *Beverley* and *Argosy* transports (the third Para battalion to remain as a mobile reserve); the four infantry battalions then to be flown into both cities. Centres of government were to be taken over, along with important utilities. With the first objective in Salisbury being the Rhodesian Broadcasting Corporation studios, with a Royal Signals team specially trained by the BBC to operate the broadcasting facilities, and a Psyops team to broadcast a constant message to the population; part of the messages being in Shona and Sindebele as well as English for people to tune into the broadcasts from Bechuanaland. Kariba was to be seized by coup de main based on the Guards Parachute Company, with heliborne elements of 40 Commando seizing the airfield, bridge and power generators. The Armoured Reconnaissance Regiment was to cross over the Kariba Bridge, making a road advance to Salisbury, 42 Commando and elements of 40 were to leapfrog down the road using the Wessex helicopters and RAF Andover and Twin Pioneer aircraft. The Fleet Air Arm strike aircraft were to act as a cab rank close-air support over the two main operational sites. Fifth Brigade was to be flown in direct from staging areas in Malta, and the RAF base at El Adem in Libya, and the USAF Idris base in the same. They were then to be followed by the artillery, armoured and engineer units of 3rd Division in an infantry role. These units were to act as holding units in Salisbury and Bulawayo. The initial strike units from Zambia and Bechuanaland were then to spread out throughout the country. The garrison in Bechuanaland to be reinforced to two battalions (not from 3rd Division) was to advance up the road to Plumtree then to Bulawayo. This was to be a BETA Force. The plan required the use of all RAF air transports available (even a squadron of obsolete Hastings aircraft was to be used as freighters bringing in supplies from Eastleigh), with maintenance being a major concern. At this time there was still a substantial logistic support system in place in Kenya—all gone by 1967. The rational behind the operation was for large numbers of lightly armed infantry to be on the ground, saturating the urban areas, to maintain control of the population, disarm military and police, as well as the civilian population. Apart from the armoured cars and some 120mm Wombat recoilless anti-tank guns, no heavy weapons were to be taken. A colonial administration was then to assume power backed up by some 1,500 British civil police. At the time we had large scale maps issued showing Rhodesia, all the names changed to that of British garrison towns, Winchester, Aldershot, Colchester, Portsmouth, Munster, Berlin, Singapore etc. Fooled no one! There was much opposition to any attempt to bring Rhodesia under control; within 16th Para at the time there was tremendous ill feeling. An example of the dislike for the operation was a Fleet Air Arm lieutenant commander commanding a Scimitar aircraft air-refuelling flight; he was married to a lady from Gwelo, and refused to take part in the build-up to the operation. It took the arrival of Major-General Tony Deane-Drummond as GOC 3rd Division in the autumn of 1966 to bring the invasion's plans to a halt when he confronted the Labour Prime Minister and Minister for Defence with the concerns of the officers and men, as well as the logistical problems confronting the operation.

Despite the plotting in London, PK was in a sanguine mood when Peter Alexander from *The Telegraph* interviewed him just before Christmas "in a simple, thatched bungalow on his farm in Selous where we spent the weekend. PK changed into a white smoking jacket for dinner." Alexander reported his host was confident Rhodesian firepower would deter a British invasion: "Our 21,000 reservists are all crack shots. They know every kopje and bush of the countryside around them. I estimate this is the firepower of six infantry divisions in the last war," he said.

Soon after the interview, on a visit to Fairfield, he told a reporter, "More than 90 per cent of Rhodesians support the government and all of them are prepared to take up arms. We could wipe out all the African states," he warned.

But Rhodesia had no seat at the UN and its passports were declared invalid. Her only friends were South Africa and Portugal. Rhodesia was ripe for communist seductions. When the African Nationalists went looking for military support they did not have to look far. Ian Smith later described how close Britain and Rhodesia were to war. "We heard from our sources that Harold Wilson was sorely tempted to pull the trigger. The matter came to a head when his service chiefs told him they were reluctant to go to war against the people who had fought so bravely at their side against the Germans. Military intervention was put on hold. If the military men had been more forthcoming I think Wilson might have done it and that would have been a catastrophe."

Happy to be in the limelight and typically opinionated, PK described Wilson as "highly dangerous, uninformed and a conceited little man" and compared Prelate Michael Ramsey's call for war to "the tragic connivance [of the British] at the destruction of Czechoslovakia in return for the useless appeasement at Munich in 1938". He also promised "scorched earth" if Britain invaded Rhodesia, on the scale the Red Army employed against the Wehrmacht. "There would be no quick-kill," warned PK. "It would be a long, drawn-out and dreadful process. No installation would be left standing. There will be a smoking ruin and a desert."

He was also quick to warn that Zambia would suffer under Rhodesia's sanctions, which proved correct as their traditional routes through South Africa closed. Copper had to be flown out and oil flown in. Road traffic was forced onto the 'hell run' overland route to Dar es Salaam.

PK's father, Major Piet, also weighed in: "Mr. Wilson, who never fired a shot in World War II, has had the impertinence to call the Rhodesian cabinet a group of little frightened men. A cabinet which contained men like Ian Smith who was shot down twice, fighting as a volunteer for Britain. You can well perceive why I, who always stood for maintaining our friendship with Britain, am completely disenchanted."

Marge Bassett remembers, "I never thought UDI would happen and was a little sad when it did. As an Englishwoman, I felt Rhodesians of every colour had been betrayed by Britain. It was a hectic time. We at the ministry were besieged for interviews. I loved my Queen and did not like what we were doing, but looking back now I suppose we had little choice. I did not like what was happening but the Queen let us down eventually."

Rita McChlery worked in the Hartley Constituency office at this time:

Most Saturdays, PK would travel 160 kilometres from Salisbury to attend to his constituents and was open to any issues people wanted to raise with him. Those Saturdays were very exciting because we were kept in touch with what was happening in the country. Apart from that it was always a joy to listen to PK; he was always so amusing. Straight to the point and his vocabulary was out of this world. He was also exceptionally kind. On my first trip to the UK he asked me how I would manage with the tiny travel allowance we were entitled to. I told him we would manage somehow. After our arrival [in the UK] there was a messenger with an envelope and some money from PK to help us along. Whenever he went overseas he would come into the office with a bottle of perfume for me; what a treat and how much joy it brought into my life ... such a thoughtful and kind gentleman and someone who loved the country as much as I did.

"PK loved Rhodesia," remembers Marge Bassett:

and would have done anything for the country. I suppose we all would have in our own different ways. We worked hard but it was worth it. I would not have missed the experience for the world. And we have been proved right about everything. He was a brave man. He had impeccable dress sense and good manners. Hugely charming and this did lead to problems with women. He had a peculiar effect on people. People would meet him and hate him and then love him. He was very persuasive and had such a keen wit; he had an excellent way of putting thoughts into words.

In the office, he always insisted on Chinese tea and special cups; bowls with lids. He loved food and entertaining. Always formal and normally black tie. He knew an awful lot of people and always had houseguests. Pride of place was reserved for his magnificent dining table from Public Works that seated twelve. Peter, from Mozambique was the cook, Luigi the butler and Farnabeck was effectively his general factotum—he could do it all. He was wonderful to his staff and they stayed with him forever.

"Farnabeck was amazing," remembers Lin Mehmel. "One is reminded of Pasepartoe in *Around the World in Eighty Days*. Instructions were cursory but Farnabeck would get the job done. Organizing a safari would be a simple: '... going to the *shatien* [bush]; elephant and buffalo—ten days' or 'I'm away for ten days, the usual. Pack an overcoat'. Overcoat was the signal he was going overseas and Farnabeck would react accordingly."

"What is not well known," recalls Marge, "is that despite the impression he created of supreme self-confidence, he was far from being unaffected by events. Particularly during his time as Minister of Defence, when the death in action of any of our troops saddened him greatly. His letters to the next of kin of every serviceman who gave his life for Rhodesia were always handwritten by him. A great friend and comfort to him in those dark days was the Rev. Peter Grant who, with his adored wife Buntie, had moved to Norton, in Minister's constituency, some time in the early 1970s. Peter became Chaplain to the RLI. I have fond memories of both Peter and Bunty. I recall at the end, when it became obvious that Rhodesia as we knew it was irretrievably lost, Peter saying that now, especially, we must 'all stand tall'."

Monica Germani, who knew him well, says his outward cynicism and apparent callousness was not the real PK; that beneath it was a "deep sensitivity and depth of thinking".

Late in 1965, the Ministry of Information was expanded to include immigration and tourism. PK could now restrict entry to Rhodesia for those he deemed undesirable and he immediately set his sights on journalists.

When Harold Wilson had the BBC install a broadcasting post in neighbouring Botswana, PK feared its propaganda potential. Initially tempted to destroy it, he changed his mind when it became clear few listened. But he warned the *Rhodesia Herald* and *Bulawayo Chronicle* to "publish at their peril". Henceforth "irresponsible" reporting would be subject to censorship. The papers responded by leaving large blanks where articles had been cut. Academics from the University of Rhodesia attacked PK in a letter to *The Times*, describing him as a "skilled propagandist who believes his own propaganda".

One of the incidents that infuriated PK was the famous 'bodies in Cecil Square' footage. Working on assignment for the BBC Ronnie Robson filmed dozing Africans in Salisbury's Cecil Square, naming them victims of Smith's police. On another occasion BBC cameramen threw money into dustbins, calling the resultant scrimmage "poverty in Rhodesia".

Peregrine Worsthorne of the *Daily Telegraph* suspected PK's ministry of manipulating events after finding astonishing peace and calm. Finally finding a large crowd and anticipating mayhem, he discovered a ticket rush for 'My Fair Lady'. On another visit Worsthorne recalls arriving

> … at Salisbury. I rang up, dare I say it, but I suppose I ought to admit it, my old friend PK van der Byl, whose name has been already mentioned. I said, "PK, here I am, visiting the colony in rebellion; can you put me up for a few nights?" And he said, drawling down the telephone, "I hope you have brought a black tie." I said, "Well, as a matter of fact I didn't think a black tie was appropriate for a visit to a colony in rebellion against the Crown, PK." And he said, "Well that is a bit difficult, because I have got a dinner party." In any case, I did arrive without my black tie and I remember being shocked to find open on the coffee table in PK's house, who was then Minister of Information (I am not sure even if he had such a grand title, he ultimately of course became Foreign Minister, war minister to all intents and purposes) a recently perused copy of *Mein Kampf*. This bears out [the] comment about the fascist element, which cannot be

overlooked. I was fond of PK, but he was a racial supremacist admirer of Hitler.

Max Hastings, masquerading as a Rhodesiaphile hunter-fisherman, repaid endless hospitality with vitriolic scorn:

> Like most of my colleagues I reported from Rhodesia in an almost permanent state of rage. We saw a smug, ruthless white minority, beer guts contained with difficulty inside blazers with RAF crests, proclaiming themselves the guardians of civilization in the heart of Africa. They killed carelessly, tortured freely and exploited censorship to conceal their worst excesses. The city dwellers, patrons of Meikles Hotel bar, were the worst, because they were the most hypocritical. Fervent supporters of 'good old Smithy', many took care not to expose their necks, preferring to 'kill Kruger with [their] mouths', as Kipling put it 70 years earlier.

CHAPTER NINE
Rebellion

To the north, Africa continued to fracture. In the Congo Joseph-Désiré Mobutu forcibly removed President Kasavubu and began to rule by decree, while in the Central African Republic President Dacko was forced out in a coup that brought Jean-Bedel Bokassa to power. Bokassa, fascinated by Napoleon, would go on to declare himself 'Emperor' and establish one of Africa's most brutal regimes.

On 3 January 1966, PK welcomed to Rhodesia three left-wing Labour firebrands on a fact-finding visit. They were David Ennals, Christopher Rowland and Jeremy Bray. Expecting chaos, seething streets and angry people, the parliamentarians found glacial normalcy. Out of 30,000 civil servants, they were disappointed to find only 36 had accepted Wilson's invitation to resign and receive compensation.

Continuing their tour, the three MPs somewhat naively attended a Salisbury political meeting and received rough treatment. The white farmers were not happy to be told by the visitors to hand the country over to African Nationalists. Amidst shouts of "Communists!" tempers flared. Rowland was hauled over a table and doused in beer while attempting to flee. Bray had his hair ruffled and Rowland, also soaking, had to be helped from the hall in a state of shock. One onlooker described him as "looking like a drowned rat".

Protesting to the government, PK told them they had broken the law by addressing a political meeting and reminded them they had spurned government help with their schedule. One of them acknowledged underestimating the depth of feeling among the whites before hastily leaving for Zambia.

After this incident, Sir Godfrey Nicholson, a senior Tory backbencher, visited Salisbury and spent time as a guest of PK. His report was positive and very different to that of the Ennals group. An irritated Wilson accused Nicholson of being influenced by PK. "It would have been better if you had perhaps remained more at arm's length from this very competent brainwasher."

PK responded with: "Regarding the British government's handling of our affairs, my difficulty is to find the brains in order to wash them."

In January 1966, Commonwealth leaders harangued Harold Wilson in Lagos for not using force in Rhodesia. Wilson mollified them with assurances that Rhodesia would succumb within "weeks rather than months". Nigerian leader Balewa need not have worried. Days later, attacked by politically motivated thugs, his mutilated body was found in a roadside ditch and another African political career had ended in grisly fashion.

On 7 February 1966, 24 ZAPU terrorists were brought before the Salisbury High Court, charged with sabotage and attempting to overthrow the government. They had been trained in Moscow, Nanking and Pyongyang and received heavy prison sentences. On the same day, PK met Selwyn Lloyd, Conservative spokesman on Commonwealth Affairs at Salisbury airport. He expressed the hope that the use of force had been ruled out by the British government.

Meanwhile, the Rhodesian press and legislature were in an uproar over tightened censorship. PK explained later:

> Sanctions upon us, information relating to sanctions-busting was incompatible with our survival. Bear in mind the printed media was foreign-owned—a dangerous predicament for any country under siege. We had to censor it. Does anyone think for one moment a fellow like Max Hastings cared one jot for the people of Rhodesia? I dare say not—he cared about furthering his own career by joining a popular chorus. I might add; the British government in Northern Ireland has seen no reason not to use censorship in like-minded fashion.

On 10 February 1966, Major Piet left the South African parliament for the last time to applause from both sides of the house.

In March PK visited Switzerland where he denied reports on discussions he had held with Edward Heath on the question of British troops being sent to Rhodesia. On his return to Salisbury PK told reporters that sanctions had been "amazingly effective" but only in "uniting all Rhodesians behind the Prime Minister".

However, there was no denying imported luxuries were hard to find and PK became a victim of his own bravado:

> I was invited to open an exhibition of locally made wine and spirits. On arrival I was given glasses of various concoctions. After the first two or three my palate was so vitiated I was unable to distinguish good from bad. I gave a stirring speech praising the quality and ordered a couple of cases of this essentially artificial Barolo wine. I spent a troubled night and the next morning found that I was partially paralyzed down the left side but did not associate the two events, thinking it was simply something that happens to all of us and in the course of the day the paralysis wore off. Some time later the Barolo arrived and I began to drink a certain amount of it every day and started to develop some alarming symptoms of migraine, headaches and nausea. I was tested for bilharzia, hookworm, amoebic dysentery and other tropical afflictions but all with negative results and only when the Barolo was finished and the symptoms had disappeared did one realize what was responsible.
>
> But now I had no wine. So I journeyed to an Indian trader in Gatooma, a Mr. Kewada, to seek his help. He said he had a small amount of imported wine squirrelled away and offered it to me but at a terrible cost. I explained I was looking merely for a *vin ordinaire* to satisfy my daily needs and preferred not to spend extravagantly on this requirement. He said he had

another idea and produced a few bottles of the dreaded Barolo! I can't drink that I explained; it gives me headaches, migraines and nausea. Funny you should say that said he; it does the same to me! Harold Wilson would have loved it!

In April 1966, the British government refused PK a visa to attend a Hussars dinner. Dropping from view, his whereabouts became a mystery. The Rhodesian press thought he was in Paris.

In the Commons, Conservative MP Mr. Biggs-Davison asked why PK had been denied entry while British politicians travelled freely to Rhodesia. He was told the ban affected representatives of an 'illegal regime'. Other rulings seemed merely vindictive. At the same time, Rhodesian-born Royal Navy pilot Rob Fynn, on orders from the Defence Ministry, was refused permission to visit his family in Rhodesia.

On 10 April, Britain received UN permission to forcibly intercept vessels suspected of violating sanctions. Under pressure from Wilson and for only the second time in its history, the UN had declared a country, Rhodesia, "a threat to world peace". Enoch Powell called the British government's premise a "… big, black, bold, brazen lie. To say Rhodesia is a threat to the peace of Africa is the same as Hitler when he said that Czechoslovakia was a danger to the peace of Europe."[44]

On 7 May 1966, PK left Paris for Johannesburg, announcing he had "completed a number of missions in several European countries" and that "Ian Smith has become an international hero".

But not long after his return there was tragedy in his Hartley constituency when terrorists murdered farmers Mr. and Mrs. J.H. Viljoen, leaving three children orphaned. PK immediately involved himself in a fundraising drive to assist the orphans. Soon after the funeral he quietly left the country again to return to Europe on a secret trip that lasted three weeks.

Despite securing a big election victory at home, Wilson's international star was waning under Rhodesian expectation. Sanctions had made

---

[44] Peter Joyce: *Anatomy of a Rebel*. Grahame Publishing, 1974

Britain £100 million poorer and he wished to be rid of this albatross. With assistance from South Africa and Portugal, Rhodesia was surviving. Wilson was unwilling to take issue with them, so realized he had to negotiate. Rhodesia, for its part, lacked recognition and international finance. South Africa's Verwoerd was sympathetic, but pushed Smith toward settlement talks.

On 23 July 1966, Major Piet suffered a heart attack and was hospitalized. "I visited him several times," remembers Lin Mehmel. "Initially he was in a private ward at Andrew Fleming Hospital. All he wanted was a glass of Chateau Yquem. So, with the doctor's permission, but without Joy's knowledge, the search began. Rhodesia was certainly not flush with imported wine of that quality. I approached the Simleit brothers at Central Cellars and told them who was in need. They not only found a small bottle but gave me a discount. In spite of his condition he complained bitterly that he was not ten years younger because the wards were filled with lovely girls. Like father, like son I suppose. He was then flown back to Cape Town with Joy and a whole entourage of support staff."

On 12 August, while Piet was convalescing in Cape Town's Leuwendaal Hospital after minor surgery, Hendrik Verwoerd was assassinated in the House of Assembly. Dimitri Tsafendas, a messenger and one-time drifter, greeted the Prime Minister then stalked him and stabbed him four times in the chest. Members of parliament rushed forward and after a violent struggle, the assassin was finally subdued. Four Members of Parliament who were medical doctors rushed to Verwoerd's aid and one gave him the kiss of life. Mrs. Verwoerd also ran down to the chamber from the wives' gallery. She kissed her husband as the doctors battled to save his life. The Prime Minister was rushed to Groote Schuur Hospital where he was certified dead on arrival. Tsafendas's motives remain unclear to this day.

On the first anniversary of UDI, during a visit to Luxemburg, PK told *Le Figaro* that of 150 terrorists who had entered the country from Zambia, only four had not been accounted for. He attributed this success to overwhelming local black support for the Rhodesian security forces. Under surveillance and constantly on the run, he was given 24 hours to leave Amsterdam. His father commented: "It is strange that the British government harbours criminals bent on destroying South Africa but squeal the moment someone asks for a chance to explain the Rhodesian position."

PK later explained how he managed to keep travelling: "The two gentlemen who were of immeasurable assistance to me in getting access to Europe in order to help break sanctions were de Marenches[45] of French Intelligence and Franz Josef Strauss, the Bavarian Premier. Strauss controlled the Bavarian border so he gave me entry to Germany and de Marenches opened the door to France. I do think the various intelligence services knew where I was but often chose not to intervene. However, there were a few times when I was thrown off trains at night and stuff like that ... frog-marched off through the snow ... very irritating. On one occasion, travelling from Paris to Vienna by train, I was sold to British Intelligence by the concierge in my hotel. I was woken up the moment the train passed beyond Strasbourg and told to come out. I held up the train for an hour or two while I rose, shaved and prepared myself. Then I was marched back to Strasbourg where I spent a very agreeable night."

"PK's trips abroad were a source of great irritation to the CIO [Central Intelligence Organization] boss, Ken Flower," says Lin Mehmel, "because Flower was mostly in the dark about his movements and for an intelligence chief, who was probably also reporting to London, this was a little embarrassing. Strauss was amazing in arranging PK's travel. In Germany there would be secret service cars behind the car carrying PK. They would

---

[45] Count Alexandre de Marenches served with the French army in WWII as aide de camp to General Juin and later helped to coordinate the US military with the remaining French divisions. He became head of the Service de Documentation Extérieure et de Contre-Espionnage (SDECE), France's external intelligence agency, and served in that position from 6 November 1970 to 12 June 1981. He is known to have predicted the Soviet invasion of Afghanistan to an American journalist who immediately reported his conversation to US National Security Advisor Zbigniew Brzezinski and left for Kabul "arriving in the same time as the Soviet tanks did" (Marenches in *Dans le Secret des Princes*). In 1986, he co-authored *Dans le Secret des Princes* (published in English as *The Evil Empire: Third World War Continues*) with journalist Christine Ockrent about his days working in secret services. In 1992, he co-authored *The Fourth World War: Diplomacy and Espionage in the Age of Terrorism* with David Andelman.

mix up the convoy then split, making it very tricky for anyone to tail PK. I was privileged to have couriered some correspondence between PK and Alexandre de Marenches who, along with Strauss and Otto von Hapsburg, PK trusted implicitly. This was done without Flower knowing. My cover for being there was sourcing documentary material for television. Flower was furious when he found out."

On 1 December 1966, Smith led a Rhodesian delegation for talks with Wilson's team aboard HMS *Tiger* on the Mediterranean. Consigned to the 'B' cabins in the cruiser's bowels, Jack Howman recalls the indignities of second-class citizenry: "The British attitude to us was one of Victorian paternalism and condescension, at times insufferably arrogant. Perhaps," he went on, "this is understandable for, in the British view, had we not had the impertinence, the audacity, to defy, indeed to challenge the power and the authority of Her Majesty's government and were we not the first of our kind for 200 years to do so?"

Surprisingly few disagreements surfaced, except around the mechanics of the return to legality. Wary of possible British perfidy and despite Wilson's bullying, Smith advised he would need cabinet approval before signing. Wilson became apoplectic and menacing, finally threatening force if Smith did not sign. Howman relates the events on the last day of the talks:

> We came into the Admiral's day-cabin, to find Mr. Wilson in an absolute fury. I have never before seen a man indicating such vicious malevolence as this man did at that moment. "You will sign these documents! I will not have Britain humiliated! You will sign before you leave this ship!" he shouted. I believe something happened to Mr. Wilson that evening, that he received a call either from his own government or from another source; that he was put on the spot, and I am convinced that he was petrified that we should leave the ship without submitting ourselves to his jurisdiction … His attitude was one of a fearful panicked man who, in seeking to ride a tiger, was trying to pull us on too.

On 5 December, after an exhaustive cabinet meeting, Smith announced fundamental acceptance of the *Tiger* principles, but refused to abandon the country's constitution. Particularly repugnant to the Rhodesian leadership was the demand that they surrender control of the country's security forces to the command of a British governor. The next day, Britain requested widened mandatory sanctions at the UN. History shows Smith was justified in doubting British sincerity. After the 1980 settlement at Lancaster House, the transition to majority rule was expedited with unseemly haste once control was ceded to a British governor. Undertakings were ignored and voters massively intimidated by Mugabe's forces, resulting in a stolen election.

The present Marquess of Salisbury considers the failure of the 'Tiger Talks' to have been a missed opportunity: "Harold Wilson was essentially a decent man," he recalls. "He told me he never understood why Ian Smith failed to agree on the terms he offered him in these negotiations."

Out of the public eye, PK completed his fugitive diplomatic rounds in Europe and returned to Rhodesia on 22 December. Shortly afterward his father was put up as the United Party's candidate for State President in South Africa. Predictably, he lost to the Nationalist candidate Dr. E.T. Donges, who was elected on 28 February.

In January 1967, Smith caused outrage saying, "The role of the European has been to protect the African from himself. History has shown that the African is his own worst master. What we are striving for is not only that the rights of the Europeans are assured under our system, but the rights of Africans will also be assured."[46]

Chipping in, PK quoted a report in Mensa's *Intelligence* magazine suggesting a study had shown the "intelligence of white Rhodesians was staggeringly high". A possible reason, the report suggested, was that

[46] Peter Joyce: *Anatomy of a Rebel.* Graham Publishing, 1974

intelligent and resourceful people are quickly stifled and irritated in a restrictive society, and it was for this reason many people left Britain for the colonies.

In March 1967, PK wrote to his father of a curious incident that occurred in his Hamburg hotel. On covert business at the time, a friendly concierge advised him that persons unknown were tailing him. PK acted quickly and "… went to my room and threw my luggage together and was out of there in 20 minutes. Three hours later I was the other side of Germany. I am now staying in private houses." Just who was tailing him in this instance was never discovered.

With sanctions-busting forming a major part of PK's brief, an unlikely opportunity presented itself in the messy squabble between Nigeria and its southern state of Biafra. The oil-rich Biafra surprised its Lagos ruling junta by seceding on 30 May 1967. It had French backing and widespread local support but survival depended on international recognition. With Britain and the Soviet Union condemning the secession, Biafra became a default ally of Rhodesia.

Finding itself at war, Biafra cobbled together a makeshift air force. Lacking expertise to run it, Biafra looked to Rhodesia, and in particular to Jack Malloch, a colourful character who flew spitfires with Ian Smith in Italy during World War II. Brought up in Umtali, Malloch, like Smith, was shot down before linking up with Italian partisans and making his way back to Allied lines. Years after the war he flew Spitfires to Rhodesia as part of the process of re-equipping Rhodesia's air arm. Before his involvement in Biafra he flew in Katanga Province for Moise Tshombe's forces, losing an aircraft to UN gunfire in the process. He would return to the Congo to support Mike Hoare's mercenaries just before UDI but then returned home to focus on sanctions-busting for the Rhodesian government. In July 1967 Malloch made his first gunrunning flight into Biafra and continued until the war ended in 1970. During this period, he spent a spell in jail in

Togo when found carrying nine tons of Nigerian banknotes. Although junior to Jack Howman, PK was given charge of West African sanctions-busting operations. He explained:

> I think there were reservations about Jack. He might be spurned and that would not be good for someone of ministerial rank. I do think I was probably better at dealing with the sort of odd-bods that were out there. Jack was very formal, straight-laced, and very direct. Nobody messed around with Jack. I got thrown out of all sorts of countries, which would not have appealed to Jack. I was also able to operate in French society because I had been there. Jack was an outsider in that context. He was a quintessential colonial.

On one trip PK travelled to Libreville via Paris where he linked up with Max Dumas, a French-speaking CIO agent, and Jean Morichaud-Beupré of the French Service d'Action Civique (SAC). Contact was made with Gabonese president Omar Bongo and relations were established between Salisbury and Libreville.

> We discussed options with Bongo who wanted to know what was in it for Gabon. I told him we had all sorts of technical expertise to offer and we could help in agriculture, tourism and industrial development. They wanted meat which we were happy to trade. I then took up another delegation consisting of Harry Oxley, Nick Spoel, Ginger Freeman (tobacco) and Robbie Roberts (Reserve Bank). Trying to get Jack Malloch more involved we put together Air Gabon Cargo and this became the foundation of the expanded Rhodesian beef industry. From Gabon it went all over the world: Congo Brazaville, Côte d'Ivoire; funnily enough quite a lot ended up in the Soviet Union. We could not

have got this all done without the help of Jacques Foccart[47] and SDECE[48] [French Intelligence]. But we could have done more. Jack Malloch had been running a shoestring operation in Biafra, Katanga and Yemen. Got himself locked up in Togo and had a run of financial disasters. The Rhodesian government helped out but there were other contributors, people with interests in Africa and the Middle East—I don't know who they were. David Young does but he's not saying. You have to understand that thanks to Jack and the opening of Gabon, all kinds of things were made possible. Meat was important. It actually kept the whole of the Rhodesian cattle industry going, which was a vital ingredient in keeping the country going. It also kept people on the land and that too was essential in keeping the country viable. This connection was invaluable for our survival. Indirectly it played a major role in the continuing defence of southern Africa; economically, militarily. It could not have happened without the French. They were a vital component.

PK recalled the events in an interview in 1995: "We got into a relationship with Bongo ... I would say it was due virtually entirely to Jack Malloch's

---

[47] Jacques Foccart (31 August 1913–19 March 1997) was French President Charles de Gaulle's and then Georges Pompidou's chief adviser for African policy, who, in 1959, founded the Gaullist organization Service d'Action Civique (SAC) with Charles Pasqua, which specialized in shady operations. From 1960 to 1974, he was the President's Chief of Staff for African and Malgache matters. Henceforth, he played a most important role in French policies in Africa, so much so that he has been said to have been, after de Gaulle, the most influential man of the Fifth Republic. He was considered to be the instigator behind various coups d'état in Africa during the 1960s. He retained his functions during Georges Pompidou's presidency (1969–1974) and was replaced by Valéry Giscard d'Estaing, a young deputy whom he had trained himself. He was then rehabilitated in 1986 by new Premier Chirac as an adviser on African affairs for the two years of 'cohabitation' with socialist president François Mitterrand. When Chirac finally made it to the presidency in 1995, Foccart was brought back to the Elysée at the age of eighty-one. He died in 1997. According to the *National Interest* review, "Foccart was said to have been telephoning African personalities on the subject of Zaire right up to the week before his death."

[48] *Service de Documentation Extérieure et de Contre-Espionnage.*

support of the war in Biafra; I mean he was ferrying all that stuff up from Gabon into Biafra. I said we should support the Biafrans, because we were battling against more or less the same lot [Britain and the USSR] as they were. We sent a whole lot of 'jim-crack' rifles with Jack into Biafra, which were well received and we were thanked by Ojukwu and his deputy. This had a pleasing result, because it pleased Bongo too. He, along with the French, was supporting Biafra. It was terrible. The Ibos there were starving and dying like flies; over half a million died. Outmanned and outgunned with their opponents being generously supplied by the British and Soviets, the Biafrans fought on in a sublime and inspired defence of independence. In Biafra the option was to submit to genocide; in Rhodesia it was to submit to majority rule but the same degree of courage was required."[49]

PK continued: "Ian Smith deserves a lot of the credit. He had the guts to do it and gave Jack and me the green light to go for it. I only fault Ian Smith for not putting the boot to the financial wet-noses like David Smith. We had to fight tooth and nail with them to keep Jack going."

Back in Rhodesia, in September 1967, documents retrieved from slain insurgents identified them as ANC (African National Congress) operatives and linked them to South Africa. The news alarmed South African Intelligence and the country began deploying police in Rhodesia in a bid to keep them out. Smith was also suspicious that Britain was helping ZAPU terrorists in Zambia and sent a letter of complaint. He did not receive a reply.

During this time, William van der Byl was frequently in Rhodesia on business. "I saw little of PK because I was running the Rhodesia fertilizer industry and did not want to be seen asking for any favours. In fact I lie; I did ask him to introduce me to [Finance Minister] David Smith on one occasion, but that was all. In my view they cocked it up quite magnificently in Rhodesia. They could have done a deal earlier on, which may have averted the war; having said that, the atmosphere there was wonderful. It was always a relief to be away from the strains and stresses of South Africa.

---

[49] *Daily Telegraph*, 10 June 1969

It was a very relaxed country. I used to stay at Meikles Hotel and always enjoyed it very much."

With a British invasion still threatened, PK told a Salisbury luncheon meeting: "Everything in the path of an advancing army will be destroyed—all amenities and all installations. Let Mr. Wilson realize this before he attempts to embark on something that can only lead to disaster. Mr. Wilson must realize that we cannot be brought down by sanctions, but nevertheless this dangerous little man, whose conceit matches his arrogance, is still determined to try and crush us."

The Soviet contact man in the West at this time was Alexander Chernyaev and his recently revealed diaries disclose the existence of a "special relationship" between the British Labour party and Moscow and a "reverential approach" of the party leaders to their Russian comrades. It is also now known that Jack Jones, who became the leader of the Transport and General Workers' Union, was a paid-up agent of the KGB.[50] When PK insisted that the Labour Pary was in cahoots with the communists, his view was widely dismissed as outrageous.

On 20 December 1967, an international incident was narrowly averted off the coast of Beira when a Royal Navy frigate fired warning shots at a French tanker making for port in violation of the British blockade. A message was sent to the British captain: "General de Gaulle might like to hear of a French ship being sunk by the Royal Navy." Hostile action ceased and the ship sailed in.

On 6 March 1968, three Africans were hanged at Salisbury Central Prison despite an appeal for clemency from Queen Elizabeth. Two had been convicted of the political murder of an unarmed white farmer. An international press storm resulted but Sir Hugh Beadle, the Rhodesian Chief Justice, said it was inconceivable that the trial judge should have recommended the law not be allowed to take its course. He reminded the public that the accused had stopped an unarmed farmer on his way home at night with his wife and child and stabbed him 16 times before throwing

---

[50] *The Spectator*, 7 November 2009

petrol bombs into the vehicle. Managing to retain control long enough to drive out of the killing zone, the farmer then died at the wheel while the mother and child were later rescued.

Days later, the BBC was forced to apologize for running a programme supposedly on Rhodesia, containing footage from Sharpeville where South African policemen had killed 71 people.

CHAPTER TEN
War and sanctions

Armed incursions in the early days of Rhodesia's bush war frequently went badly for the insurgents. In one incident in the late 1960s, David Scammell, a National Parks game ranger, discovered tracks of hundreds of people while patrolling the Chewore Wilderness Area looking for poachers. This being suspicious, he raised the alarm. No incursion of this magnitude had ever taken place before and troops from the SAS, RLI (Rhodesian Light Infantry) and RAR (Rhodesian African Rifles) were mobilized immediately. The terrorist camp was located and the attack went in with brutal effect. For the first time, the older regular black soldiers saw their much younger white countrymen in battle and they were amazed. A black sergeant-major who had seen action in World War II remarked of the young RLI troopers: "They have the faces of boys but they fight like lions."

PK visited the Zambezi Valley to see for himself where the battle had been fought. "It was somewhat disappointing," he commented, "that numerous corpses were not found, but there was clear evidence that a large number of terrorists had been killed." He used the opportunity to compliment Scammell on his skill and fortitude.

Group Captain Peter Petter-Bowyer, in his book *Winds of Destruction*, recalls PK visiting troops in the Zambezi: "Following the Vampire strikes against Hadebe's group, PK decided to visit the site. He was not really known to the men in the field at that time and his arrival at Karoi for his helicopter flight to site was quite an eye-opener because his dress was so appalling. Below his Australian bush hat he wore a pink shirt with bright blue tie, khaki shorts with black belt, short blue socks and 'vellies' [veldskoene, lit. bush shoes]. His strange dress in the bush was often discussed. I honestly think he did this from time to time simply for the shock effect. He knew the Zambezi Valley like the back of his hand, having walked it extensively on his hunting expeditions."

Petter-Bowyer continues:

> When the RLI and SAS got to know him better, PK became very popular with the soldiers. His ridiculous accent appealed to them just as much as his strange dress. He often requested to be taken on patrol so he could "shoot a terrorist" but asked that care be taken not to get him "lawst". After he became better known to the air force, he arrived by air at Thornhill to attend some official function or another in Gwelo. Station Commander Group Captain Ken Edwards offered the Minister lunch in the officers' mess after his official function was over. PK said he had an awful headache and declined the offer. However, when he returned to Thornhill, he told Ken that he had changed his mind and would love to take up the earlier offer of lunch before flying back to Salisbury. Not surprisingly, the caterers were in a bit of a tizzy for receiving such late notice but, as always, they presented a superb meal.
>
> There were many officers and wives enjoying Saturday lunchtime drink in the Grog Spot when John Digby walked in wearing PK van der Byl's very smart Homburg hat. He had found this on the table in the entrance hall to the mess. "Surely the Minister, with his British Army background, knows better that to leave his hat in the entrance hall of an officers' mess, when its rightful place is in the cloakroom!" Digby said. Having made his point, John placed the hat on my wife's head. Beryl immediately sat on the bar counter and posing in an exaggerated manner, made some statement in PK's affected accent. She was still doing this when Eddie Wilkinson whipped the hat from her head and, before he could be stopped, poured a full pint of beer into it, causing instant loss of shape. Some officers took sips from the hat before it became the object of a roughhouse rugby

match during which it shrivelled and shrank into a shapeless mess. Once the match was over, the hat was unceremoniously driven down one of the horns of a kudu trophy hanging on the wall. When the Minister was ready to leave, his headache immediately redeveloped because he could not find his prized hat. Group Captain Edwards tore into the Grog Spot to see if anyone had seen it. Everyone pointed to the kudu horns. PK took off for Salisbury in a thundering bad mood and John Digby phoned officers at New Sarum to brief them on what had happened. A whole group of them rushed off to find hats and gathered at Air Movements in time to meet the Minister. As PK emerged from the Dakota, everyone doffed their hats in greeting. Unable to respond, the Minister's annoyance and headache worsened. Fortunately, he was humoured sufficiently to accept the offer of a drink in the mess where his headache dissipated before his departure for home in good spirits.

John Digby took all the Saville Row hatmaker's details from the destroyed hat and, through his brother in London, had a new Homburg made. When Terry Emsley was persuaded by John to present the new hat to PK, the Minister vowed never again to leave it unattended in any place other than a hatbox in the boot of his car.

PK van der Byl stood out in any situation. For all his eccentricities and flamboyance, PK was a bright politician who spoke fluent German. I heard it said that he very cleverly saved Rhodesia many millions of dollars by 'confiding', very loudly, with a fellow passenger on a Lufthansa flight out of Germany. This was done to make sure that an agent—whether British or American, I do not know—sitting behind him could hear his words. He knew the agent was trying to establish the purpose of his visit to Germany—and PK wanted to oblige. This was because he had just received confirmation from home that the new Rhodesian Mint had successfully started pumping out high-quality Rhodesian dollar notes. By boasting loudly about the German firm that was about to deliver Rhodesian currency through an agency he named, he triggered a UN action that blocked the deal. Thanks to PK, this 'UN sanctions-blocking success against Rhodesia' not only saved millions in foreign currency at UN expense, it heightened another of the country's self-sufficiency triumphs.

Ron Reid-Daly, who later formed and commanded the Selous Scouts recalls an early encounter with PK: "I was with the RLI then and we were doing border control in the Zambezi Valley. I had a patrol deployed on the Hunyani River and I went to check on all the men. I made my way to their position to pay them a visit and found them a in a high state of hilarity which did not amuse me one bit. We were supposed to be fighting a bloody war! It was midday and I then realized that not only were they taking it easy, but these buggers had also been drinking. I was bloody pissed off. To add to my anger, the next thing I saw was an impala hanging from a tree. We were not allowed to shoot for the pot without permission, so on top of the fact that they were pissed it looked like they had been poaching too. Just as I was about to explode, the sergeant spoke. 'Sir,' he said, 'it's not our fault. The minister, Mr. van der Byl, came here to see us and invited us to his hunting camp for lunch and we've just come back. When we were there he filled us up with brandy, beer and all sorts of booze. Being a minister I felt we could not refuse an order. Then when we left, as a parting gift, he gave us this impala.'"

Nick Howman, then a serving soldier, remembers a similar incident: "We were based at Bumi Hills for a while during the war when we received a message from Army HQ that a VIP was flying in. We were ordered to secure the airstrip, which we did. The plane landed and out stepped PK, complete with hunting rifle and smartly dressed in a safari suit with cravat. He then went off with Rupert van der Riet for a few days' hunting. On his way back, a freshly shot impala was dropped off at our base as a thank-you from PK."

On 29 March, the UN broadened sanctions again, but by now even Harold Wilson understood the measures had been counterproductive. Forced to survive on their own, Rhodesia's industrialists could now make goods which were formerly imported. Self-reliance and a captive market brought economic growth. British pique remained high—on Armistice Day, the Scots Guards were forbidden to play at a service commemorating the Rhodesian dead of two World Wars.

To the alarm of Rhodesians, in April 1968 Kenneth Kaunda commenced seizure of white-owned farms and businesses in Zambia. This would lead to the collapse of the country's agricultural economy, but was widely applauded by the black political class. At the same time, Enoch Powell warned that uncontrolled immigration into the United Kingdom would lead to conflict and "rivers of blood". For this, Edward Heath promptly sacked him. "Of course Powell was dead right," PK would later remark, "but he was way ahead of his time and very few in the United Kingdom were comfortable with the truth. That remains the case today."

On 13 September 1968, with Jack Howman moving sideways, PK was promoted to Minister of Information, Immigration and Tourism. Angus Graham who had fallen out with Smith, was dropped.

By this time, PK was a celebrity and was frequently called on for TV appearances. Always charming, he cultivated the fashionable white hunter mystique. "He was indeed one of a kind," says Lin Mehmel, "and the beauty of it was that you could not typecast or easily read him. In many ways, he was a contradiction in terms. He was equally at home tracking elephant in the bush, in the smartest clubs or in well-informed debate with a prime minister of a European country."

Michael Hartnack, writing for the *Despatch Online*, recalls that many saw him as "a 19th-century-style connoisseur, a man of culture and an aristocratic statesman".

To The Point magazine ran this description: "He has an air which is easily mistaken for arrogance and a knack for making enemies, whether among Victoria Falls hoteliers or those representatives of the overseas press whom he classes as 'scoundrels and ragamuffins'. There is, however, a liberal streak in van der Byl. His views on the rights and role of the coloured communities of southern Africa would startle many on the right."

Chris Whitehead, writing in *Rhodesian Personalities*, describes his manner of speech as "an aristocratic English nasal drawl [with] Imperial English mannerisms".

While his accent bemused Rhodesians, it rankled Afrikaner politicians 'down south'. Despite his eccentricities, he had become an uncompromising and highly opinionated politician. Few opponents took him lightly, particularly when he suspected "the whiff of surrender".

Commenting on his promotion to full minister, PK described politics as "a family bad habit". On why he had left South Africa: "It does not do to live in the shadow of one's father and even though I hold him in tremendous respect and have learned a lot from him, I wanted to go my own way." Discussing his conflict with the press, he said, "I admit I have interfered, but I did so because I considered it necessary. I doubt I shall have to do it again because the Board [of the Rhodesian Broadcasting Corporation] is now running things in the best interests of Rhodesia."

As a cabinet minister, PK continued his covert travelling, selling Rhodesia:

> I was a sort of agent I suppose and of course I used my contacts for sanctions-busting. I merely opened doors and left the deals to better qualified people. This paid dividends and our economy showed remarkable growth in adverse circumstances. The French were very important in this regard as were the Germans but the French were less rigid. Franz Josef Strauss, in his capacity as Minister of Finance in the German government at the time, was a terribly important figure. He single-handedly delayed the full imposition of German sanctions for two years. We were very short of motorcars in Rhodesia and this, along with keeping our helicopters flying, was one area where I was able to help but alas my attempt to get us recognized proved fruitless. It must be said, however, that the French were never

anti-Rhodesia nor were the African Francophone countries. My father warned me not to be taken in by the Afrikaner Nationalists. "I know these people [the Nationalists]," he said. "They are not the descendants of the warrior Boers—the Smuts and de la Reys—they're a lot of half-baked intellectuals; a lot of frightened little men who have let the genie out the bottle and can't get it back in. They are full of big talk; not one of them has seen a shot fired in anger, let alone been shot at. When the thing goes against them, which it will, when the crunch comes—they're going to drop you [Rhodesia] in the shit!" Sadly he was proved right.

On 20 September, Wilson sent a Foreign Office official to Salisbury to invite Smith to new talks off Gibraltar. PK had just had a narrow escape on a hunting trip in northern Mashonaland:

> We were stalking a herd of buffalo which was in an enclosed neck of land against a river. We knew that if disturbed the only way out was over the ground we were standing on. This did not cause any worry as we were prepared to get out of the way quickly. But what we did not realize was that a lion was also after the buffalo and was between the herd and us. I selected a fine bull and fired but at the same time disturbed the lion. Naturally it wanted to get out and came the only possible way which was straight toward us. The African carriers, my guest and I all took to our heels and scattered. The lion continued the chase for about 20 metres and then broke through the line of carriers and disappeared into the bush. This is what I expected but it was an exciting moment. We returned to the buffalo, which rose as we approached but a second shot finished it off. Had it been a matter of life and death I would have shot the lion but I did not have a license. Although the lion came within 15 yards of me, I did not fear for my life.

Around this time PK met a professional big game hunter, Rupert van der Riet. A rugged individual and a crack shot who later developed the Rhodesian safari industry, he became one of Rhodesia's most famous hunters. An early favourite for a medal in trap shooting at the 1972 Munich Olympics, he and the Rhodesian team were subsequently banned after pressure from black American athletes.

The two men became lifelong friends and together would hunt big game, mainly buffalo and elephant, in areas within the Zambezi catchment area, Omay, Sengwa and Chete. "He was very good with a rifle," remembers Rupert. "A very fine hunter; he preferred a .465 double on safari."

"They never talked politics," recalls Verity van der Riet. "I think this was a time for PK to distance himself from all that he was dealing with as a minister."

At the end of September, PK travelled to Spain after he received news that Prime Minister Salazar of Portugal had suffered a stroke. Rhodesia had lost a staunch friend. Into his place came political activist and former law professor Marcello Caetano.

"PK travelled to Madrid to see some friends, one of whom was Paula Khuen-Lutzoew," remembers Lotti. "As it turned out, she had been invited to a party which she did not wish to attend, so organized for PK to go in her stead. This outing was to have important ramifications because it was at this gathering that he met many of the people who would invite him into 'The Circle'[51]. It was a Christian, conservatively inclined think tank made up primarily of scions of important European families. They were involved in the maintenance and strengthening of European power and were active in Africa, where they deplored creeping communist influence. It was out of that event he built many of the contacts that would be of so much value in helping Rhodesia survive. I am not sure, but probably present there that night was Juan Carlos, the future King of Spain."

As reported on 21 October 1968 in the *Rand Daily Mail*, "the key man, Information Minister PK van der Byl" was still finding ways to export

---

[51] Officially the CEDI: Centro Europeo de Documentación e Informatión

Rhodesia's products. The paper listed tobacco (to East Germany); asbestos and pig iron (Rumania); iron and steel (Argentina); corned beef (Greece); maize (Europe) and gold (Switzerland).

In October, he flew to Lisbon to meet senior Portuguese government officials, triggering a protest from the British Foreign Office. Initially shielded from the press, he finally explained he was on a private visit to see friends in the Algarve. Three days later he arrived back in Lisbon and, much to the fury of the press, promptly disappeared. One journalist saw the lighter side: "But he will again politely outwit reporters as the Cheshire Cat fooled Alice. He will vanish quite slowly, beginning with the end of his tail and ending with a grin, which will remain some time after the rest of him has gone."

In another encounter, a hostile young American reporter queried PK's right to question US policy on Rhodesia: "What do you know about America; have you ever been to America?" she asked. Enjoying himself, he implored her to help him remember the name of the "fancy university on the east coast of the United States where I studied". When the flummoxed American suggested the name 'Harvard', he yelled excitedly, "That's it!"

PK returned home three weeks later, having addressed The Circle and invited them to Rhodesia for their next conference. His talk had covered African civilization "which is as authentic to them as European culture is to Europeans". He also predicted dire consequences for Rhodesia if people "expected Africans to swap civilizations and suddenly behave like Europeans". Africans, he said, had their own system of democratic consensus, which was, in many ways, as effective as the Europeans'. Quizzed by the press, he described the CEDI as an international organization committed to opposing communism and supporting Western civilization.

On 9 October 1968, new settlement talks took place aboard HMS *Fearless*. Wilson changed his tack and was markedly more hospitable this time, even upgrading Smith to the Admiral's cabin. Accompanying Smith were Jack Howman and Des Lardner-Burke. Although progress was made, nothing had been signed when the talks broke up four days later. Sticking points for Smith were the right of appeal to the Privy Council and a mandatory blocking quarter in the House of Assembly. This was, in his view, a "second-class" form of independence; but importantly Wilson had softened on the interim powers of the governor.

"PK told me he became quite outspoken and wanted Ian Smith to accept," says Lotti. "He said, 'Let's just play the British government at their own game; accept the damn thing then ignore it.' But Ian just did not have a devious bone in his body and tactics of that sort were anathema to him. Ultimately of course, the talks ended in no agreement."

By the end of 1968, the Johannesburg *Sunday Times* reported Rhodesian tourism was flourishing with bookings surpassing pre-UDI levels. The paper identified PK as key to this revival, congratulating him for his hard line on shoddy hoteliers and negative newspapermen.

With the suspected influx of British intelligence agents, PK, ever in the mood for the lighter side, proposed spy-spotting package tours. Prizes could be offered for successful identifications, he suggested.

Despite obvious adversity, with the help of assisted immigration packages white numbers in the country had grown to 237,000—the highest in history. Asked why he was not doing anything to attract black immigrants, he said such a move would "… be like bringing coals to Newcastle".

This comment drew predictable fire but he was soon in hotter water with feminists. "I have never met a woman with an original idea in her head," he said, adding, "no woman could do my job because she would have to command a large staff of senior men who would object, and I would agree with them entirely."

His subsequent non-appearance at a dinner of the Business and Professional Women's Club was duly noted by the *Rhodesia Herald*. "He had been called away to the comparatively safe task of tracking a wounded buffalo," the paper reported, and in his opening remarks the guest speaker, Mr. N. Brendon, conceded that 'Mr. van der Byl's absence might have something to do with the fact he did not own a bulletproof vest'." Unperturbed, he next offended the Italians. Asked what he thought of Italy he said, "It is a marvellous country and a particularly splendid one to conquer."

In early 1969, retired judge of the British High Court, The Rt. Hon. Sir Wintringham Stable PC, MC, visited Rhodesia on a fact-finding tour, meeting politicians across the political spectrum, including PK and Ian Smith. In his report he wrote: "During my month's stay in Rhodesia, I travelled many thousands of miles and had contact with a considerable number and variety of people. I found a law-abiding and orderly society; I never encountered a scowl, much less a rude word or unhelpful act from an African. I have heard Rhodesia described as a police state. I saw very few policemen and none of them armed."

Following a period of diplomatic quiet between London and Salisbury, Smith began moving toward a republican constitution, believing "people would be more ready to approach us … if we have completely broken away from Britain and the Crown". He announced his intention to adopt a constitution designed to lead to legislative parity between white and black.

Despite these lofty goals, the *Rhodesia Herald* found much to criticize, insisting Smith had chosen white rule over moderation. Nonetheless, white voters overwhelmingly supported Smith's referendum on the matter. Days later, Humphrey Gibbs resigned the governorship and returned quietly to his farm, and the next month the Residual British Mission closed its doors, ending the last semblance of diplomatic ties. The UN Security Council failed to pass a resolution calling for the immediate use of force by only one vote.

Writing in the *Daily Express* before Christmas 1969, John Monks reported Rhodesians were now "thriving, that Santa Claus was laughing at sanctions and that the shops were bursting with quality merchandise". The United Nations Sanctions Committee grudgingly reported that economic activity in Rhodesia was now higher than it had been at independence in 1965.

Aggressively questioned about reports that the Rhodesian government hanged people "secretly", PK replied: "Rhodesia is a civilized country and would not have anything to do with public executions."

CHAPTER ELEVEN
Republic declared

In mid-January 1970, with the capitulation of Biafra, the Nigerian operation came to an end.

A month later PK suffered a heart attack.

"He came back from cabinet," remembers Marge Bassett. "The Secretary for the Ministry was with him and he said PK was unwell. I took him some water and could see he was pale but he was putting on a brave face. He complained of a pain in his arm so I phoned the doctor and took him to hospital. It turned out they had misread the ECG the day before and he had suffered a heart attack. He was hospitalized at Salisbury Central Hospital for six weeks."

On 2 March 1970, Rhodesia became a republic.

The Queen suspended the grant of 'Royal' to the Rhodesian Air Force and the Rhodesia Regiment and the Queen Mother resigned as Honorary Commissioner of the British South Africa Police.

But support for the ruling party was never greater and Smith swept all 'A' roll seats in the April election.

It was clear Wilson and Smith had stalemated, but fresh hope arrived in June with a new Conservative government under Edward Heath. Heath had been critical of Smith, but more so of Wilson and expressed a determination to break the impasse.

On 16 July 1970, PK addressed the 10th Congress of the Rhodesia Tobacco Association. "The stability and real backbone of a country depends on a settled and prosperous rural population because they, more than any others, have their roots spread deeply and irrevocably into the soil of the land. Farmers are the most immovable and reliable element of any country's population. Without them the country will collapse."[52]

In late 1970, PK set up a new sanctions-busting operation in the Middle East through a man introduced to him by his hunting friend Piet Bosch. Bosch was related by marriage to Marandellas farmer Chris Landon, brother to Tim Landon also referred to in the left-wing press as 'The White Sultan'. (At the same time Chris Landon, when not farming in Rhodesia, ran a tea-trading business in Mozambique where he worked with Americo and Antonio Felizardo. Later, with the accession to power of Samora Machel, he and his associates were expelled from the country. Using his Canadian passport, he became a covert emissary for PK, and spent considerable time helping Jack Malloch. One of his tasks was to source spare parts from derelict Hawker Hunters in the Middle East for the air force. Of great significance, he and Antonio Felizardo later helped Ricky May of the Rhodesian CIO establish ties with the embryonic MNR, or Renamo, the Mozambican National Resistance Movement.)

Canadian-born Tim was a Sandhurst graduate before joining the Hussars. While at Sandhurst, he became friendly with Qaboos, the son of the Sultan of Oman. They remained friends and met again when Landon was deployed to Oman in the late 1960s as part of the British effort to combat the Soviet insurgency in the Dhofar region. Initially deployed in the south, he later joined the British-orchestrated plot in Muscat to remove Sultan Said bin Taimur. He persuaded Qaboos to cooperate in the intrigue which saw the Sultan deposed and exiled to London in July 1970. With Landon close at hand, Oman under Qaboos was radically transformed from fiefdom to a modern and prosperous country.

"I met Tim for the first time on the steps of parliament," PK recalls. "He was sitting there with Chris and Pete. We talked and it did not take long for

---

[52] 38 years later, economist John Robertson wrote of Zimbabwe's ruinous land 'reform' under Mugabe: "None of [the ZANU-PF apologists] mention the fact that land reform closed down Zimbabwe's biggest industry, or that this industry had been a highly successful contributor to the country's economy largely because of the adoption of methods and technologies that had evolved all over the world in very recent years ... The effect of land reform has been to reduce farming activity to patches of small-scale subsistence cropping, often using outdated cultivation practices and almost always on a small fraction of the land that was 'recovered' from large-scale commercial farmers; the whole programme has been a disaster."

me to realize this was a man I liked and with whom I could do business. This was the beginning of the Oman connection and Tim Landon played a huge part in helping Rhodesia survive. He really stuck his neck out for us on many occasions."

"Tim had a tremendous presence," Lotti recalls. "He was understated, quietly spoken and a good listener. He was also very bright indeed."

"The Omani connection was an interesting one," recalled PK. "The early depredations along the east coast of Africa were almost entirely Omani. The slave trade was run by the Omanis. Mozambique was named after the chief 'wog' of Oman—Masa an wa Mbikwe. The Omani people had an ancient, emotional tie to Africa and Tim Landon worked on that very cleverly. Just like Francophone Africa looks to Paris as the centre of the universe, you get these extraordinary historical-emotional connections which influence decision-makers. I do think this had a lot to do with the Omani involvement in Rhodesia. Whether it was a pining for a glorious past I don't know, but there was a connection there which did not apply to the Saudis at all. If it had come off and we had won through, it would have put the Omanis in a strong position."

On 27 July 1970, Rhodesia lost a faithful friend when Portugal's Antonio Salazar died. Unapologetically anti-communist and autocratic, he ruled Portugal with an iron fist from 1932 to 1968. "I was tremendously fond of Dr. Salazar," remembered Ian Smith. "He lived very simply and chose his words very carefully. He loved it when I told him that between Portugal and Rhodesia, the socialists running Britain would never get the better of us, as long as we stood together."

In January 1971, General Idi Amin toppled the government of Milton Obote amid applause from Whitehall, opening a new chapter in the saga of African tyranny. Back in Rhodesia, dealing with matters sartorial and as a man of style, PK felt qualified to speak on deteriorating dress standards: "It has been said manners maketh man. With equal truth it can be said that 'clothes proclaim the man'. While I would hate to see a complete dropping of standards, female trousers are here to stay and have to be accepted and that includes shorts along with that excellent invention, the mini skirt."

"People in Europe are confused between wearing as much as possible or as little as possible. In the famous [restaurant] Maxim's in Paris, they have a rule which seems to work very well. If you are properly dressed you are shown to the right-hand side of the room; if not you are taken to the left-hand side. Surely we can follow that example here in Rhodesia."

Forgiving the Mediterranean-type mores of resort towns Kariba and Inyanga, he recalled a wartime incident in Cairo when a stark-naked British officer was seen pursuing a woman through a hotel. "At his court-martial it was successfully pleaded that an officer in action need not be in uniform. In this case, it was agreed that he was properly dressed for the occasion."

Addressing dignitaries at the Rand Easter Show, PK reminded the West how Rhodesia guarded the line against communist expansion. Rhodesia's fall, he warned, would have grave implications for South Africa and the Free World.

On 1 May 1971, Franz Josef Strauss arrived in Bulawayo for a two-day stay. Writing to his father, PK described the portly Bavarian as "a very intelligent and powerful personality" and noted some of his after-dinner witticisms:

On African Nationalism: "When the natives are prevented from oppressing and killing each other, they complain that they are denied freedom and self-determination."

On the Cold War: "We know for certain that the Russians have several hundred ICBMs aimed at different targets in Germany. The Americans have pulled back their advance bases so we are in the middle. In the event of a conflict, we Germans will have the privilege of being killed by nuclear bombs without the satisfaction of knowing who they belong to."

On the Americans: "The Western world is ruled by the Americans ,who are the most powerful, richest and kindest fools history has produced."

PK also wrote to his father of the impending visit of Otto von Hapsburg, describing him as "by far the best informed man I know". In June, PK announced plans to develop a 200-mile game-conservancy strip between Victoria Falls and Kariba Dam wall, which was later shelved for security reasons. Opening an art exhibition in June 1971 he acknowledged personal limitations but declared: "As far back as the Impressionists, right through to the present day we have seen the melancholy spectacle of the so-called artistic temperament running amok and degenerating into licence of the worst sort, including downright charlatanism."

Lotti recalls: "PK did not know a lot about art but, as with most things, he had strong opinions. He would deliberately say within earshot of an artist he disliked: 'Well, you know dear chap, there were only ever two decent painters produced in Africa: Thomas Baines and the Bushman.'"

Addressing a meeting in the southern Lowveld at Nuanetsi, he provocatively declared that "without the positive effects of sanctions, Rhodesian industrialists would be 25 years behind".

In October, the press was exercised by the arrival of a mystery jet at Salisbury airport which whisked PK and a small group away on a flight serving French Champagne, which had not been seen in Rhodesia in a long while. Later that month, he took his father hunting in Matabeleland en route to Victoria Falls to open a new branch of CABS (Central African Building Society). Peter Bieber, a close associate, remembers the trip: "While visiting PK for the CABS opening in the Victoria Falls, Major Piet suffered an abdominal problem which required extensive surgery, and I received a distressing call from the old man. On this occasion he asked me to take over the finances on Fairfield and gave me power of attorney in this regard. I continued to look after the farm until the late 1990s. It was through my friendship with Major Piet that I became friendly with PK.

"I first met Major Piet in October 1966. We became friends and in early 1969 we cruised to South America together aboard the *Rena del Mar*. When I returned to South Africa later that year, the stock market was collapsing. I took over the Old Mutual unit trusts and acted on occasion as Board Secretary when Major Piet was Deputy Chairman."

Back at the negotiating table, Smith found dealing with the Conservatives almost as frustrating as with Labour, but encouraging signals flashed with Whitehall replacing terms like 'majority rule' with 'responsible rule'. Visits by Lord Goodman and Foreign Secretary Douglas-Home were well met with Smith and Home establishing excellent personal relations. To the surprise of many, where Wilson had failed, an agreement bringing the imbroglio to an end was signed in November 1971 on the understanding that 'it was acceptable to the majority'. Smith agreed not to campaign for the document's acceptance as long as Britain expedited the process.

"It was agreed that the commissioners would arrive in the country within two weeks," said PK. "I was present when this agreement was made. Immediately afterwards I went to my office and was talking to Hostis Nicolle and a few other people. I told them what had been agreed and Nicolle asked if it was in writing and been signed. The answer was no. He said, 'Well then, it's worth nothing.' He was precisely right because the Foreign Office gerrymandered and delayed the agreement till it became unrecognizable. Meantime we had agreed to stay out of the debate so we sat twiddling our thumbs while Bishop Abel Muzorewa trashed the agreement. Sadly this gave the impression to many Africans that the government was impotent and weak. The outcome would have been very different if the agreed timetable had been kept."

Lord Pearce's commissioners arrived some months later amid growing concern about British commitment. The surprise departure of Commissioner Lord Harlech midway through the process fuelled Smith's doubts. He wrote in his memoirs that it was "most unusual in the middle of such an important exercise. We wondered why but were told it was for personal, family reasons".[53]

It emerged Heath sunk the Rhodesia settlement in exchange for Liberal support for UK entry into the European Common Market. Liberal leader Jeremy 'Bomber' Thorpe had long sought Rhodesia's fall and Heath traded this irresistible scrap. Thorpe considered white Rhodesians homophobic and an embarrassing relic of a shameful imperial past. Recalls Hilary Squires:

It was October 1971 when I first met PK. It was at a candidate selection committee meeting. A vacancy had been left in the

---

[53] Ian Smith: *The Great Betrayal: The Memoirs of Ian Douglas Smith*. Blake Publishing, 1997

Top: Fairfield House toward the end of the 19th century.

Above: Lotti's grandfather, Emperor Charles of Austria, the last ruler of the Austro-Hungarian Empire, who died in 1922.

Centre right: PK as a toddler, with George, Prince of Wales (at right).

Right: PK with a fine kudu bull.

Top: Jan Smuts, Joy van der Byl, Louis Esselen, Major Piet and Mrs. Smuts

Centre left: PK at Bishops, second row, second from left.

Above: PK and Maureen Egland.

Left: The 1942 christening of Princess Irene of Greece and Denmark, wearing the van der Byl christening robe. The Greek royal family was in exile in South Africa during the war. The father, King Paul of the Hellenes, is behind Constantine II, while his queen, Frederika of Hanover, has her arm around Princess Sophia.

Above left: PK in Egypt during World War II, next to his father, Major Piet.

Above: PK as an officer of the Hussars, *Photo* John Dodgson

Left: PK with his tank crew, Italy 1944.

Below: PK reclines in his Jeep in Carinthia, Austria, April 1945.

Top: The April 1947 Royal visit to South Africa. King George VI and Queen Elizabeth meet Major Piet and Joy van der Byl. A young Princess Elizabeth can be seen on the right of her mother.

Above left: Early days tobacco farming in Selous. PK in front of his farmhouse.

Above: PK looks askance on the Salisbury tobacco floors.

Left: PK (far right) having tea with service chiefs in the bush during early counter-insurgency operations, c. 1966.

Top: Early Zambezi Valley operations. On PK's left are F/Lt Ian Harvey (who later served with distinction during the Bush War) and Supt Sanderson (BSAP).

Above: PK on an outing with National Parks and Information Ministry personnel. Max Dumas is on the right.

Above: PK with the world-record elephant he shot in Angola.

Centre left: Fairfield House.
Photo Neville Clayton

Above: Formal portrait, the Deputy Minister of Information, March 1964.
Photo Basil Shackleton

Left: PK at a Portuguese National Day garden party, with the Portuguese Consul-General, Dr. J. de Freitas (centre), 10 June 1965. At left is 'Boss' Lilford.

July 1965. Cardinal Colombo (right) and Mr. Zadotto chatting to PK during their visit to Rhodesia to inspect Catholic missions and hospitals in the Kariba area.
Photo Tony Pierce-Roberts

Prime Minister Ian Smith signs the UDI proclamation, 11 November 1965. He is flanked on the left by D.W. Lardner-Burke and C.W. Dupont and on the right by W.J. Harper and Lord Graham. Middle row from left: J.H. Howman, P. van Heerden, B.H. Mussett, J.J. Wrathall and G.W. Rudland. Back row: A.P. Smith, I.B. Dillon, L.B. Smith, I.F. McLean, PK van der Byl and Brig A. Dunlop.
Photo Basil Shackleton

Dillon, van der Byl, Dunlop and L. Smith after the reading of the UDI proclamation.
Photo Basil Shackleton

Top left: Clifford Dupont signs the Oath of Allegiance to HM Queen Elizabeth, Queen of Rhodesia, and loyalty to Rhodesia, 17 November 1965. *Photo* Basil Shackleton

Centre left: PK van der Byl, D. Williams (Deputy Director of Information) and Ian Smith hold a press conference, 17 November 1965. *Photo* Basil Shackleton

Below: 11 December 1965. Rhodesian Front, Hartley Constituency Council. Back row from left: A.F. Ward, M. Cohen, J.P. le Roux, J.O. Pascoe, K. Boyce. Middle: J.I. de Wet, W.A. MacCallum, G. Heyns, D. Holtzhausen, B. Keevil, L.W. Lewis, G. Thomas. Front: H.F.N. Light, P.K. van der Byl MP, H.J. Visser, Mrs. D. Zaleski, S.N. Eastwood, M. Skea. *Photo* Branson

PK at the funeral of Mr. and Mrs. Viljoen, 23 May 1966. The Viljoens were cruelly murdered by terrorists. *Photo* Alan Allen

Below left: March 1968. PK, as Deputy Minister of Information, visits Warrant Officer Herod (1RAR) in hospital. Herod was wounded in action during Operation Cauldron in the Zambezi Valley. *Photo* Roy Creeth

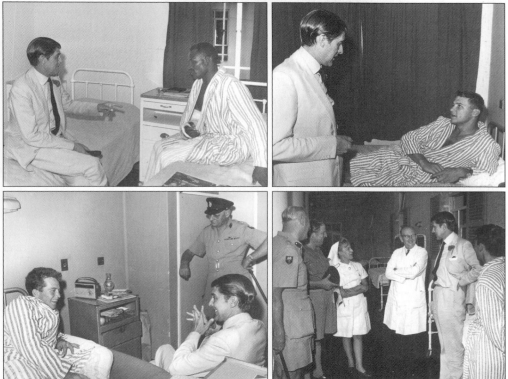

Centre right: PK chats with SAS Cpl C.J.J. Liebenberg, wounded during Operation Cauldron.
Photo Roy Creeth

Above left: PK chats with SAS Tpr Donald Junner, wounded during Operation Cauldron.
Photo Roy Creeth

Above right: PK doing the hospital rounds after Operation Cauldron. The patient is Gunner Mande, the medical officer is Dr. Laidler and the nurse is Sister Vye. *Photo* Roy Creeth

Top left: Dr. Richard Jaeger, Vice President of the German Bundestag, and Mrs. Jaeger seen here on 1 May 1968 with PK, on a private visit to the Victoria Falls. *Photo* Roger Bull

Top right: 4 October 1968. PK admiring a fine set of buffalo horns. *Photo* A.W. Gray

Above: PK—suave, debonair and sophisticated—in his element, mixing with European aristocracy. *Photo* Foto Nagy, Munich

Centre left: Joy and 'Major Piet' van der Byl, taken sometime in the '70s. *Photo The Argus*

Left: Lin Mehmel, PK's confidante and family friend.

Above: PK poses with his trackers and a trophy buffalo.

Left: PK takes tea with SAS captain, Mick Graham, in the northeastern operational area.

Below left: PK tours the operational area in the northeast of Rhodesia, here seen with pilot F/Lt Pete Simmonds.

Top: With senior military commanders on a visit to the operational areas. From left: Lt-Col Dave Heppenstall (RAR), Lt-Gen Peter Walls, AVM Frank Mussell and PK.

Centre left: PK shows signs of strain.

Above: Archduke Otto von Hapsburg, PK's longtime friend.
Photo Estudio Reicar, Lisbon

Left: PK with Monika Hapsburg.

Above: PK on a trip to Kariba with the Rt. Hon. Julian Amery.

Right: Lord Richard Cecil, KIA.

Above: From left: Piet Bosch, PK, Qais Zawawi (Omani foreign minister), President John Wrathall, Tim Landon and Chris Landon.

PK chats with Mr. J. Gondo MP (left), member for Kunyasi, 6 August 1970.

PK visits the offices of the Ministry of Information's newspaper, *The African Times*, which boasted a readership of over a million. Here he looks over a script with Gervaise Chitewe and Benson Funyama. *Photo* Basil Shackleton

PK receives the Grand Officer of the Legion of Merit from President Clifford Dupont, 19 June 1971.

4 August 1971. PK at the Nkoni Cattle Club, Tjolotjo Research Station field day

Top left: PK visits Domboshawa Training Centre, 10 March 1972. Here he chats to Messrs. A. Kadyevu and A.C.S. Gulu from the Mobile Film Unit of the Internal Services of the Ministry of Information, Immigration and Tourism. *Photo* Alan Allen

Top right: One of PK's favourites, Warrant Officer Gibson Mugadza (RAR) was awarded the Bronze Cross of Rhodesia for valour in action, January 1975. His final appointment before retirement was RSM School of Infantry, 1980. PK was instrumental in opening up the commissioned ranks to black soldiers.

Above: Rhodesian Front Parliamentray Caucus, June 1974. Front row from left: D.C. Smith, P. van Heerden, L.B. Smith, M.H.H. Partridge, B.H. Mussett, P.K. van der Byl, D.W. Lardner-Burke, I.D. Smith, J.J. Wrathall, J.H. Howman, I.F. McLean, A.P. Smith, I.B. Dillon, R.T.R. Hawkins. Second row: D. Divaris, G.R. Hayman, R.E.D. Cowper, J.J.L. de Kock, E. Broomberg, A.G. Mells, J. Christie, S.H. Millar, C.F.S. Clark, A. Skeen, J.A. Newington. Third row: B. Ponter, A. McCarter, R.B. Hope-Hall, A.L. Lazell, D. Fawcett-Phillips, R. Cronjé, H.G. Squires, A. Holland, A.J.W. MacLeod, P.F. Shields. Fourth row: J.J. Burger, W.E. Stuttaford, A. Mosely, E.A. Sutton-Pryce, T.I.F. Sandeman, E.M. Micklem, H.D. Tanner. Back Row: R.G.S. Simmonds, J.P.B. Nilson, C.E. Barlow, J.C. Gleig, G.R. Olds, D.A. Hamilton-Ritchie, D.J. Brink. Inset: W.M. Irvine.

Above left, above right and below: PK, as Minister of Defence, visits the operational area in the northeast of the country.
Photos Simon McBride

Left: PK with General Peter Walls and Air Vice-Marshal Frank Mussell. *Photo* Simon McBride

Top left: PK presents 2Lt Roddy Smith with the Sword of Honour. School of Infantry, Gwelo, February 1975.

Top right: Lotti with Marge Bassett, PK's long-serving secretary, on the occasion of her award of the Meritorious Service Medal, February 1979.

Above: PK, as Minister of Defence, inspects an RLI passing-out parade, Cranborne Barracks, 1976. The officer on the far left is Lt Tom Simpson, and partially obscured is the RLI Commanding Officer, Lt-Col Peter Rich.

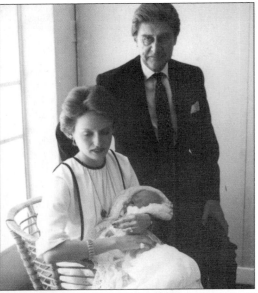

Top left: Lotti's and PK's wedding, 31 August 1979.

Top right: Pieter Vincenz's christening, 1981.

Above left: Valerian's christening in Cape Town, September 1982. From left: Lady Stella Bailey (godmother), Lotti and Valerian, Cardinal Owen McCann, Joy van der Byl, PK and Pieter Vincenz.

Above right: Family photo, 1985.

Left: Three good friends: Franz Joesph Strauss, the Bavarian premier (at left) with Alexandre de Marenches, former head of French Intelligence, and PK, 1987.

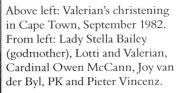

Top left: On safari, 1985. PK and Lotti with Valerian and
Pieter Vincenz in front.

Top right: PK with David Dimbleby, 1999.

Above left: The 1988 family Christmas
card.

Above right: The 1994 family
Christmas card.

Left: Casimir van der Byl with
Archduke Otto von Hapsburg, 2007.

Top left: Original artist unknown. Copied by Lin Mehmel for members of the immediate family.

Above: Ian Smith and Lotti, 2007.

Left: From left: Kata Landon, Ian Smith, Lotti, the author (behind Lotti), Ron Reid-Daly, Valerian and Pieter Vincenz, 2007.

Below: PK's funeral, November 1999, on the hill overlooking Fairfield.

Salisbury Central constituency by the resignation of Tony Ellison who was under a cloud arising out of a conviction for some statutory provision in relation to his business. PK was on the selection board along with Angus Graham and Wickus de Kock. My first impressions of him was he was something of a dilettante, a bit foppish, anxious to carry the war to the anti-RF Argus Newspaper Group and impatient with the restraints placed on his antipathy by the laws of defamation. As far as I knew he was then a bit of a political lightweight. Later I would discover that at the level of grand strategy, in the realm of international affairs, he had a very good head. I was not in the same league as him in that arena. The contacts he made, developed and nurtured during his time as Minister of Foreign Affairs, were of inestimable value in breaking UN sanctions. I remember thinking of him as a latterday, small-scale Metternich, more concerned with building bridges and securing alliances that furthered his country's interests; he worked effectively behind the scenes and at a personal level. He had the most astonishing range of contacts across the international scene of anyone I ever knew. Apart from his attending annual grouse shoots with the King of Spain, his association with the Sultan of Oman, facilitated by Tim Landon, was the key to accessing exports through the Middle East. His friendship with Bongo was the subject of much discussion and, when he was decorated by the Gabonese president, there was much mystery surrounding the award. One irreverent suggestion was that is was for surviving a night with Madame Bongo!

In October 1971, Archduchess Adelheid of Austria died. She was a friend of PK's and an academic with an abiding interest in Africa. Lotti recalls, "She was highly intelligent, a journalist with very strong views and very involved with Otto's work."

"Before she died," recalls her brother, Otto von Hapsburg, "she told me she was leaving her good friend PK van der Byl to me to look after. That is how I grew to know PK and the Duke of Montrose who was also in the Rhodesian cabinet. At the time, I was member of the European Parliament for Bavaria. Up to then my primary interest was in the Portuguese and in helping them maintain their presence in Africa. I worked closely with Adriano Moreira who was a close adviser to Dr. Salazar in his position as Minister responsible for the Overseas Territories. He understood very well the strategic value of a Portuguese presence in Africa and how important Rhodesia was to them. It was against this background that I met PK and became involved in helping the Rhodesians. All I can say is, I did as much as I could for them. They were great people and PK was a great man. He was very flamboyant but to be like that takes courage and he was a courageous person. He dearly loved Rhodesia and would have done anything for his country."

PK's friendship with Otto increased his profile within The Circle. "The Circle de Pinay," recalled PK, "played a major part in Rhodesia's affairs. Established by Antoine de Pinay and Konrad Adenauer [German Chancellor], it was initially a conservative Christian/Catholic collection of notables who met unofficially a couple of times a year to decide Europe's response to Communist expansion. After meetings members would then return to their respective governments and try to influence policy. Members included lot of devilishly important people like de Pinay himself, Carlo Pesenti, Prince Casimir Wittgenstein, Alfredo Sanchez Bella [a Spanish minister], Julian Amery, Jessie Helms [US Senator], Franz Josef Strauss, Giulio Andreotti [Italian Defence Minister] and Alexandre de Marenches [head of French Intelligence]. Meetings invariably took place in Franco's Spain."

"Alexandre de Marenches," according to Archduke Otto, "was absolutely brilliant and very brave: a long-term thinker and one of the greatest minds that I have encountered."

"For some reason de Marenches had little sympathy for South Africa," PK recalls. "He thought Hendrik van den Bergh, head of BOSS [South African Bureau of State Security] was a complete half-wit."

"PK got on immediately with Franz Josef Strauss," recalls Otto, "and their friendship had many positive consequences for Rhodesia. CEDI also helped de Gaulle in Algeria establishing the Afro/European link. Most of our members identified the communist threat in Africa and wanted to do what they could to oppose it."

"Later, my friendship with the King of Spain helped enormously," recalls PK. "He didn't get directly involved but our friendship gave me cachet with the rest. I used to stay with him and we went shooting together. As a result, Rhodesian passport holders were allowed into Spain. "There was a Jap called Tanaka but I was the first real 'wog' admitted to The Circle. Otto opened every door for me and God alone knows what a difference that made to saving Rhodesia. Through him I got access to the top Belgians, Germans, Italians, even the Greeks, although their colonels were not terribly Catholic. There were also a few intellectuals; writers and poets, but mainly political people. Andreotti helped us screw that bugger Agusta of Agusta Bell to make good on helicopters he owed us. A general summoned Agusta to a meeting and our helicopters arrived two weeks later." PK continued:

> I was able to talk Rhodesia at these meetings and most empathized with us. Strauss almost single-handedly delayed sanctions for two years. He also helped us in breaking sanctions. When the meetings moved to the UK and the US, I was unable to attend because I was banned from those countries. Kaulza de Arriaga, who commanded the Portuguese Army in Mozambique, was a member so we had a good chance there to talk about mutual problems. As an 'Old Boy Network' it had few equals. Strategically, we in Rhodesia were not terribly important to the French so their support for us with Bongo was puzzling, but in a cynical world never totally discount the emotional factor. It still plays a part in great affairs. And there is no doubt we were seen as an attractive cause; we were seen as brave and decent people. Not a bigoted lot of sods full of bullshit and bravado

like the South African Nationalists. We had an emotional appeal to people like Strauss and indeed to many in England; people like the Salisburys who undoubtedly inhibited the worst vicissitudes of British action against us. Rhodesia reminded the French of their Algerian experience; they felt for us. Funnily enough Bongo did not like the South Africans but he liked the Rhodesians. Somehow we had a better rapport.

Recalls Lin Mehmel:

Partly thanks to Circle contacts, we managed to get America to lift sanctions against importing Rhodesian chrome in 1971. PK could not get into the country but some of us, including myself, did manage and thanks to Senator Harry Byrd and Buddy Fulton-Lewis, the 503 Byrd Amendment, repealing the law banning the import of Rhodesian chrome, was passed. This was a very significant development and a boon for the country. I persuaded Senator Byrd to visit Rhodesia, which he did, and PK could not have given him a better reception at Bath Road. That was the beginning of a lifelong friendship. At the time, Senator Byrd was also in close contact with Dr. Anton Rupert. Also, with the help of some members of the Circle we managed to get our sugar into Germany. I was very involved in this exercise. Only PK could have mixed so easily in the Circle milieu. He gained their confidence and so much flowed from that with their help. Later, at PK's behest, I would also work with Senator Jesse Helms on the sanctions issue. He was instrumental in sending many groups and people to Rhodesia to meet PK and learn firsthand what was going on in the country.

Back in South Africa, convalescing at Groote Schuur hospital after his Victoria Falls trip, Major Piet was amused by an article in the *Sunday Express*. It reported that Princess Alice, sole remaining grandchild of

Queen Victoria would visit South Africa as the guest of Mrs. Joy van der Byl, 'widow' of the late Major Piet. The Major quickly responded to the editor: "My doctors at Groote Schuur have asked me to inform you that while your report might be an evident anticipation, it is at the moment a gross exaggeration. While I have quoted the doctors, as an ex-politician, I do not expect you to take my word for it."

As far as farming was concerned, PK's record remained patchy. "He had the ranch near Bulawayo by this time," remembers William van der Byl, "so quite a lot more money had gone in. PK then said he wanted to do citrus. I blew my top and said, 'Get what you have sorted out first, and then do citrus.' The ranch was run by a very nice Irishman who told you what you wanted to hear, and it never did very well. It was eventually taken over by Nick Prilieux."

"I sat down with PK," remembers Peter Bieber, "and we had a long hard look at the farm financials. He was meeting his repayments but that was all, and I had to tell him to sell one of the farms, which he agreed to do. PK needed a good income but was never a spendthrift or wasteful. He was stylish, but not in an unnecessarily extravagant way. Unfortunately, he was not a very good businessman."

In March 1972, PK addressed 6,000 black administration trainees at Domboshawa Training Centre, suggesting Africa and the world would do well to copy such facilities. Shortly afterward he controversially suggested the 1971 British agreement should be scrapped, unless full independence was granted. On the defensive, at the Party Congress later that year, he weighed his successes (France and Germany) against the overwhelming failure to secure Western recognition.

"There can be little doubt," says Lin Mehmel, "that both PK and Ian Smith underestimated the depth of the malice that would be visited upon the country after UDI. Both men believed, naively, as it turned out, that reason and fair play would eventually prevail among the democracies but the world had moved to a completely different mindset and the old values and rules had been abandoned."

In April, PK drew fire from the British press for denying William Davis, editor of *Punch*, a Rhodesian visa. Defending his decision, he described the magazine as "a vitriolic, left-wing political journal with very little humour except of a debased sort; that had been openly and viciously hostile to Rhodesia and everything we stand for."

Responding to accusations that he had acted with immaturity he said, "… to keep anyone out, irrespective of what damage their writing may do to our image or however untruthful, biased, distorted they may be is one thing. But frankly, if it is a sign of maturity to condone slander, pornography, permissiveness and the undermining of public morale, I prefer to retain my immature, wide-eyed innocence." He further criticized Britain for welcoming and giving Bishop Muzorewa a platform to hurl insults at the Rhodesian government and in September 1972, PK withdrew Abel Muzorewa's and Canaan Banana's passports. Banana called it "an act of cowardice". (Banana, then a darling of the UK media, went on to become the first president of Zimbabwe in 1980, a position he held until 1987. He was convicted in 1998 on eleven charges of sodomizing members of his security detail and sentenced to a prison term.)

While Rhodesia was gaining little traction, elsewhere the president of newly-named Zaire, Mobutu Sese Seko, let it be known he was willing to trade with the country. "This connection was thanks to Hans Germani," PK recalls. "Hans had been with Mike Hoare's lot in the Congo and become very close to Mobutu. This was how we managed to start moving our beef into and through Zaire. Germani and Hoare had helped Mobutu to power, so he was beholden to them."

CHAPTER TWELVE
PK goes to war again

On the fighting front the insurgents were forced to change tactics. They had been identified in the Zambezi Valley by moving in large numbers and wearing 'figure 8' patterned boots. To counter this, they moved their focus east to Mozambique, seeing this as an easier access point into Rhodesia. Fighting their own liberation war against disinterested Portuguese colonial forces, Samora Machel's Frelimo fighters welcomed the new combatants.

As a result, on 21 December 1972, a revitalized enemy stalked a remote farmhouse among the lush fields in the Centenary district of the northeast. In the dead of night they attacked. Their target was the de Borchgrave homestead which was raked with rockets and machine-gun fire, wounding one of the children and wrecking the house. Marc, the father, reached for the phone only to find the line had been cut. His wits about him, fearing a vehicle ambush, he slunk out the house with his rifle and ran the two miles to a neighbouring farm to raise the alarm. Security forces responded while the de Borchgraves moved to their neighbours for sanctuary. But the reprieve was to be short. Two nights later the terrorists struck again at Whistlefield Farm where the de Borchgraves had sought sanctuary. Marc and another one of his children were wounded. An RLI reaction team coming to their aid hit a landmine, resulting in the death of a trooper. The war for Rhodesia had been rejoined in earnest and the Rhodesians were being punished in their homesteads.

While the war in the east of the country escalated, tragedy struck at the Victoria Falls with the murder of two Canadian girls on holiday by drunken Zambian soldiers firing across the river. PK, as Minister of Tourism, was outraged and called on the Canadian government to, at the very least, demand an apology from the Zambian Government but Canadian

External Affairs Minister, Mitchell Sharp declined. He would only go so far as to say the Canadian government "was still not satisfied" with the explanation it had received from Lusaka. In Ottawa, an opposition MP suggested that if Rhodesians had committed the offence, the Canadian government would be "ranting and raging, morning, noon and night". PK issued a statement urging tourists not to be deterred, but called the killing "a disgraceful and monstrous interference with people's freedom, and proves the Zambian army is out of control … An RBC crew went to the Falls to film the aftermath and the search for the bodies but the incident received little coverage as it did not suit the international media view of Rhodesia. Mr. Dryber, father of one of the girls, came to join the search but the bodies were never recovered."

Shortly afterward, PK 'parachuted' Costa Pafitis into Rome to work covertly with well-placed Rhodesian sympathizers in the ongoing sanctions-busting campaign. Pafitis remembers:

> I joined the Ministry of Information soon after UDI. My father owned the Ambassador Hotel where I was working but I hankered after a job in the public sector that would bring me in closer contact with what was going on in the country. I liked PK instantly; his refinement and intelligence were impressive and I think he saw in me someone who could fill certain roles and look after specific people; I was often assigned to the Khuen-Lutzoews. The fact that I am also Greek might have helped. His family's close association with the Greek Royal Family was part of his history and I think this made him empathetic to people of Greek extraction. I'm sure my Sandhurst training also helped; PK liked military people.
>
> Not long after I joined the ministry, PK sent me to Pretoria to undertake press relations for John Gaunt, who then represented Rhodesia in South Africa. One of my more memorable tasks on behalf of PK was to go and buy a bottle of Joy perfume for his mother every Christmas. He would pick up the bottle on his

way through to his family every year. After five years there, I returned to Salisbury, but only briefly before being sent to Italy. PK said he was going to have to resort to "a bloody Greek to deal with the bloody Italians". PK had excellent contacts there through The Circle. I got in because of my Greek passport. My cover was artistic; I claimed to be researching a comparison between Italian and Greek art. I told the Italians theirs was far superior and had little trouble with the authorities thereafter. PK came to see Andreotti frequently. I was given the number of General Michaelli, then head of Italian Intelligence, and told to call if I ever got into trouble. The book *The Salamander* by Morris West was set in this time and place and I'm sure the 'salamander' was, in fact, Andreotti protected by Michaelli. I was introduced to a group of operatives who I contacted through The Circle when I needed something done. They were very efficient and helpful.

Adding glamour to my situation was the person who provided my contact to The Circle. An exquisite lady, a former Miss America, her name was Jeanine Leigh Avery Kahn and she was connected to someone high up in the Italian hierarchy. She was also linked to the film industry and it was through this connection that Ursula Andress came to the Victoria Falls and made the film 'Africa Express'. I went to the premier with PK in Rome. These, looking back, were my finest days and I have PK to thank for this, and also for where I got to in my career. Thanks to him I was awarded the Member of The Legion of Merit based on the citation he wrote; something I'm terribly proud of, but all really thanks to PK.

On the occasion of my presentation to the members of The Circle there was a bevy of German starlets present who were at that time training in Italy; the most beautiful girls. Jeanine, the former Miss America was also there and she did all the introductions. The function finished at about eleven o'clock that evening and she was all for having a night out, but I slipped out and went to my room. Barely had I arrived there when Jeanine called to announce she and some of the girls were anxious to go out and wanted company. A little rattled, I called PK in his room and told him in a respectful tone that there were girls below looking for a night on the town and told him I was little unsure as to what to do. There was a brief silence before PK resolved the issue: "Well, the answer is elementary, Costa," he said, "we will simply feed them and then fuck them."

One of my principal duties was to maintain lines of communication with Italian industry. Rhodesia had a history of using Italian technology. Kariba Dam and the Rhodesian Iron and Steel Corporation are two examples, but in addition our air force trainers were Sia-Marchetti and we would eventually receive Agusta Bell helicopters. In order to maintain business ties, it was my job to get entrance to the country approved for Rhodesian representatives who had been listed by the British as targeted individuals denied access to Europe. In my work there, the South Africans were very kind. Having no diplomatic status, communication with Salisbury was awkward and they invariably allowed me use of their facilities. The head of South African Airways [SAA] was also very kind to me. SAA crews helped me ferry documents back to Rhodesia.

One of my other tasks was to try and recruit Italians; mainly people who had recently left Libya, to settle in Rhodesia, but this did not bear much fruit. We tried the same in Malta where there was high unemployment but with little success.

PK was incredibly effective when he arrived on the scene. He had a knack for flattering people with his detailed knowledge of their respective histories. Often he knew more about his host country than they knew themselves, which people found fascinating. This turned to adulation when he told them how glorious their respective pasts were. He could interface with virtually any nationality, and more than hold his own. In essence, he was the consummate foreign minister, as he subsequently became. An aristocrat in a sense, he did not endear himself to all, particularly those who saw him as aloof and a bit of a snob but he could not be ignored in any context. And behind it all was a very genuine individual and a man who offered total loyalty to those with whom he sided.

On one occasion we went and visited the place where he had been posted in Italy as Intelligence Officer in the Hussars. There was a wedding on at the time and we approached the gathering. PK, as ever beautifully turned out in blazer with a handkerchief puffed out of his pocket, immediately turned heads, one of which belonged to one of the bridesmaids; a very pretty little girl who seemed unable to take her eyes off him. I suggested to PK that he might want to get to know her better but he demurred on account of his height. "I doubt," he said, "that I could breed with anything that close to the ground."

Despite speculation that PK's star was fading, Smith retained him in a cabinet reshuffle in May 1973. After the reshuffle Smith took his ministers to Kariba for a tiger-fishing match with a National Farmers' Union team. Smith won the biggest fish but PK left early to host a five-day visit from Franz Josef Strauss.

In August 1973, a subdued Abel Muzorewa met with Ian Smith. Unsure of his political future he recanted his earlier opposition to the Home agreement. Smith took heart from this meeting, as internal black agreement was still a British prerequisite.

For PK, one of the great tragedies of the Rhodesian imbroglio was the failure of the world to attach any importance to the role of the traditional leaders in the country's body politic. Scorned as white puppets and stooges, he argued that these people were in every way more representative of the majority of the black populace but his entreaties invariably fell on deaf ears.

Addressing a group of chiefs at an installation ceremony in October

1973, he spoke bluntly, referring to ZANU as terrorists: "These are not simply black people who come to attack the white man because, in fact, at the present time, they are destroying the property of more Africans than they are of the Europeans. They are, on the contrary, hardened criminals who have come to spread terror and to try and take the country from all of us and to run it only for their benefit. Where this has happened in other parts of Africa the situation has become very grievous."

Later that year, PK tabled a new Broadcasting Bill which transferred control of the RBC to a restructured board. This drew criticism from independent politician Allan Savory, a former Smith man who had resigned in the wake of a land expropriation exercise in the Matetsi hunting area near the Victoria Falls.

At the same time, to step up sanctions-busting, PK helped facilitate the government purchase of a Gabon-registered DC-7 for Jack Malloch, and his efforts soon paid dividends. By the end of 1973, statistics showed the country's GNP had doubled and the national workforce had grown by more than 200,000.

In August 1974, PK's political star was on the rise again with his promotion to Minister of Defence, replacing the dependable Jack Howman. Smith, probably looking for a spark, had opted for PK's energetic, hands-on approach. "This elevation to Minister of Defence was, I think, the highlight of his life in politics," says Lotti.

South African writer Al Venter met him around this time and remembers PK: "I got to know PK quite well. Through him, I engineered Republican Press into doing four 24-page supplements in *Scope* and its opposite Afrikaans number soon after he became Minister of Defence in 1974. I took a crew of four into Rhodesia and we were there for months, most of it at the 'Sharp End'. He was a marvellous guy. I was actually at lunch at his delightful Cape-style home in Salisbury (with fellow minister Wickus de Kock) when I collapsed with malaria. PK was quite alarmed at my condition at first and called to Wickus to pull out the 'Witblits' brandy! I'd been in the Valley (on the Mozambican side) and came down hard, so that my family was called to my bed at the Andrew Fleming Hospital.

It took three difficult months to get over that one. When I recovered, he personally drove me back to the Monomatapa Hotel in what I thought was his Rolls."

In his new post, PK was keen to familiarize himself with conditions at the front line and paid a visit to the Fireforce base at Mt. Darwin. As fortune would have it, the siren went soon after his arrival, signalling an enemy sighting and troops were activated.

Lieutenant Richard Passaportis, then a young subaltern in 1 Commando, RLI, recalls the day:

> I sprinted to the chopper which was already winding up and jumped into my seat behind the pilot, ready to fly, when I looked across and was dumbfounded to see none other then the Minister of Defence sitting opposite me. Immaculately clad in starched shirt, shorts and stockings, he looked very calm. Then I looked at his weapon and to my horror noticed he was carrying a heavy hunting rifle. This troubled me. We were only in four-man 'sticks' and I needed all the firepower I could muster. He was sitting where my machine gunner should have been sitting, carrying his gun and 500 rounds rather than a handful of especially hand-loaded cartridges. I implored PK to give up his seat and to let me take my gunner because I was leading the ground attack and would have to make sure I did not falter. I asked him to make way but promised I would have him brought in on the 'second wave' so he could have a crack at the enemy. He immediately obliged and we flew to the enemy position, previously identified by a hidden OP (observation point). We hit the ground running but found nothing. A little pissed off, I remonstrated with Mick Hardy, Selous Scout commander of the OP, suggesting he had screwed up—there was nothing to be found. He was adamant he had sighted the enemy.
>
> There was a sense of anti-climax as we searched the bush, but with the arrival of the 'second wave' choppers I became

terrified something might happen to the Minister of Defence. I had arranged for him to go with a 'stick' which included Trooper Chillcott—a 'boy soldier' we were also keen to keep out of harm's way—as far from the action as possible. All was quiet when suddenly there was an almighty bang that broke the silence and all hell broke lose. As luck would have it, the 'gooks' were hiding in a wash-away under an overhang on a curve in a dry riverbed and were discovered by none other than Trooper Chilcott and the Minister of Defence. As Chilcott fired a rifle-grenade into their position, he was hit in the face by a mortar bomb thrown by the enemy mortar man, which broke his jaw and floored him, leaving PK to blast away at the enemy, which he did with great gusto.

Happily the engagement ended successfully, apart from a wounded Chilcott, and PK was thrilled with his performance. On our return he led us straight to the pub and ordered ten cases of beer. It was like winning the lottery; the troopies were ecstatic and none will forget the experience. PK was in hilarious form and he kept pace with the best 'groggers' the RLI could produce. It was this sort of engagement with those fighting the war that earned him total devotion from Rhodesian servicemen.

Throughout the years I knew him he was incredibly kind to me and my family. On occasion I was invited to dine with him in Salisbury and they were always special occasions for me. He was always interested and interesting. It was a sad day for Rhodesia when he was sacked as Minister of Defence.

"He conducted himself extremely well in this portfolio," says Costa Pafitis, "because he almost literally led from the front. This is why he so endeared himself to the soldiers and airmen. He was physically very brave, a bloody good hunter and a fine marksman."

But clouds were gathering on Rhodesia's eastern border as Portuguese resolve in Mozambique wavered. Lisbon wanted the empire but the financial strains were telling, the economy was struggling, their sons were dying in far-off places and international criticism was mounting. Accused of atrocities (most subsequently proved to be false) General Antonio Spinola, Portugal's new leader following the coup that ousted Marcello Caetano, looked for a way out of their African entanglement.

Sensing a major strategic shift, Smith wanted an alliance with South Africa and Portugal to defend everything south of the Zambezi River but the winds of change were blowing hard. Vorster was reticent and Samora Machel's dream of a Marxist dictatorship in Mozambique was at hand.

Wanting another mandate, Smith went to the polls in July 1974 and swept the board. During the lead-up, PK encountered a formidable lady while out campaigning. Champing at the bit while she awaited question time, the solid lady took a deep breath, drew herself to full height and began: "Mr. Chairman, last Rhodes and Founders holidays I went to the Vumba ..." when PK interrupted, "My dear lady, if only I had known!" This brought the house down and the angry questioner flounced out the hall in fury.

Ron Reid-Daly recalls:

His appointment as Minister of Defence was an immediate tonic for us. Morale improved immeasurably throughout the armed services when news of this development filtered through. I loved the guy. He was eccentric, outrageous at times but what a fantastic sense of humour he had. Whatever he did, he did with gusto and enthusiasm. Soon after his appointment I remember he phoned Peter Walls and asked him to have a uniform made up for him. It must be said that PK and General Walls never really hit it off. He wanted the uniform made to his own specifications with an English-style high collar and buttons in all the right places. Having found out that the RLI were wearing shorts rather than longs, he asked for something along the same lines, but smarter. He then arrived for a visit in a helicopter in a camouflage, cavalry-type shirt and these beautifully tailored shorts, out of which came these long thin legs. He was carrying a heavy-calibre hunting rifle; a .450 I think. It all looked bloody funny but I tell you he could walk and he could shoot. He then spoke to the local army commander and said, "Right, what patrols are going out because I'm going with and I need to kill something as soon as possible." There was a lot of "but … but … but" from the army commander, but PK cut him short: "Don't but me … I'm the Minister of Defence and I'm telling you to send me out into the field."

Those hard-arsed RLI 'troopies' looked at PK very sceptically. Part of the problem was they couldn't understand his accent—they thought he was talking another language. The patrol headed off and scepticism turned to admiration when he walked the troopies ragged; they came back with a very different view of the man and that was really where it all started. He became a bit of a legend. The men of the RLI were devoted to him.

Flight Lieutenant Pete Simmonds recalls some of his experiences with the new minister:

I was posted to No. 7 Helicopter Squadron in 1974, by which time the civil war in Rhodesia was well on its way. On this occasion I had just completed a four-week trip on operations in Mt. Darwin in the northeast of the country and was looking forward to ten days' rest at home, away from the war. On my first day back at New Sarum Air Force Base I wasn't pleased when my boss, Squadron Leader Eddie Wilkinson, told me that an Air Task had come in and there was no one left on the squadron to do it but myself. There had been a recent cabinet reshuffle in government and Mr. PK van der Byl had just become our new Minister of Defence.

PK, as he was affectionately called, had decided that the best way to get to know the military and to show how serious he was in his new portfolio was to tour the front line. My Air Task was to fly him around the northeast operational area. We only had Fireforces from Mt. Darwin eastward and south down to Fungwe in the Mrewa district. A Fireforce was a group of five or six troop-carrying helicopters led by another gunship helicopter. They were designed to carry a quick reactionary force to any troublespot that could be identified by the Security Forces. I had been tasked to spend one night each in Mt. Darwin, Marymount Mission and Fungwe with PK while he got to know the various army commanders and their men in each place.

Eddie Wilkinson briefed me to take an Alouette II for the job, to fly low in the operational area so as not to be shot at, but not so low as to frighten the Minister. I was then to drop him back at the squadron where the Commanding Officer of New Sarum would be waiting to greet him before he drove home that Friday. I hadn't met PK before, but had seen him on television and was therefore aware of his colourful, eccentric character. But I can't say I was ready for him when I did meet him for this trip. On the Tuesday my flight engineer, Steve Stead, and I prepared the Alouette II with enough fuel to fly us safely to Mt. Darwin. Steve and I had a tiny bag each with clothes and toiletries for three nights in the bush plus a stretcher each, packed under the back seat of the aircraft. The two of us took up very little space in the aircraft.

PK duly arrived on the Squadron with Wilkie in attendance. His car drove up to the helicopter and introductions and handshakes took place. I noticed that the new Minister had somehow managed to find a full set of smart camouflage clothing for the trip. His attire was conspicuous in that he wore no rank on his shoulder at all, but his green and khaki longs were different because he held them up with a brightly coloured red and yellow stable belt. He had kept the belt from his earlier days as an officer with the 7th Hussars during the Second World War in Italy. He must have dug deep in the attic for that belt. Then his bedroll was hauled out of the car boot and I wondered if we would ever get it into the tiny Alouette II. It was bigger than a 44-gallon drum and it was obvious he intended to be comfortable. Then two large bags came out of the car. One must have had clothes in it and the other, much heavier, clinked suspiciously, but somehow we managed to squeeze it all into the cabin. He was also hanging on to what looked very much like an elephant gun. He was well known for elephant hunting and was determined to bring it. No one suggested he change it; he wanted to put 'his gun' to good use on this trip.

The chopper was frightfully heavy but we managed to take off and flew away north over Borrowdale. We then passed over the granite hills and valleys of Dombashawa and on to Bindura, before descending to 50ft. above ground level for the rest of the trip to Mt. Darwin. Right from the start PK was chatty and excited, but he let me know within ten minutes of leaving New Sarum that he was to be dropped in the Botanical Gardens near his house, off Second Street Extension, when we returned on the following Friday. Wilkie had been explicit that he must be brought back to New Sarum where he would meet the Station Commander, but PK was insistent that he would be dropped near his house and wouldn't accept the instructions I had been given. I thought it was odd that he should be worrying about the end of his trip before it had begun but, as he said with a little ceremony in his very English accent, "It's all been organized, Peter! I've arranged for people to meet me there, so it cannot be changed, we must land in the Botanical Gardens!"

Ten minutes from Mt. Darwin, I warned Operations on the radio that we would be arriving soon and discovered that a contact was in progress west of Mt. Darwin. 'The King', Colonel Dave Parker, was running operations in Mt. Darwin and suggested we change frequency so that the Minister could hear the 'punch-up' taking place over the radio. PK was delighted when we changed to Channel 2 and immediately badgered me to join the contact. He wanted to be put down on his own in the contact area with his elephant gun: "On high ground please, Peter, as I like to attack downhill. I'd like to bag one of these chaps and this is an ideal opportunity, don't you think?" All this was said seriously in the strangest of accents, and Steve Stead was gagging in the back of the aircraft.

There was no chance I could do what he asked of course, but I felt I owed it to him at least to ask The King if we could fly at height over the contact area for a look at it from a distance. Colonel Dave Parker was adamant in his next instructions: "Get the Minister to Mt. Darwin, NOW, Simmo. He is not to be allowed anywhere near the contact; I will get him as close as he needs to be on the map in my Ops room when he lands!" PK heard the transmission and looked disappointed. All the while Steve kept a straight face, seemingly oblivious to the goings-on of pilots, officers and ministers around him.

After we landed, PK saw out the rest of the contact in the ops room and spent the afternoon poring over maps, tactics, and strategies and getting to know the men involved in the war. He enthusiastically chatted to soldiers and managed to attract even the roughest troopie's attention with them saying they wanted to "*kyk* this new oke" [look at this new guy]. That evening he endeared himself in the officers' mess with his quaint stories and three bottles from the clinking bag. The Minister knew a thing or two about winning us over and we were well lubricated by his Scotch whisky, fine wine and beguiling character.

The following day he wanted to visit Karanda Mission on the way to Marymount Mission. The King had told him that we had taken some seriously wounded soldiers there recently and that the renowned American surgeon at the mission had kindly patched them up before sending them on to Salisbury General Hospital. He had probably saved the soldiers' lives. Since we were never really sure whose side any of the missionaries were on, it was considered a good idea to encourage them by sending the Minister to thank them personally for their action. We were not expected and landed unannounced at the airfield where the Karanda Mission pilot was attending to his Cessna. When our blades stopped turning he wandered over and I persuaded PK to leave his elephant gun in the aircraft. The pilot didn't know who PK was so I told him this was the Minister of Defence for Rhodesia, and explained why we were there. He was most impressed with all this and insisted on calling PK 'Your Highness' for the rest of the visit. Steve Stead and I made no effort to correct him and it seemed PK had no intention of putting the pilot right either. He obviously preferred to maintain his 'no rank on the shoulders' stance and his new 'Your Highness' title. It seemed to me that it actually suited him. The pilot showed us to the surgeon who was appropriately thanked with a little pomp before we moved on in a cloud of dust to Marymount Mission.

Halfway there we flew over a couple of African women carrying huge suitcases on their heads as they walked along a lonely path in the middle of nowhere. PK immediately wanted to check them out "in case they are carrying weapons of war". This was a Minister like no other we had seen before. He was determined to be directly involved. He was a contact waiting to happen. No other senior politicians had been this far into the bush before and frankly, even the good ladies from the Border Patrol Welfare Fund had ventured deeper into the operational zone than any of the ministers I could remember. I felt there would be no harm in letting him have a look in the suitcases and, who knows, they may have contained something they shouldn't. I looked for a suitable area and landed. I asked the long-suffering Steve Stead to accompany PK with his own weapon for the suitcase inspection. Steve's face gave nothing away as he galloped away with his FN after the Minister, who was by now bounding through the bush with his enormous gun held menacingly at the ready. By the time I got airborne and overhead the offending suitcases were open on the ground, and the African ladies were standing nearby with their hands up in the air. PK was 'hoiking' colourful clothes out of the suitcases with the barrel of his gun. There was clearly nothing sinister hidden away in the suitcases and PK's disappointment was obvious, even from the air. We left the ladies to continue their haulage and moved on to Marymount Mission.

If Karanda was a mission prepared to treat our troops in an emergency, Marymount was the opposite. The missionaries were openly hostile. This was most unfortunate, because with their endless supply of donor funds they had built a huge swimming pool, which we weren't allowed to use. A certain Father Ignatius refused to let us near this most enticing pool. He was well known to many of us for marching angrily about in his white socks and sandals, complaining about the many inconveniences of having military people around his mission. He never missed a chance to send letters of complaint to the long-suffering army commanders camped at the nearby airfield.

Major Brian 'Robbie' Robinson commanded the SAS base at Marymount at the time, and his men were operating over the border in Mozambique. It crossed my mind that the Minister may not win over as many hearts and minds at this place as he had the previous day. They had lost a man in action, SAS Corporal Storie, and no matter how professional the SAS were about their very specialized job, they were still a tight-knit force of human beings. Having lost one of their own, they would have been in no mood for nicety visits and polite chats with strange ministers. Robbie was a tough master and the type of man who would have normally preferred that politicians stay in

Salisbury with their suits and lengthy discussions while he was left unencumbered to fight the war.

I couldn't have been more wrong and was underestimating PK's charm. He was fully aware of Corporal Storie and while sensitive to this he was determined to let these soldiers know they had a supportive representative in government who was thoroughly on their side.

When we landed, he wanted to address the few men in camp and he did this sensibly. PK then mentioned to Robbie that he was tired of his camouflage longs and he wanted to look more like the rest of us with the standard khaki shorts, no socks and veldskoen shoes. The Quartermaster was summoned by Robbie and a short while later the Minister walked back into the Ops tent wearing a particularly tight pair of short shorts, displaying spindly, white legs. Brian Robinson saw the shorts and suggested that perhaps they were a little too short and that he might want a larger size. In front of all the assembled men, PK looked down and announced, "You are quite right of course, Brian; my cock sticks out of these ones!" It certainly lightened the mood and he was winning them over fast. After a change into more suitable trousers, more discussions about tactics, strategies and troop movements took place. PK then insisted on spending the night on ambush somewhere in the bush to "bag one of those buggers".

We had an early meal with him in the mess tent and more bottles came out of the musical bag. He then set out with a group of Rhodesian African Rifles men to ambush a known terrorist track. It rained that night and I really hoped, while I was tucked up in my dry bed, that PK would get a chance to finally use his gun. It didn't happen and yet he still returned chirpy and unfazed by the wet night he had endured in the bush. He had found a *demo* [African hatchet] while out there which he had decided to keep as a souvenir: "A rather good specimen, don't you think?" He then had breakfast and a sleep before we were supposed to leave at midday.

Brian Robinson had had more luck with Father Ignatius than previous commanders, having cajoled a precious half hour's swimming each evening. This privilege was to be temporary, and all pool rules had to be 'strictly adhered to'. The rule list was exhaustive and barely allowed swimmers to get wet. Staff at the mission had pool access most of the day. Students had a couple of hours under supervision and a restricted number of thoroughly washed soldiers were allowed in from 5.00 p.m. until 5.30 p.m. with "no noise, please".

After his rest, PK was outside the Ops tent looking a little tired when he asked about ten or 12 SAS men around him if there was anything more he could do to help them before he left. The question was asked in the context that he might do something for them back in Salisbury as the Minister of Defence, and most present were content to say that nothing was required. His action on ambush duty the previous night had already won their respect. One troopie, however, seized the moment and explained the swimming pool problem, describing Father Ignatius as "a member of the enemy".

PK sized up the situation immediately and his answer was simple. He waved his hand in the air and said, "Go to Ignatius and give him my regards please, corporal. When he understands who I am, explain to him that from now on my troops will have free access to the pool, that he will be allowed to use it from 5.00 p.m. to 5.30 p.m. and if he doesn't like the new rules, I'll deport the fellow." We left Marymount Mission a couple of hours later much to Father Ignatius's relief, with the complete support of every soldier within a hundred miles.

Lin Mehmel remembers the visit as part of a group given permission to visit and film the army camp as part of the ongoing psychological warfare exercise on a 'need to know' basis. "By the time we arrived at Marymount, PK was already there. You could hear him bellowing some distance off in the makeshift Operations tent. I could tell he had every intention of being overheard, saying, 'You can't tell me, dear boy, that the nuns spend their entire day in the swimming pool. Aren't they supposed to pray or something of that order?' There was a mumbled reply from the army commander before his voice boomed out again. 'Well then,' he shouted, 'we'll have to establish just precisely when they actually hose down the nuns and plan accordingly.'"

Peter Simmonds continues:

A commando from the Rhodesian Light Infantry was manning Fungwe Camp. It was under the command of Bruce Snelgar, with five helicopters at his disposal. The camp was based on a low granite kopje at the western end of the Fungwe airfield. I radioed ahead that I was landing there in ten minutes with a VVIP on board. I had elevated PK from VIP to VVIP in my radio transmissions and as we flew over the camp, Joe Sysloe—who thought I was lying about my passenger to make myself sound important—lined up five bored men to give me a formation 'brown eye'. PK saw the bare bottoms facing skyward as we flew by before landing and asked me disdainfully if my compatriots usually welcomed me like this. Bruce Snelgar looked after PK for the rest of the day and the last of the clinking bottles were gratefully consumed on top of the warm granite kopje as the sun went down that evening. It was a particularly red sunset and we were comfortable late into the night, with the heat radiating out of the granite rock on which we were camped. I sent a message back to my squadron commander, saying I would be dropping the Minister off, at his insistence, near his house in the Botanical Gardens.

The next morning Bruce gave me a telex saying that this would not be allowed. The Commanding Officer at New

Sarum had planned it all and he was to be dropped in front of the reception arranged for him in front of the HQ building at New Sarum that afternoon at 5.00 p.m. I wasn't going to argue with PK about this and by now I was sure that, as Minister of Defence, his orders outranked everyone else's anyway.

We left Fungwe at 4.00 p.m. and flew out of the operational area and back over Avondale to PK's chosen triangle off Second Street Extension in the Botanical Gardens. Air Traffic Control had been warned of my flight and asked me if I was proceeding to New Sarum, which they were expecting. I told them that I most certainly was going to New Sarum but would be landing in Avondale briefly on the way. They didn't bother informing New Sarum of this stop, so no one had the chance to prevent me from landing at the Minister's preferred landing zone. When we touched down at PK's landing spot, all became clear. The adjacent six-lane highway was packed solid with Friday evening traffic. This traffic all but stopped with the arrival of our camouflaged war-zone helicopter.

Two servants dressed in freshly ironed, starched whites were standing to attention, waiting for us at the side of the landing zone. The enormous bedroll went on to the head of the first servant and the bags were carried by the second, while PK led the entourage away from the chopper.

He was wearing his newly acquired shorts and a fair amount of soot from marching through the bush and sitting in ambush; the *demo* was hanging off his left shoulder and his elephant gun was prominent in his right hand. He threaded his way through the traffic waving to the drivers as the new Minister of Defence was seen to be doing his work.

He must have won many votes that day and mine was one of them. I was in the quagmire for not having taken him to New Sarum, but by then there wasn't much that could be done about it. It was a fantastic trip during which Steve and I had many laughs and we both found ourselves missing him by the time we took off for New Sarum.

On a sad footnote, The King, Colonel Dave Parker, was killed in a helicopter crash while carrying out a Christmas visit to all troops in the operational area in 1975. Major Snelgar was awarded a medal for gallantry when he single-handedly cleared a cave full of terrorists, winning him the Silver Cross. In 1979 he was killed in a helicopter while flying as an airborne commander along with the pilot and gunner.

Some years after our visit to Marymount, bloody tracks from a wounded terrorist were followed into the mission. No terrorists were ever found because the mission staff had hidden them away. Later still, Father Ignatius was riding on his motorbike in an area a few miles from the mission. A Communist TMH–46 landmine as big as a cake tin had been planted by a terrorist in the road he was on, intended for a military truck. Father Ignatius detonated the landmine and was blown to pieces.

CHAPTER THIRTEEN
Mozambique goes Marxist

In September 1974, after a trip to Cape Town for talks with the South African government, PK told the RF Congress in Bulawayo that a second battalion of the RAR was being formed. On reducing the call-up burden he was blunt: "We will do this only when we have eliminated terrorism. We are not running a containment operation. The policy is to eliminate terrorism and until then we are going to need more manpower, not less."

Later, PK flew with CIO boss Ken Flower to Lisbon to seek clarification on Portugal's intentions toward Africa. "Soares, the acting Foreign Minister, told me the Entente Cordiale with Rhodesia was effectively over. This was very disagreeable news. There would be no further assistance," recalled PK. Portugal wished to leave Africa and its focus now was on making the best deal possible with Frelimo.

Flower and PK made another unsuccessful attempt to change minds in Lisbon in December. Ken Flower recalls: "PK [was] at his mercurial best, putting [future Portuguese Prime Minister and President] Mario Soares's effete young secretary right when he queried whether his [PK's] ancestry was 'Hollandaise'? 'Dutch, young man,' he replied, 'not a sauce. But my ancestors shook the grime of Holland off their shoes three and a half centuries ago for Africa and have never been back since.' Then he asked me to slip a pornographic book into [SA intelligence chief] Hendrik van den Bergh's pocket in the hope it would compromise him when arriving back in Johannesburg."[54]

At a Christmas party in December 1974, 200 soldiers were served dinner by PK, Colonel Dave Parker (commander of 1RLI) and General

---

[54] Ken Flower: *Serving Secretly.* John Murray, 1987

Peter Walls. Afterward, PK performed creditably in a 'down-down' beer-swilling contest.

Talking to reporters later who questioned the emergence of a rowdy culture among young Rhodesian men ("brash, bullying young men", as one journalist described them) , he was forthright: "Youth of Rhodesia; there's nothing to touch them, they're bloody marvellous. We are bloody proud of them! Far from being bullies, they show the greatest degree of chivalry. As far as my own experiences are concerned, Rhodesian youth are more courteous, kindly and respectful to others than any contemporary youth anywhere else."

Pressed to explain a psychiatric evaluation which linked male Rhodesian aggressions to sexual outlet, PK was ambivalent: "Not being a psychiatrist, I don't know what that all means, but if it means that if not chasing terrorists he would be chasing women rather than practising ballet or the harpsichord, I have no difficulty with that person. I do not condemn interests in the arts but I do think the average young Rhodesian is more geared toward manly recreational pursuits. I understand him being more inclined to going out into the bush to shoot rather than to an exhibition of watercolours."

PK was understandably unhappy to be denied access to the Selous Scouts by General Walls, despite being the responsible minister. Ron Reid-Daly remembers:

> He was seriously pissed off, but that's the way it was then; not even the country's Minister of Defence was allowed near us. At that point we were trying to pass ourselves off as a tracking unit to keep the 'pseudo' role secret. I reported to General Walls and he reported to the Prime Minister. The Minister was not in the loop. This rankled PK. It was a Monday when I received a call from the Chief of Staff, General Rawlins. His PA put me on the line and it was a concerned voice I heard. "Ron," the General said in worried tone of voice, "what have you done?" I said far as I knew, I'd done nothing. Rawlins was sceptical. "Well, you must have done something, because you and I have

been summoned to see the Minister. We have to be there at half past two this afternoon." I could make nothing of this surprise request. We lunched at Army HQ, and then travelled to the ministry by car. Along the way, the General asked me again if I was sure I had done nothing that required me to explain myself to the Minister. I searched my mind and replied in the negative.

We arrived at his office and were seated at a long table before being served tea in beautiful China cups by his secretary, Marge Bassett. PK then made a regal appearance and did his best to put us both at ease, but the fact is we were both bloody nervous. Then he broke the silence to tell us he had decided to summon us to his office after considerable thought. Rawlins expressed understanding but asked, rather nervously, why the summons had been issued. There was another silence and then a bark. "The reason, General," PK replied, "is because we're losing the bloody war, General!"

Rawlins was taken aback. "Oh dear, sir," he said, "I thought we were doing rather well."

"No, we're not," said PK, "we're fighting with the gloves off … it is now time to get in and kill these people or all will be *lawst*."

Rawlins answered quickly and said, "But, sir; that's what we're doing."

PK said, "No, we're not; we're killing the wrong people … we have to get in and kill the people who are helping the enemy!"

Rawlins was very taken aback and there was a silence while he pondered the Minister's outburst. "But that would be murder," the General replied.

PK was unmoved: "I don't care what you call it, just do it."

Then he turned on me. "And what the hell are you doing?" he asked, accusingly. Respectfully I replied, informing him I was not allowed to tell him what I was doing.

With that he exploded. "I'm the Minister of Defence," he said, "and you can't tell me what your regiment is doing?" He was now very angry and I reminded him I was a soldier, a mere major, and simply following orders from General Walls. He understood this defence and I assured him we were making progress with innovative counter-terrorism tactics. This mollified him a little.

A T/A (Territorial Army) engineer serving on the Mozambican border remembers an encounter with PK: "One day he arrived at the camp. He was immaculately dressed in regulation army kit. However, unlike our 'normal' kit, his had obviously been tailored and everything was beautifully pressed. His FN rifle was also polished and shiny. Despite this parade ground appearance, PK went out on patrol with one of the infantry patrols. I was on the patrol and nothing much happened. His peacock-like appearance didn't impress the troopies much, but his decision as Minister of Defence to go out on a live patrol gained the respect of all."

By now he was carrying an AK, but even this raised issues. "PK loved real action," remembers Brian Robinson, "and I think he would dearly have loved to have been more involved in an operational sense. He took a particular liking to carrying an AK which posed a problem for me because I did not want the troopies to think the FN was inferior because it was not the Minister's choice. I asked him very politely if he wouldn't mind changing his weaponry. He was very understanding and agreed to do so."

PK urged aggression at every opportunity. "Step up use of the bayonet. That's the most effective propaganda, the bayonet. You can't divorce propaganda from action … You see, hearts and minds are very much conditioned by what happens militarily."

Later he caused consternation for advocating 'drumhead' trials where field commanders would have authority to execute enemy prisoners. "That way," he later said, "villagers would have seen that justice was being done. We were up against an extremely violent enemy—we had to meet them with violence but we never really took the gloves off. A terrible shame in my view. Army commanders told me Rhodesian soldiers would resist orders to form firing squads. I said poppycock; they'll stand in a queue waiting for their chances."

Despite military successes, Rhodesia was feeling the pressure of South Africa's new Détente policy by the end of 1974. Vorster badly wanted South Africa accepted into the community of African nations. While accepting the general concept, Smith worried that Rhodesia was the bargaining chip and warned Vorster that apartheid and not Rhodesia, was the real problem. Vorster told him he was out of touch and, just to remind him where real power lay, stopped a shipment of munitions and supplies to Rhodesia. In December 1974, a reluctant and wary Smith agreed to an immediate ceasefire and allowed the release of political detainees. One of those released was Robert Mugabe. The *quid pro quo* guaranteed by Vorster was that Zambia and Mozambique would bring to an end the armed incursions but this did not happen and the Rhodesian defenders lost ground as their restraint was ignored and incursions continued.

In an interview with *Die Transvaaler*, PK acknowledged the need for political change in Rhodesia but said it must be evolutionary: "... under no circumstances will we send hundreds of our young men to the border to face death or maiming if we then sacrifice everything they are fighting for". Later he stated his view that "... Rhodesian troops have become the finest and most effective counter-terrorist troops in the world."

Recalls Costa Pafitis:

> Some people thought PK was overstating the case when he spoke so highly of the Rhodesians, but I don't think so. Remember he was South African but he seemed to think the Rhodesians were cut from better cloth. I think he liked the unity of purpose and was happy to be away from the English/ Afrikaans animosity of his homeland. He absolutely loved the country and its people and that certainly included the majority of blacks whom he cared for deeply and with whom he had an incredible rapport. Most of them revered him. But having

said that, when the work was done he knew how to misbehave. Once I was ordered to the airport to collect a female friend of PK. My car was a small Triumph Herald which was slow and rattled, so I was a little floored when I arrived at the airport to see a glamorous lady standing next to 14 suitcases, all about as big as my car. As it turned out, she had just left Ethiopia where she had been a guest of Haile Selassie, who I think had had more to offer than we did. Loaded down to the rims we rattled back into Salisbury and she did not look too impressed. Eventually we shuddered to a halt in PK's driveway and I waited nervously, knowing that PK's girlfriend was inside. Cucumber cool he swept out of the house resplendent in white tuxedo and welcomed the new arrival with all his normal charm while I looked on anxiously. Then showing her toward the door while all the servants humped her cases he turned to me quietly and whispered. "I say old boy, are you attached?" A little taken aback, I replied that yes, in fact, I was now a married man. "Oh dash it!" he said, "how very inconvenient." Then he took his leave to deal with the muddle unfolding inside.

In January 1975, Major Piet died and PK attended his father's funeral at Fairfield. Also in attendance was future president P.W. Botha, who had begun his political career as a heckler. In this role he had previously harrassed Major Piet when on the campaign trail. Obviously there were no hard feelings for the man who later aquired the moniker, *Die Groot Krokodil* (The Big Crocodile). Among the condolences received was one from John Vorster, describing the major as "a colourful person and a sincere friend of many people", while De Villiers-Graaff, Leader of the Opposition, said: "Oom Piet, as he was affectionately known to many thousands of South Africans, was a gallant soldier, a very successful farmer, distinguished businessman and astute politician, who, with the passage of the years, became South Africa's most beloved elder statesman."

On his return PK took the salute from the men of 1RLI at Cranborne

Barracks. About this time a mysterious letter came into the hands of PK at the Ministry of Defence. Written by Angolan Governor-General Coutinho ('the Red Admiral') to Agostinho Neto, Marxist leader of Angola's MPLA rebels, it confirmed PK's worst fears of the grand communist design on southern Africa:

Comrade Agostinho Neto,

The FNLA and UNITA insist on my replacement for a reactionary who will play ball. If this becomes concrete it will be the end of our plans to give power only to the MPLA. There remain those movements of 'clown' whites who give support to the Portuguese colonialism and imperialism, which is only faithful to the imperialists.

The same imperialists contradicted our secret talks in Praga which Comrade Cunhal signed in the name of the PCP [Portuguese Communist Party], so that we can, under the glorious PC controlled by USSR, spread communism from Tangier to the Cape and from Lisbon to Washington. The implantation of the MPLA is vital so that we can break down that bastard Mobutu, puppet of imperialism, so that we can take possession of Zaire as well.

After the last secret meeting we had with comrades of the PCP we decided to advise you to give immediate execution of the second phase of the plan. Did not Fanon say that the inferiority complex would only be removed after the killing of the colonialists? Comrade Agostinho Neto, you will now give secret instructions to the troops of the MPLA to terrorize in any way the whites: killing, looting and burning in the hope to provoke their abandoning Angola.

Starting with the children, women and the aged in order to restrain the courageous and the strong. So strongly are those white dogs tied to the land, that only terror will make them run. The FNLA and UNITA will stop receiving support from the white capitalists and their military experts. We remain awaiting the resignation of the whites and their capitalists, and then we can rebuild a new socialist state or something similar should this be difficult.

Yours sincerely,

Antonio Alva Rosa Coutinho
VICTORY IS CERTAIN

On 16 February, at a meeting in Cape Town, Vorster threatened to withdraw helicopters and ground forces from Rhodesia if Smith dragged his heels on Détente. PK was incensed when Smith briefed his ministers in Salisbury, given the insurgents' non-compliance with ceasefire requirements. When Smith and PK were later summoned to Pretoria and told to release a political detainee, the South African press queried Vorster's double standards, considering Mandela and Sobukwe's ongoing incarceration, but this point was simply ignored by the South African PM.

On 25 June, with Rhodesians looking on anxiously, an independent republic was proclaimed in Mozambique under Samora Machel. Marxist excesses followed as homes and businesses were declared state-owned and thousands fled Machel's gulags and work gangs. By 1976 an estimated 50,000 inmates filled concentration camps such as Inahassune north of Maputo and Massacaze near Beira. The Catholic Church, once strong Frelimo supporters, were driven underground and baptism was banned. The legal code was abolished, replaced by military tribunals and legal representation was proscribed.

At her angry husband's side throughout this destructive process was Samora's wife Graça[55] and Armando Guebuza,[56] the man who would oversee the forced relocation of hundreds of thousands of peasants in a

---

[55] Now married to Nelson Mandela

[56] Present president of Mozambique

disastrous exhibition of social engineering. Brief resistance from a group of abandoned settlers, politicians and disaffected militarists was quickly crushed by Frelimo cadres with the help of Portuguese troops. One of those fleeing was Monica Germani: "People have no idea of that time because it has been written out of history but it was the same as the Congo. If you were white you fled with your life and not much else. It was a terrible time."

Two days after Mozambican independence, PK was invited to review the passing-out parade of A Company 2RAR, the last at Methuen Barracks before the RAR moved to a new depot at Balla Balla. Brigadier Dave Heppenstall remembers: "I think it was Mike Shute who came up with the idea that we should get PK an RAR blazer tailored by his own tailor in Salisbury as a presentation on the parade. The tailor was sworn to secrecy and duly made the double-breasted blazer. After the inspection, PK returned to the saluting dais where he was approached by the adjutant and ordered to remove his immaculate charcoal-grey suit jacket. He did so extremely reluctantly but the look of delight on his face when the RAR blazer was put on had to be seen to be believed! When the parade marched past, PK was seen standing to attention but fingering the bottom of his new blazer (a perfect fit) with both his hands. He was absolutely delighted with it and wore it for the rest of the day."

Later, cheering African soldiers carried him shoulder-high from their canteen to his car, and then pushed his car all the way to the gate in a spontaneous gesture of affection and respect considered one of the highest honours the RAR soldiers can bestow upon anybody. "It was one of the proudest moments of his life he told me later," says Marge Bassett. "The name they gave him, *Mhurwi a'kashinga* [brave fighting man], also came as a great honour to him." But there was uproar in the Rhodesian and Zambian press in July 1975 when ANC (African National Council) Publicity Secretary Edson Sithole accused Rhodesian agents of poisoning him prior to a flight to Lusaka for talks with the Zambian government. Suspicions were heightened when it became known another senior ANC member, Enos Nkala, was also sick on the plane.

Badgered by black MPs to answer the charges, PK told parliament: "We don't practise opposition by elimination."

"What about [recently assassinated] Chitepo!"[57] they shouted.

PK refuted Sithole's claims of having only tea and biscuits before the flight. "My information is that he had large quantities of beer and baked beans for lunch followed by brandy on the plane." One can only assume that he was being less than sincere when he warned that "baked beans can sometimes produce regrettable symptoms, although they are seldom serious.

"Furthermore," he explained,

> he has an extremely complicated private life and one of his lovers has let on she sometimes spikes his food with a 'love potion' in order to hold him and this might account for occasional bowel discomfort ... there was grave dissension between a woman he is living with and another woman friend of a more transient status and on at least one occasion I understand a certain amount of blood has been spilt.

He went on to mention that Sithole was also probably nervous of seeing Kaunda after several "intemperate outbursts directed at him".

In August Leo Ross, PK's old friend and Secretary of Information, died. A former District Commissioner and World War II comrade, PK's eulogy described him as embodying all of the characteristics of Kipling's 'thousandth man'. He recalled meeting him in 1965 and "... there developed one of the greatest and most fruitful friendships of my life".

On 8 August, PK aimed another broadside at diminishing South African support for Rhodesia: "The terrorists who are trained and equipped outside our borders and who invade our country with the willing help of other governments are here for a much wider purpose than the overthrow of Rhodesia. They are here to represent a force which sees Rhodesia as just

---

57 Herbert Chitepo, a prominent Nationalist leader, had recently died when a bomb exploded under his car in Lusaka. This set off bitter internecine fighting within the movement.

one more stepping stone to victory over South Africa, because they see South Africa as a vital key to the security of America, Europe, and the rest of the Western world."

This did not go down well in Pretoria and the South African press reported that Vorster was upset with the Rhodesian government—particularly PK—for scaremongering South Africa into supporting the Rhodesian war. The press also noted PK's absence from recent delegations to South Africa. Later that month in a gesture of obeisance to Vorster, Rhodesian ministers met Black Nationalists for talks on a train carriage on the Victoria Falls railway bridge.

PK went armed with a pistol in a shoulder holster. Taking his seat at the conference table next to Smith, he nudged the Prime Minister and allowed his jacket to flair, giving Smith a sneak view. "Just in case these terrorists get out of hand, sir," he explained touching the pistol, "I'll be able to give us some covering fire."

"An exercise in futility," recalled PK. "This was Vorster wanting the world to see him as a peacemaker. We knew it was not going to work but we had to go through the motions. It was most unpleasant—a whole gang of politicians and terrorists jammed into a carriage around a long table. The terrorists were on the Zambian side where they had an area set aside for them to drink and eat and we were on the southern side. At the end of the day their side looked like a recently occupied country; everything had been drunk and eaten and all sorts of stuff was broken. The whole lot of them were rendered incapable of doing anything constructive at all."

Ken Flower recalls in his memoirs that "... aggravating the situation was the intrusion of such intermediaries as Mark Chona, the intrusion yet again of Lonrho and Ian Smith's deliberate inclusion of PK van der Byl who could be relied upon to upset the South Africans, Zambians and the ANC." According to a government official, who was present on the sidelines, PK was irritable from the start:

He was hosting a dinner party in Salisbury on the Friday and was annoyed when Vorster asked everyone to stay another night in the hope something could be salvaged. PK was sitting in the carriage with both delegations at their seats around the table when he demanded a telephone be brought to him. This was not usual and all the attendees, including Kaunda, were listening when he angrily dialled a number. It soon became clear his mind was far from furthering Vorster's Détente exercise and bringing lasting peace to southern Africa when he loudly addressed his major domo at his house in Salisbury.

"Farnabeck," he said loudly, "where the fuck have you been?"

Farnabeck must have mumbled a reply when PK carried on. "*Ezwa* [listen/understand] … to me now," he said. "No bloody dinner tonight … *mena ikona buya* [I cannot come] … no dinner tonight … *Ezwa*? So you put that fish back in the fridge … *Ezwa*? The fish must go back in the fridge or it will go rotten!" He waited to hear Farnabeck's reply but it was not forthcoming and he was very worried about his fish so he shouted louder. A total silence followed with all the black nationalists looking on like stunned mullets but PK was oblivious to them; he was trying to get the message through to Farnabeck, terrified his fish would be out the fridge too long and go rotten. When Farnabeck still seemed confused he shouted even louder: "No, you fool! The bloody fish … put the bloody thing back in the fridge. *Mena ikona buya* for dinner tonight … I am staying here with these bloody people!"

Finally, happy that Farnabeck had understood the message, a visibly flustered PK looked back down the carriage at the faces of some very confused nationalist leaders who were not at all sure they could believe what they had just heard.

Eventually, realizing his hopes had been dashed, Vorster left the venue in disgust, unhappy his plans and hospitality had been abused. On his return to Pretoria, in what must have been a fit of pique, he recalled all South

African men and equipment from Rhodesia. Adding to his woes, events in Angola were unfolding fast and an opportunity had arisen for South African troops and CIA-sponsored UNITA fighters to capture Luanda. PK comments:

After our relationship deteriorated following the Victoria Falls debacle, I went to Pretoria to see Vorster. Before seeing him, however, I saw General Hendrik van den Bergh in the morning and in the course of conversation mentioned to him I was concerned about the situation in Angola. South African troops were within canon-shot range of Luanda but were not advancing. Van den Bergh explained that they were uneasy about an assault because they feared heavy casualties, so the situation was not a straightforward one. I pondered this and told him things were pretty quiet in Rhodesia and I'd be happy to let him have the RLI, a battalion of RAR and some of the chaps from the SAS. I said my chaps would go in there and take Luanda in 24 hours with South African air support. I explained we would simply capture it then give it back to the South Africans who were then at liberty to hand the country on to Holden Roberto, Savimbi or whomsoever they selected, but this way we would guarantee Angola did not go to the MPLA and the Soviets. I said we would be in and out, and for the record would never have been there. He said he would put this suggestion to Vorster. I made it clear to van den Bergh that if they did not move on Luanda within ten days, Angola would be lost.

I saw Vorster later in the day and we sorted out our other difficulties whereupon I pressed him about my offer of help in Angola. I reiterated time was of the essence. Vorster did not like my approach at all and completely rejected the offer. Sadly I was right and a country that might have been in the Western orbit was lost. The entire history of south–central Africa would have been dramatically altered if the Rhodesians had been allowed to go in. Angola was then handed over on a plate to the MPLA and the South Africans withdrew.

In another meeting with Connie Mulder, then South African Minister of Information, I suggested we draw a line along the Kunene in the west and the Zambezi in the east and pool our resources in a joint endeavour to keep the enemy north of that line. He said we Rhodesians would have to do that alone— South Africa would not be party to such a thing. These were two massive errors of strategic judgement that have had a profound impact on Africa and the world.

CHAPTER FOURTEEN
Selous Scouts attack

Following reports in the *Sunday Express* that Vorster had lost patience with PK, Smith was forced to take Rowan Cronjé in his place on a trip to South Africa on 20 October 1975. Vorster had no problems with Cronjé, who probably made a determined effort not to upset the irascible South African leader.

With the food poisoning controversy barely over, suspicion again fell on the Rhodesian government when Edson Sithole disappeared in December. Last seen walking out of the Ambassador Hotel in Salisbury, he was never seen again and his disappearance remains a mystery to this day. PK and Hilary Squires officially denied government involvement in Sithole's disappearance when asked to submit statements in a High Court hearing.

Just before Christmas 1975, a saddened PK flew home from Fairfield on receiving news that a helicopter crash had claimed the lives of General John Shaw, Colonel Dave 'The King' Parker, Captain John Lamb, Captain Ian Robertson and Sergeant Pieter van Rensburg. David Parker was earmarked for bigger things and his loss was a considerable blow to the war effort.

In January, PK holidayed in Spain on Quintos de Bernuy's farm near Malpica de Tajo castle and went partridge shooting with the King of Spain. He returned home following a headline-grabbing outburst by President Samora Machel in which he threatened to mobilize "ten million blacks to attack the whites". A visibly relaxed PK suggested: "The real reason for these histrionics is the fact that he is in an extremely difficult and critical position himself. The Mozambique economy has been devastated by wholesale nationalisation and the purge of white Portuguese has caused huge economic distress. He is looking for a scapegoat."

At the same time, word reached Salisbury that Soviet tanks were being offloaded in Maputo harbour, bound for Mugabe's ZANLA. PK demanded a statement from the Foreign Office.

Minister David Ennals, whose visit to Rhodesia had ended so badly at the hands of the farmers ten years earlier, was blunt when he said Rhodesians could expect no British assistance in their "racial war". PK replied that while there was no expectation of assistance, it was nonetheless ironic that London, not Salisbury, insisted Rhodesia was still a British colony. As a colony, shouldn't Rhodesians expect protection, he asked? He added that, in his opinion, Rhodesia's "fatal blunder" was going to Britain's assistance when they were under German attack. Later he announced the postponement of army commander Peter Walls's retirement.

On 3 March, Mozambique received £15 million from the British government and immediately declared itself on a war footing with Rhodesia. "It is quite unbelievable and grotesque," PK said, "that a Marxist terrorist regime should be financed by the British government in order to destroy what was once part of the British Empire."[58] He then spoke of the presence of over 5,000 terrorists in Mozambique and announced that the size of the regular army was to be increased.

Asked by a reporter what would happen if the terrorists reached town, PK replied simply that, "We will shoot them". A clandestine visit to Johannesburg on 6 March occasioned much speculation, but he would only say, "I have been watching bowls and that Kyalami thing [the South African Grand Prix]."

In April 1976, Harold Wilson resigned, handing power to Jim Callaghan claiming mental and physical exhaustion. Those in Rhodesia who hoped the change would bring a warming of relations between London and Salisbury would be disappointed.

In April, PK was interviewed at his home by Al Venter who wrote this report: "He lives alone in a rambling mock Cape Dutch house. Considering he holds the vital defence portfolio, security is markedly absent. He drives to and from his office in his own car without an escort or guard and the

---

[58] Paul Moorcraft: *A Short Thousand Years*. Galaxie Press, 1979

house, security-wise, is indistinguishable from any other in the street. His table offers excellent fare, some say the best in Rhodesia, with a tendency toward French cuisine. Lunch is usually followed by cognac. He answers most questions without reference to notes or an aide. He has a remarkable memory and can often recall what was actually said years earlier."

Meanwhile, PK criticized the British press for glamourizing a train attack by insurgents. "The terrorists derailed a passenger train and killed three unarmed tourists. That was hardly the most gallant battle since Borodino. Rather than the headlines we saw ... I should like to see 'Murdering terrorists dispersed by man and his wife', which is exactly what has just happened. The killing of the tourists was a monstrous crime."

On life under sanctions, he lamented being unable to visit his tailor in London.

Discussing his hunting trophies with an American female journalist at his home, he was asked if he was concerned about guerrillas in the bush. "My dear child," he replied, "gorillas these days are found only in remote parts of the Mountains of the Moon. If you mean terrorists; yes, but worried, no."[59]

On 27 April, Smith announced the inclusion of black ministers in government; a move universally derided as windowdressing.

In May, addressing a passing-out parade of RLI recruits at Cranborne Barracks, PK said, "To you falls the honour of exacting the most terrible vengeance for our comrades and compatriots who have been maimed and mutilated by the terrorist beasts."

On Cuba's possible intervention: "We will beat the life and soul out of them." He accused the US Congress of "cowardly and treacherous behaviour in opposing the efforts of President Ford in his bid to contain Soviet expansionism in Angola".

June saw the Soweto riots bring international criticism of Vorster's government and, amidst growing genocide in Uganda, Idi Amin declared himself 'President for Life'. While Soweto hogged the headlines, Amin's

---

[59] *The Telegraph*, 19 November 1999

genocidal actions drew little or no criticism from the Commonwealth, the UN or any world leaders.

But the war was taking a financial toll, and July 1976 brought a 40-per cent increase in defence spending, while PK infuriated the Catholic Commission for Justice and Peace by saying "… they [the terrorists] will be bombed and destroyed in any manner which the commander on the spot considers to be desirable". The clerics also took strong exception to his offer of amnesty to African villagers "if they beat the terrorists to death".

The Commission had long criticized Smith's government. Its Chairman, Carmelite Bishop Donal Lamont from the Umtali Diocese, had written to the *Rhodesia Herald* in 1970, calling the architects of the republican constitution the "real terrorists" who should be held accountable for "this enormous crime". He would continue to be a thorn in PK's side until his deportation in 1977 following a conviction for aiding and abetting terrorists. He returned to newly independent Zimbabwe in a triumphal flourish immediately after independence in 1980, but his stay was a short one. Assaulted by two of his black priests for reasons never made clear, he was badly beaten and had to seek specialist medical attention in what was then apartheid South Africa, after which he returned to Ireland.

On 9 August, the Selous Scouts carried out a spectacular raid on Nyadzonya, an insurgent camp in central Mozambique. Commander Ron Reid-Daly went to great lengths to keep its planning secret. He had been warned by the Rhodesian Special Branch that their associates in Portuguese Intelligence were convinced Flower was a British agent. Reid-Daly sought one-on-one approval from General Walls. Laying a map down on the floor in the General's office, the General was taken aback by the scale of the target and the degree of risk, but was persuaded by the feisty Selous Scout commander to back the attack. It was estimated the camp contained 5,000 insurgents. In an effort to disguise the provenance of the attacks, the raiders disguised themselves as Frelimo and travelled by road and bush track in a mobile column. An estimated 2,000 insurgents perished while the Selous Scouts returned intact.

Unsurprisingly, the world press insisted the camp was a refugee facility and accused the Rhodesians of atrocities. PK challenged the UN to send a fact-finding mission and asked why Mozambique itself had not called the UN. Edgar Tekere, then a senior Mugabe lieutenant, later scoffed at these allegations. Asked by David Dimbleby if Nyadzonya was a genuine military target he replied in the affirmative adding, "… they knocked us flat". But once again Pretoria took the news badly. The day after the attack, Ambassador Harold Hawkins received a rollicking from an angry Vorster followed by the withdrawal of South African helicopter crews on 26 August.

"This," said PK, "after he had given public assurances that South Africa would stand shoulder to shoulder with us. When the press tackled me about rumours that Vorster was about to do this, I questioned their motives and asked what made them think a man of integrity like Vorster would do such a thing."

Vorster, asked about PK, declared he would have nothing further to do with that "dreadful man".

An unrepentant PK called Reid-Daly to congratulate him and asked for a full debrief. With some trepidation Reid-Daly complied:

On my arrival at Milton Buildings with Rob Warraker, who had commanded the assault on the ground, PK personally came out and ushered us in. I tried to skim through the events baldly but he would have none of it.

"Ronald, dear chap," he drawled. "You say you simply drove through all those places in Mozambique. How on earth did you get away with it?"

I explained we made our vehicles look like Frelimo's to which he exclaimed: "Good Lord, how extraordinary. But what about the base? I can understand the vehicles—devilishly clever—but how did you get into their base in broad daylight?"

I explained we were disguised as Frelimo, to which he replied 'You mean you wore Frelimo uniforms? Good God, good God!" he said. He was absolutely overjoyed. I knew then the

Scouts had a friend for life. PK had been a supporter of ours and I was pleased we had more than vindicated his faith in us and our concept. I always knew that PK would be there for us. He was an extremely loyal man.

It was after the Nyadzonya raid that I received a call from PK asking me yet again if he could visit us at our barracks. I had to tell him the answer was no but that we had a reception facility outside the main cantonment and I told him he would be welcome there.

"Delighted old boy,' he said. "Delighted."

The following evening he pulled up in his car with his driver. I had my guys waiting but by this time the booze was flowing and everyone was getting nicely pissed. This did not worry PK. He came straight in and joined the party. I introduced him to the troops and he asked if he was expected to address the gathering. I told him that would be appreciated and he asked me what he should say. I said, "Just tell them that they're fucking good at what they do and they'll be thrilled." I knew this would mean a great deal to the African soldiers in particular.

PK quickly launched himself into a stirring speech but his diction and accent left Basil Moss, the Shona translator, struggling for words. The next thing he was quoting in French from Napoleon Bonaparte and my black soldiers were now completely lost; they had never heard of Napoleon, and Basil was again left scrambling for words. He looked at me for help and I said, "Just tell them they're fucking good," which he did, and everybody was thrilled with PK's speech.

With us at the time were some 'tame' [captured and 'turned'] female gooks. They were having a ball strutting their stuff on the dance floor. I said to PK, "If you really want to make an impression on this lot, you better go and dance with them." He was up in a flash, twisting and turning. It brought the house down. They absolutely loved the guy.

Saxon Logan came out at this time to interview PK for *The Spectator* magazine. "What a character. He reminded me of Dracula. I recall his aide putting his head round the door and saying: 'Minister, the Belgian First Secretary is here from Pretoria,' and PK said, 'I am busy being interviewed for *The Spectator*; throw the man a bag of nuts and tell him to wait.' The Belgian diplomat (who must have been covertly visiting Rhodesia at the time) must have heard him, but it didn't worry PK at all. He was a terrific guy."

Costa Pafitis recalled another 'Dracula' moment at the Gatooma Hotel:

We sorted ourselves out in our rooms and then PK and I went for a walk in the park nearby. While doing so a young boy came running toward us and stared at PK. "Gee, sir," he said, "are you related to Dracula?" PK glared back at him with one nostril flaring prior to being nasty and said, "Yes. Listen, you scruffy little bugger. I *am* Count Dracula and if you don't piss off I shall eat you."

Pieter Bieber recalls his times with PK:

At this time I was visiting Rhodesia frequently on Old Mutual business. I saw quite a lot of PK. His 'military command' thrilled him. He loved his soldiers and I think they loved him. I had one very exciting outing when he took me in a helicopter to visit the troops in the field. I thoroughly enjoyed his company at all times. He had a wonderful turn of phrase and was a superb raconteur; he had strong views but his position was always well thought out. He liked to dominate conversation. I don't think he was an intellectual but he was a deep thinker, melancholic at times. He had gravitas; he would walk into a room and all would know he was there. He was loyal to his friends. He knew a lot of people but had only a few friends for whom he would have done anything. Knowing him certainly enriched my life.

He was frightened of nothing and it showed; I remember him going after a huge cobra on the farm once armed only with a rock. I thought he was mad.

Phillippa Berlyn asked him in 1969 if he believed in meritocracy. His response was:

> As Professor Joad used to say, it depends on what you believe is a meritocracy. Naturally one believes in merit but firstly one has to find a way of assessing merit. I have considerable reservations about streaming children in schools by ability. One often finds that those who had the best of university training are never heard of again and others who one never heard of at school run the place.
>
> It is difficult to know the difference at a certain stage between a balanced judgment and assessment based on the retention of experience and knowledge as opposed to pure intelligence. It is very dangerous to be dogmatic in this regard. When it comes to meritocracy, in that it is aimed at African-European relationships, one must be ever wary of confusing book learning with education and education with civilization, because they are not the same. I believe meritocracy must contain as a major ingredient, civilization.
>
> After all we live in the age of absurdity. If there's no swing toward sanity I see little hope for the world. A possible exception to this is Enoch Powell—a brilliant speaker striking a strong chord of response among people at all levels in England.

On 26 August, PK wrote to *The Times* in conciliatory tone:

> If Her Majesty's government is genuinely concerned and wishes to help, let Britain exercise the responsibility she constantly claims by using her undoubted influence on the Commonwealth

countries of Tanzania and Zambia to discourage them from harbouring and training terrorists. Let Britain too cease to give aid to Mozambique and condemn a country whose forces are constantly making incursions across our border and attacking non-military targets.

Cannot relations between our two countries be regularized in the same spirit of magnanimity and reconciliation that was evident in 1785? Her Majesty has pointed out in relation to the American declaration that it was "very much a bilateral affair between us". The same applies to our assumption of independence in 1965, and it is to Britain that we look for help, not hindrance, in combating the expansionist ambitions of communist powers in Africa.

There was no response from the Crown or the British government.

CHAPTER FIFTEEN
PK fired

Despite apartheid in South Africa, Foreign Minister Hilgaard Muller's stated policy for Rhodesia was black majority rule, and as a starting point for a new beginning the sidelining of PK was demanded. "I was assured [by the South Africans] if we wanted to maintain ... the smooth supply of our requirements, I would have to get rid of PK in Defence. Clearly I had no option," wrote Ian Smith.[60] On 9 September 1976, in a sudden reshuffle, PK was dismissed as Minister of Defence.

"There is no doubt that PK irritated Vorster," says Lin Mehmel. "Both Smith and PK let Vorster know he was too trusting of black leaders. History shows they were right; Vorster was led a merry dance by people like Kaunda."

PK's firing led to press speculation that Smith felt threatened by his Defence Minister's popularity. While this is almost certainly untrue, no one believed the official line that he was being "freed up to work on foreign affairs and constitutional matters".

Said PK:

> Vorster called Ian Smith and said, "Get rid of van der Byl or I'm turning off the tap." It was as simple as that. To make it worse for us, Pik Botha then leaked a story to the press with a big spin on it, explaining how the 'peace-loving' John Vorster had forced my dismissal in the interests of peace and Détente. I remember walking in to see Ian Smith with a copy of one of the papers and this angered him greatly—the fact that we were

---

[60] Ian Smith: *The Great Betrayal: The Memoirs of Ian Douglas Smith.* Blake Publishing, 1997

now being humiliated in public. He explained he had no option on Defence but asked me to retain Foreign Affairs.

My relationship with Vorster deteriorated over the years. Back in 1964 when I first met him and he was Deputy PM we got along famously but as his views changed in the face of growing isolation, he decided he needed to buy some time and could use Rhodesia for this purpose. In this process, he got to dislike me more and more as time went on.

My time in Defence was the best thing I ever did. I enjoyed it enormously. Having been a soldier myself I felt comfortable but I did want to hit the enemy harder earlier and I don't think we were innovative enough.

I wanted a couple of black RSMs in the RAR made up to company commanders. Tambare and Wurayayi were very capable men. Recognition would have been not only for their military virtuosity but also for what they had been through in order to serve their country. Their families had been subjected to awful reprisals: children abducted and killed, wives raped— all truly horrible stuff. I wanted to give them carte blanche to kill terrorists in their home areas. This didn't go down well with people at Internal Affairs and, indeed, with some of our senior commanders. I missed people like General Shaw and Colonel Dave Parker at times such as this—they were very open to new ideas.

Writing in the army magazine *Assegai*, PK described his tenure as "stirring and exciting" and bade "farewell with the deepest sorrow".

Toward the end of 1976, Rhodesia became the target of Washington's 'shuttle diplomacy'. With Gerald Ford seeking re-election, an American-driven solution in southern Africa became desirable. To get Smith's attention Ford's diplomatic troubleshooter, Henry Kissinger, persuaded Vorster to cut supplies of fuel and munitions. To force the insurgents to deal, Kissinger visited Tanzania and Zambia, assuring them Smith would concede power after a phased but short-term transfer. According to the American Secretary, Nyerere and Kaunda sanctioned the plan and Smith was summoned to Pretoria.

It was left to Kissinger to read him the death rites and he later conceded it gave him no pleasure. He was in no doubt Smith desperately wanted the best for his people and understood why he was fearful of black majority rule. A man whose face bore the scars of another war fought in defence of the country that now sought his destruction, he recognized he was looking into the eyes of a supreme patriot. Kissinger offered palliative financial and political incentives, remarking later, "Ian Smith made accepting the deal worse by acting like a gentleman."

"Ian Smith was terribly depressed following this meeting," remembered PK. "In a way it was the beginning of the end but he understood this was probably the best deal we could have hoped for. Some in the party, Barlow and others, were extremely unhappy and that was understandable. We argued here as we argued elsewhere for a qualified franchise, which I think is applicable everywhere. One man one vote takes you to the lowest common denominator and produces poor quality politicians and disaster. The irony is that in reality there is really no vote at all in Africa."

Smith broadcast details of the agreement on 19 September 1976 but everything broke down when the five Frontline African leaders rejected the proposals. PK was angry: "It was now up to the Western powers, particularly America and South Africa, to sort it out." He went on to say, "They have agreed to the settlement and we have agreed to it. But in typical African nationalist fashion they have shown their unreliability and untrustworthiness. It would be totally unreasonable to expect us to change when the proposals were theirs, not ours, and we accepted them as did the rest of these people."

But there was some reward in the form of fresh deliveries of war supplies from South Africa to Rhodesia, as Vorster was well aware that the collapse of the Kissinger deal was no fault of the Rhodesian government.

Later, with the Kissinger agreement dead, the British government called a new conference for 20 October in Geneva. Doomed, in PK's eyes, to fail, it saw the Rhodesians holding out for the Kissinger terms to be implemented (a phased short-term transfer) and the insurgents demanding an immediate transfer of power. Included in Smith's delegation to travel to Switzerland were PK, David Smith, Mark Partridge and Hilary Squires. Looking back, Squires recalls:

> If PK had a weakness it was in his aversion to fine print. Details didn't interest him. "Leave that to the officials," he'd say. Fortunately we were backed by highly competent officials so maybe it didn't matter. PK and Smith were close and were happy to spar on occasion, but he was never presumptuous or offensive. An amusing incident occurred during our first lunch at the Hotel du Rhone. Most of us were out of our depth with the menu so followed PK's recommendation for (very bland) Lake Geneva perch. Eventually the Old Man [Ian Smith] said he would try some, but only because he was guided by PK who, he felt, should know because he was the Minister of Foreign Affairs. PK twittered on about the "delicious fish" and finally asked the PM if the fish wasn't "absolutely marvellous". I'll never forget Ian Smith's face. He growled, "I've had better bloody fish out of my dam in Selukwe!"

"At dinner, early on I was told by the Prime Minister to order the wine," recalled PK. "I did so, but on tasting it concluded it was corked and promptly sent it back. Ian Smith was horrified. Quite a few of the other diners were watching our table and he hated drawing attention to himself. He was also not one to waste anything and would have far rather drunk the wine than send it back. That was just Ian Smith's nature."

Ivor Richard chaired the conference which was more remarkable for ill-discipline and gift headlines than achievement. Watching from London,

Lonrho boss 'Tiny' Rowland[61] bankrolled much of his protégé Joshua Nkomo's bill, and promoted his alliance with Robert Mugabe in the Patriotic Front (PF).

Kissinger had warned Smith to be wary of British malfeasance. The Rhodesians took exception to being called the "Smith Delegation". Richard referred to the militants as "liberation movements" while PK called them "terrorists". Smith later likened Mugabe's men to a "bunch of gangsters" and flew home furious when it became clear Richard was unable to do so much as enforce an agenda. Leaving the mercurial PK in charge perhaps best illustrated Smith's exasperation.

Talking to the Swiss media, PK had reporters sniggering when he said most rural Africans could be forgiven for thinking that black majority rule was "something you find on a menu", and called the Mugabe delegation "itinerant, temporarily unemployed terrorists", with Mugabe himself a "bloodthirsty Marxist puppet who has threatened to arraign anyone associated with the [government]". Referring to "the deplorable spectacle of four black delegations quarrelling like cat and dog over what would be the carcass of Rhodesia", he accused Britain of "reckless frivolity" in its handling of the conference.

With Mugabe persistently arriving late, PK one day demanded an apology and provoked the future prime minister. "Foul-mouthed bloody fool," screamed Mugabe.

---

[61] Of Dutch/German/British parentage, born Roland Fuhrop in an Indian internment camp in 1917, Tiny Rowland became a member of the Hitler Youth before moving with his parents to England where he was schooled. After the outbreak of war Fuhrop changed his name to Rowland and served briefly in a non-combatant role in a service corps. Hostilities over, Rowland visited Southern Rhodesia and laid the seeds of an African conglomerate that would grow expeditiously and soon wield enormous influence the length and breadth of the continent. Keen observers of this meteoric development insist it was achieved only with solid financial and diplomatic support from the British government. It has also been suggested that the multinational was, in fact, a front for British Intelligence and for the projection of British influence by corporate means. Having selected Nkomo as his 'man' to rule an independent Zimbabwe, Rowland was grooming him for the top job, but ultimately Robert Mugabe would prevail.

Pat Bashford of the opposition Centre Party was typically critical of the government delegation and said PK's performance was "archaic and dangerous and obviously intended to show how a white man deals with cheeky people".

Christopher Hitchens went further. Writing in the *New Statesman*: "In a short and sheltered life, van der Byl is the nastiest man I have ever hit upon." When David Spanier of *The Times* asked him why the Rhodesian government did not publish the names of the terrorists it hanged, he replied "It's an academic question because they are normally dead afterwards." Spanier described PK as "a man calculated to give offence".

A former colleague recalls two amusing incidents during the Geneva fiasco:

> We Rhodesians had an internal telephone channel which was ours alone to use during press conferences. When a pair of Mugabe's people walked into the room one day, PK looked askance. Wild and woolly, they were guerrillas fresh from the Mozambique bush. Phoning me for information he pushed the wrong button and broadcast to everyone: "I say, who on earth are those two devils that have just walked in with tea cosies on their heads?" Ivor Richard spat his pipe out amidst the outrage and pandemonium.
>
> Another involved Rex Nhongo who torched his hotel room. Recently arrived from Mozambique he was unprepared for the Geneva winter. Turning every heating appliance, including a stove, to maximum, he fell asleep in his bed, but something ignited the furniture. With the room ablaze he was forced to leap off a balcony in whatever sleeping attire he was clad in. Later there was a delightful cartoon of PK holding an outstretched blanket below with a big hole in it urging Nhongo to jump. With the militants claiming foul play, Ivor Richard challenged PK to explain his role. Flicking ash from his cigar he pronounced, "It ain't me wot done it."

On 7 December, Smith returned for a few days before withdrawing his delegation and flying home. On the 14th, Foreign Secretary Anthony Crossland announced the conference had been postponed indefinitely.

"The whole thing was a bloody farce," PK recalled. "It was supposed to be about the implementation of the Kissinger accord and the allocation of $2,000 million in reconstruction finance promised by the Americans. Ivor Richard didn't have a clue. The nationalists wanted immediate power. A pity how it all turned out really because it would have allowed people who wanted to leave the country to do so with a bit of money to start a new life."

Returning to Foreign Affairs, PK experienced difficulty in coordinating the competing factions:

> Quite a lot of Rhodesian foreign policy was conducted by the CIO. Ian Smith listened carefully to Ken Flower. He did not distrust his policymakers but conducted a lot of policy off his own bat. With South Africa it was one-on-one between the prime ministers. The generals could also bypass me and go straight to the PM. It wasn't done out of malice, but they knew they could get away with it and I was often left in the dark.
>
> Ian Smith was quite secretive. What he considered important, he kept to himself. Relations with South Africa, England and Portugal were his. The rest was kind of a hurly-burly thing with wogs, foreigners and God knows what; which he neither understood nor liked. He was marvellous actually. He condoned much of my activity without necessarily supporting it.
>
> Harold Hawkins in South Africa used to send his reports to Ken Flower and Ian Smith and not to me. He was a bad man, Harold Hawkins. There was a thing called the Iron Triangle or something which was an extraordinary buggers' fraternity of Towsey, Flower and Hawkins.

Costa Pafitis concurs: "Hawkins was reporting to Flower at all times and Flower to the British, so in a sense he was also a British spy. While not defending Flower I understand what he took to be a dilemma. The Brits were saying to him you have to rein in these mad gung-ho Rhodesians who want to fight the world or else they're all going to perish. He made a value judgement to play both sides which was disastrous for Rhodesia, so history may be hard on him."

Professor Richard Wood has recently discovered a British telex from Pretoria, sent in October 1976, as the Geneva Conference began. It stated that Harold Hawkins had just handed them a 'Top Secret' CIO report on the current situation in Rhodesia. Wood does not rush to judgement but cannot imagine why he would have done this at the behest of anyone other than the British government, and notes he makes no mention of this delivery in his daily reports to Cabinet Secretary Jack Gaylard.

With efforts to break sanctions and make political friends in Africa continuing, PK found himself talking to Zaire's strongman, Mobutu Sese Seko:

I originally met Mobutu through Hans Germani who was Mike Hoare's intelligence officer during the Congo troubles. Not a lot came of it. I met up with him all over the place. Brussels, Munich, Kinshasa. I once went up to Gbadolite, his rather extravagant retreat on the border. What a trauma to get to the place. I was housed in Kinshasa in some sort of village they had built for an OAU conference or something. I was ferried around all night by cockroaches bigger than lobsters; then we flew in a bloody Hercules. All the important people were put in the front. I was there under the guise of the Chef de Delegation Federale Allemende and surrounded by Franz Josef Strauss's *pistoleros*. It seemed the entire diplomatic corps was on their way to see Mobutu. We were all seated in jump seats, then they opened the back and thousands of savages armed with bicycles, chickens, dried fish and sort-of tied-up pigs streamed on to the plane. And then it took off—bloody nightmare! When we were airborne this very lanky, tall savage in a rather grubby shirt came down the aisle and engaged a lot of people in conversation. I said to my German companions, "Who is that savage?" They said it was the pilot. I said who the hell is driving this bloody aeroplane? Enquiries were made and it turned out to be Idi Amin's Minister of Defence. Bloody terrifying.

I offered to do a lot of things for Mobutu. He had all these modern fighter jets lying in disrepair. I offered to send our chaps to fix them, hoping to spirit a few back to Rhodesia in the process, but I got no support from cabinet. Mobutu was a very welcoming bloody scoundrel but I was better pals with his right hand axe-man, Bulla Nyati. When we were in Geneva for the talks Mobutu's people were staying at his villa on the lake. Nyati was switched on, wore pin-striped suits, spoke everything beautifully; several wog languages plus French, German, Russian, excellent English. He had been in jail with Mobutu and had been governor of Katanga where I once visited him He sent me home loaded with fine South African wine. Very generous bloke.

In December 1976, PK was put up for membership of the Turf Club by Robert Salisbury.[62] "I think my father knew this was going to cause uproar and felt like making a bit of mischief," says James Cecil.

Private Eye wrote: "Hysterically pro-Ian Smith like every good Cecil is brought up to be, 'Titch' [Robert Salisbury] has created a mini scandal by putting up for membership one of the nastiest politicians even Zimbabwe has thrown up—none other than the despicable PK van der Byl, at the time Foreign Minister in Smith's rebel regime and a horror movie traitor more qualified for the Tower than the Turf."

Robert Salisbury recalls: "PK attracted a great many signatures and his candidacy was only withdrawn when Peter Carrington threatened to resign if he were elected."

---

62 Who would later become the 7th Marquess of Salisbury.

At the same time, Rhodesian Special Forces were raiding Mozambique at will to the fury of Samora Machel. He exhorted the international community to destroy Smith while simultaneously deporting 28,000 white Portuguese and incarcerating 150 priests in concentration camps. America's UN Ambassador William Scranton on a visit to Lusaka announced a tightening of Rhodesian sanctions and the stepping up of aid to "liberation movements" opposed to the "Smith regime".

Days before Christmas 1976, a large group of workers at the Honde Valley Tea Estates in the Eastern Highlands were brutally shot and bayoneted to death in front of their families. Told it was punishment for working for the white man and that their wages were so low they were better off dead, the insurgents then disappeared back into Mozambique. Rhodesia was shocked as word of the atrocity spread. PK called it "an act of unspeakable brutality". The UN voted overwhelmingly to tighten sanctions and Britain increased aid to Mozambique and liberation movements.

In early 1977, PK challenged the UN to honour its charter by allowing him to defend an allegation of military incursion made by Botswana. The request was simply ignored and the Botswanan version of events was unanimously accepted. Ivor Richard described the situation in southern Africa as potentially as dangerous as the Second World War. Nationalist leaders called for the Rhodesian forces to surrender, prompting PK to say, "We will fight to the last man and the last cartridge."

In January, US President Jimmy Carter appointed Andrew Young Ambassador to the UN in return for Young's support in garnering the black vote in the southern states. A friend of African liberation movements, he did nothing, however, as Mengistu Haile Mariam shot his way into the Ethiopian presidential palace, declared himself president for life and initiated murderous reprisals.

With the abandonment of the Geneva proposals Smith, at something of a loss, began seeking an internal settlement. Notwithstanding PK's horror of amalgamating the army with PF (Patriotic Front) cadres and the fear of "Mugabe's people's courts", he confirmed Rhodesia was "irrevocably committed to majority rule". It was also announced that the Land Tenure

Act that set aside certain areas of the country on racial lines, would be scrapped.

This whiff of liberalism saw 12 Smith MPs abandon the party, but PK refused invitations to join them. Hedging the new RF stance on majority rule, PK defaulted to a "qualified franchise" position and the requirement for two-thirds Legislative Assembly approval. He warned of a white backlash if change was too hectic.

In March, Cuban troops marched into Zaire's Katanga Province, having previously fought UNITA forces in southern Angola. As a result PK found an unlikely ally in Kenneth Kaunda, who referred to the Soviet-surrogate presence as "a tiger with its marauding cubs".

When Fidel Castro and Soviet President Podgorny subsequently toured southern Africa, PK described the trip as "calculated arrogance ... not even Hitler went strutting around Eastern Europe like this, waving an olive branch in one hand and an AK-47 in the other".[63] He derided Podgorny's "zone of peace" while simultaneously organizing the invasion of Shaba Province. "It's the normal Russian dichotomy. They probably feel they can get away with it." He urged support for the internal settlement which would be a "blow to Russian ambitions".

Speaking about the new Carter team he was scathing: "Not a single one knows a thing about [Rhodesia] or has set foot here or has spoken to the moderate majority. It has the air of staggering absurdity about it. They seem to be more occupied with kicking us while we're down than being constructive. US policy is designed to bring Robert Mugabe to power and he will make Idi Amin look like an amateur."

Reports by the BBC and *The Observer* that the Rhodesian Army was responsible for the murder of seven Catholic missionaries at Musami Mission drew the following from PK: "I have never come across anything so contemptible ... unscrupulous people are maintaining a lie to keep the name of that 'practising Catholic' Robert Mugabe snow-white. Will the BBC also suggest the IRA murders are being committed by British troops?

---

[63] Paul Moorcraft: *A Short Thousand Years*. Galaxie Press, 1979

These are cynical times but surely we have reached the absolute depths."

In April, PK joined Ian Smith and David Smith in South Africa for a disappointing first meeting with new Foreign Secretary David Owen. The Rhodesians doubted his sincerity, although Chairman John Vorster believed Owen was a big improvement on his late predecessor, Anthony Crossland.

With Andrew Young enthusiastically increasing UN sanctions, James Callaghan promised to jail former cabinet minister, Lord Angus Graham, the Duke of Montrose, if he returned to Scotland to attend a gathering of the Highland clans. At the same time, a 'secret' ZANU document indicted Ian Smith, Mark Partridge, Bill Irvine and PK van der Byl for "for crimes against the people and the State". PK was identified as "being a vigorous supporter of the war who has suggested our troops be shot in the streets".

To Rhodesian dismay, despite increasingly hostile and erratic behaviour from Samora Machel, Western aid was increased to Mozambique. At the same time, British newspapers reported more than 90,000 dead in the ongoing genocide in Uganda with Idi Amin directing and participating personally in the slaughter. This left Buckingham Palace in the embarrassing position of having to rebuff a planned visit by Amin and his huge entourage in his capacity as head of the OAU. It was widely noted that the Foreign Office had previously welcomed him into office upon the ousting of Milton Obote. Opening the new Tsanga Lodge rehabilitation centre for convalescing soldiers in the Inyanga Mountains PK said:

> In this hall we are in an atmosphere of superb courage where one of the most gallant countries in history has produced a race of men and women whose fortitude has become a byword. This new race is a great and splendid thing and one can have no greater pride than to be able to say "I am a Rhodesian". This is a breed of men the like of which has not been seen for many a long time and which may yet perhaps, by virtue of the example that it sets, go some way toward redeeming the squalid and shameful times in which we live.

The following month, July 1977, PK travelled to Europe to attend the wedding of Andrea, Otto von Hapsburg's eldest daughter, and was seated alongside her cousin Charlotte.[64] "We chatted quite a lot," remembers Lotti, "but my English was very poor. He invited me to come to Rhodesia which was very kind of him but I explained I would not be able to do that for a while."

A successful Rhodesian raid on the Mozambican town of Mapai raised morale but drew widespread international condemnation, with the US State Department calling it a ploy to draw Cuban intervention and internationalize the war. Carter warned white Rhodesians not to expect to be rescued by American troops. PK said: "Our intention is to protect our citizens—both black and white. Western countries are so besotted and debauched with détente it is difficult to know if there is anything at all they are prepared to fight for."

The raid saw David Owen asking for British troops to break Smith but discovered parliament had no stomach for it. He then called for the immediate dissolution of the Rhodesian government. Smith remarked that Owen could not be very busy if he only thought of "retribution for Rhodesians".[65]

On 4 August, talks at New Sarum air base between Rhodesia and South Africa confirmed South Africa's "full backing of the internal settlement". PK later said: "We know beyond any shadow of a doubt that their intention [the British and Americans] is to impose an intolerable settlement upon us. We must have unity among white Rhodesians while closing ranks with our black Rhodesians so as to resist the hostility of our enemies."

On 31 August, Smith went back to the polls, sweeping all seats once more. Andrew Young and David Owen arrived in Salisbury the next day. Smith called Owen "one of those petty little men trying to fill a job which is too big for him, using an arrogant posture in the hope this will impress his

---

[64] Princess Charlotte Maria Benedikta Eleonore Adelheid von und zu Liechtenstein

[65] *Umtali Post.* 22 September 1977

audience".[66] Demanding the immediate handover of the security forces to the Patriotic Front,[67] Smith was horrified. PK called the plan "totally outrageous; the imposition of Anglo-American-Russian unconditional surrender on an undefeated people who are not enemies".[68]

Owen wanted Field Marshal Carver brought in to take command of security matters. PK called it a "MacArthur solution" which wouldn't work without "first dropping a few atom bombs".

Soon after his appointment as Commissioner Designate by Owen, Carver asked Lord Valentine Cecil, then an army captain, to brief his staff on his recent visit to Rhodesia:

> His staff were not keen to listen to me but a field marshal is a field marshal so I went. The atmosphere was tense. The meeting took place in an office specially set up for Lord Carver at the Foreign and Commonwealth Office. I went to start my brief in the military fashion by describing the ground and found the maps were pre-UDI and did not even show Kariba Dam, which was an area relevant to terrorist activity. When I asked if they had anything more recent, they told me that was all they had because new ones were only available in Rhodesia and they could not purchase them for fear of breaking sanctions. However, they agreed to accept any new ones as a gift so I immediately picked up the phone and was astonished, given the state of the lines in those days, to get through to PK's secretary who immediately put me through to him. He asked me where I was and when I told him he said, "Poor you, how absolutely ghastly." I explained my problem and he was most helpful, agreeing to send new maps to the Foreign Office, which he did.

---

[66] Ian Smith: *The Great Betrayal: The Memoirs of Ian Douglas Smith*. Blake Publishing, 1997

[67] A newly formed alliance between Robert Mugabe's ZANU and Joshua Nkomo's ZAPU

[68] *The Times*, 11 November 1977

Asked why Rhodesia was seen as the enemy, PK replied: "Largely because a great lamentable degeneracy has gone through the Western world where patriotism is something to be scoffed at and honouring your father and mother and other old-fashioned values are looked upon with derision. Where loyalty, if it costs you, is looked upon as a reckless indiscretion." Support came from Enoch Powell, who declared: "Patriotism is having a nation to die for and being glad to die for it all the days of one's life."

Evening Standard sage Max Hastings declared Owen's plan sound, accusing Rhodesians of defending "platoons of delightfully obedient servants" and "gaily umbrellated patios" rather than Western civilization. "The only real question that counts is where the displaced whites are going to go ..."

He went on: "The biggest mistake successive British government made was to treat Ian Smith and his ministers as reasonable men." He referred to PK as "a sort of white caveman who talks of mowing down the blacks in the streets", and in his book, *Going to the Wars*, describes him as a "grotesque parody of a Dornford Yates English gentleman", writing that "the appalling van der Byl, this dreadful man ... occasionally amused himself by potting at blacks from his helicopter with a hunting rifle".

In a letter responding to this allegation, PK's son Valerian wrote: "This suggestion of murder never happened, and is a figment of Hastings's warped imagination. I cannot help but wonder how many other stories this apparently venerated reporter imagined in his climb to the pinnacle of the British print media."

Former Rhodesian Air Marshal Norman Walsh comments: "I am also outraged at the assertions made by Max Hastings." He continues: "A few points: We did not allow anyone to fire a personal weapon from the helicopter; this also applied to troops on board. The reason for this was the danger of firing into the rotor blades in turbulence or if the pilot had to make a sudden turn or evasive action of any sort. The only weapon fired was the gunner's weapon and then only in close liaison with the pilot who controlled weapons firing."

Hastings also suggested "providing the blacks with military assistance to support their campaign [against the Rhodesian government]. Such a policy could bring about an overnight extraordinary transformation in our relations with the Third World. At the very least we can spare ourselves further diplomatic humiliations by sending no further negotiators to Salisbury until [Ian Smith] concedes publicly that he is willing to discuss the handover of power to the black Africans to whom it rightly belongs."

Unbowed, Hastings would later comment:

> The tragedy of Zimbabwe makes some of us search our own consciences, back to the years of white supremacy. I was among visiting correspondents who reported on the guerrilla war, until I was deported by the Smith government in 1976. Some British acquaintances with long memories say to me today: "Don't you feel pretty stupid, when you see what Mugabe has done? You were one of the silly buggers who thought his thugs were freedom fighters."[69]

Continuing his rebuttal of Hastings's comments, Valerian van der Byl asks:

> Why did my father and Mr. Smith fight as volunteers *against* the crimes he accuses them of? Ian Smith was at the controls of his Spitfire leading a squadron against ground targets when he was shot down by German gunners in northern Italy. He immediately linked up with Italian partisans to continue the fight. My father saw action against the Nazis in Europe with an armoured brigade of the 7th Hussars. Historian Sir Max Hastings may not be aware of these facts because at that time he had his soft lips curled around his mother's nipple ingesting the milk that would nourish a highly imaginative mind. The irony is the men he grew to castigate played a small but courageous role in defending the freedoms he would later

---

[69] Max Hastings: *Going to the Wars*. Pan, 2001

prove so skilful at abusing. What he also chooses not to relate is that this "near-fascist and his cohorts" reached an agreement with Sir Alec Douglas-Home in 1972 and Dr. Henry Kissinger in 1976 on a peaceful transfer of power to the black majority. Both these agreements were subsequently scrapped for reasons beyond the "near-fascist's" control and they had to get on with the task of running the country while trying to maintain law and order. Eventually the "near-fascist" handed over power himself and ordered those who exercised "ruthless force" (the Rhodesian army, police and intelligence services) to manage an extremely orderly election that sealed their own uncertain fate. Over 60 per cent of the populace voted and the poll was pronounced free and fair by British officials.

Hastings called the transfer of power to Mugabe a "notable achievement for British diplomacy". I would suggest "British duplicity" is nearer the mark. Mrs. Thatcher first promised to recognize the 1979 election then recanted, and then allowed Mugabe to participate in the 1980 election despite widespread voter intimidation by ZANU-PF cadres. Lord Soames, then governor during the transition, admitted later in person to Ian Smith to being deeply embarrassed by this breach of promise, a matter over which he personally had no control.

Hastings was guilty of selective reporting, magnifying Smith excesses but avoiding "liberation army" outrages. Victims included thousands of black innocents, missionaries and farmers, their families and workers and, in two disgusting incidents, the occupants of civilian airliners shot out of the sky, their survivors murdered on the ground.

Hastings wondered how the returning "freedom fighters" would react to the new political dispensation and access to the white man's—no doubt in Hastings's view, undeserved—wealth. Well, the first question was answered when they went into Matabeleland soon after independence and massacred

20,000 suspected malcontents. Britain deemed the operation a "legitimate national security concern". I have no doubt Sir Max would have concurred. The second question has just been emphatically rejoined. The "fighters" have sacked the country, destroyed the economy, cowed the populace, forced roughly one third of the citizenry to flee and, of those that remain in the blighted land, roughly half face imminent starvation. But Sir Max can take heart; one of his old heroes Didymus Mutasa, a senior Zimbabwean minister, recently explained to the world press that if half the population were to die of starvation then that would not be a "big problem". After all, he reminded his audience, they would probably be opposition supporters.

My father may have been "ghastly" and "among the ugliest figures in the history of Africa" and all those other pungent epithets with which Hastings chooses to lace his prose, but I must point out: no one starved in Rhodesia. Harold Wilson's government, (which almost ordered an invasion of the country) acknowledged it was the best-administered country in Africa, and the army over which my father ministered consisted of 70 per cent black volunteers who fought valiantly, alas vainly, to save the country from ruin. The genesis of this attack lies in the fact that he was wrong about Robert Mugabe and wrong about my father.

Respected Zimbabwean journalist and former Smith critic, Michael Hartnack, gives Hastings and like-minded folk similarly short shrift:

> This country [Zimbabwe] is a heartbeat away from the clutches of brutal, uneducated warlords with none of Mugabe's flair for power-broking ... They may be egged on, at least initially, by the same shallow and dilettante element in the churches and the universities and the news media who will today go

to ruthless lengths to silence any implied suggestion that they bear responsibility for making this regime what it is and, incidentally, turning a promising provincial schoolmaster into a political Jekyll and Hyde. It is noteworthy how many of the 'progressive' academics who were here 1980–2000, pouring out a stream of books and learned articles in praise of Mugabe, have now quietly slipped away. They have gone off to make exhibitions of themselves in fresh idealistic crusades on behalf of other unfortunate societies.

CHAPTER SIXTEEN
Internal settlement

Feeling increasingly isolated, Smith and PK met Lonrho boss Tiny Rowland in the officers' mess at New Sarum air base to explore his ideas. An erstwhile adversary and a man Smith remained wary of, he nonetheless quickly agreed to Rowland's idea to meet Kaunda in Lusaka. Rowland was at pains to assure the two Rhodesians of their safety, but they were apparently unconcerned. They liked the idea and wanted to get going. The next day they flew to Lusaka.

Effusively hospitable, Kaunda took them by helicopter to State House, insisting it was time to end the pain and suffering. Kaunda was pleased to hear Smith wanted 'his man' (Nkomo) brought into negotiations as soon as possible and the mood was positive, but this changed during lunch when Kaunda phoned Nyerere and was told in no uncertain terms not to compromise Mugabe's position. A testy afternoon session followed and the talks collapsed.

"Rowland was very keen for us to make a deal with Nkomo," recalled PK, "and this was worth considering, but sadly it came to nothing. Nkomo was very reliant on Rowland, as were many African presidents. Kaunda was perfectly friendly but Nkomo was never produced, although I think he was waiting nearby. I had a particular connection to Kaunda because the man who helped him get to where he did was a fellow by the name of Gore-Brown, who was a friend of my father. It was at Gore-Brown's house in Northern Rhodesia that I shot my first lion as a child. Kaunda was very fond of Gore-Brown because he had helped him too, so when he discovered I knew Gore-Brown that lightened the atmosphere."

Soon after this meeting, another problem loomed in West Africa. With President Bongo set to become Chairman of the OAU, Rhodesia had become an embarrassment to Gabon. Jack Malloch's aircraft had to be moved and his operation mothballed.

"Libreville was symbolically important to us in Rhodesia. It was never particularly lucrative but it was the one real foothold we had in 'African' Africa," recalled PK.

As a result, a new operation was opened in Oman with Tim Landon's help. Called Cargoman, the airline was launched with Omani government cooperation. PK recalled:

> The Brits must have known Jack was going in and out of there but I'm not sure they knew exactly what he was carrying ... that he was carrying 'hardware'. But one must remember Oman was of critical importance to the British. At that time, the Straits of Hormuz was strategically one of the most important places on earth and the Brits were well ensconced there, so they probably thought it was not worth the risk upsetting the Omani establishment in a disagreement over Rhodesia. We were small potatoes in the greater scheme of things.
>
> Unfortunately it wasn't a great success. The whole thing was too imaginative for my colleagues. I was amazed at the attitude of these Arabs. They look upon the 'nigger' as the lowest of the low—total contempt. I tried to introduce them to some of my black associates. I said to Omar once, "Look, I've brought some of our chiefs to see you." He said, "Nonsense! They're the people our fathers used to brand with numbers on their faces. You keep them; we don't want them."
>
> We also did a bit in Egypt. We were on good terms with General Kamal, the Egyptian Intelligence boss who went on to become Defence Minister, then Prime Minister ... a bald-headed bastard of the most dangerous disposition. Ken Flower had set that up. Ricky May was at the one meeting and I had Piet Bosch with me. I remember it well because I had the most frightful squitters and was feeling like death.

Jack Malloch deserved better from the Rhodesian government. He was underfunded and had little support. He may have gone to the CIO or Ian Smith for approval but I was happy for him to just get on with it. I encouraged him to just get on and do it. There was so much shit flying anyway, a bit more wouldn't make the slightest bit of difference. "Go out and get business, dear Jack," I said. My philosophy was that any country with which you could get involved can only be of benefit—so long as it wasn't an enemy of our friends.

In November 1977, potential pro-consul Lord Carver flew in. Prewarned of his hostility toward the Rhodesian government, Smith chose to ignore him and spent the day watching cricket. But strutting the local stage, Carver wanted to make the point that he outranked the Rhodesian generals and arrived in his field marshal's uniform. Accompanying him was UN-appointed Indian General Prem Chand who was quickly nicknamed the 'Samoosa Scout'. If David Owen's plan had worked, Carver would have assumed command of the armed forces and to all intents and purposes, the country.

While Carver and Chand toured the country, they were quite unaware that ComOps, Combined Operations, was planning two huge strikes into Mozambique, and on 23 November all hell broke loose when less than 200 soldiers attacked a ZANLA base in Chimoio. Two days later they hit another camp to the north called Tembué. When the dust settled, 3,000 insurgents were dead and approximately 5,000 wounded. The Rhodesians lost two dead and ten wounded.

The international community was outraged and almost predictably insisted the targets were refugee camps while calling for the Rhodesians to be held to account. Facing down the popular view, opposition leader Margaret Thatcher called for a more conciliatory approach toward Rhodesia, but PM Jim Callaghan vowed to intensify the pressure.

Wading in, PK issued a "formal challenge" to the British government "to publicly state, frankly and unequivocally, which should prevail: the wishes of the people of Rhodesia or the vested interests of outside elements, since the two are henceforth irreconcilable. It is now apparent," he stated, "that Britain's famous six principles for a Rhodesian settlement have been proved a hypocritical fraud."

Later Smith was forthright about the British Foreign Secretary:

Owen, like virtually all the English politicians I dealt with, was unable to look at the Rhodesian problem in a genuinely objective way. More important to him than finding a solution to the problem was his desire to punish us. His insistence on handing over the army to Mugabe and Nkomo was nothing more than a scheme to exact retribution on Rhodesians. We had poked them in the eye and it was his aim to get even. The best way for him to cut our throats was to help Mugabe or Nkomo acquire power.

Kissinger, compared to the British, was a pleasure to deal with. He seemed very genuine in his desire to reach an understanding that took the interests of all into account. I have nothing but respect for him. If the British had approached our problem in the same spirit I think our history would have unfolded with a great deal less tragedy, but they were terribly vindictive and they took treachery to a new level.

At the same time, Andrew Young, seemingly obsessed with matters of race, was asked by a reporter from *The Times* if he thought Mugabe was a violent man. "Not at all, he's a very gentle man," he replied. "In fact, one of the ironies of the whole struggle is that I can't imagine Joshua Nkomo, or Robert Mugabe, ever pulling the trigger on a gun to kill anyone. I doubt that they ever have." Later he said: "I find that I am fascinated by his intelligence, by his dedication. The only thing that frustrates me about Robert Mugabe is that he is so incorruptible."

With the failure of the Kaunda initiative and seeking alternatives, Smith increased pressure on African leaders within Rhodesia to find an internal political solution. While exploring this avenue he instructed his military men to hit the terrorists hard enough to bring their leadership to the negotiating table with constructive intent.

"I'm often asked why we, the politicians, were not more aggressive," remembered Smith. "Why we did not give freer rein to our chaps to go and hit the enemy where it hurt most. The answer is the South Africans had a gun at our heads. Without them we were finished, and they were still determined to ingratiate themselves with the black leaders to the north. They looked at all our military actions in that light and if we pushed our luck we ran the risk of having them pull the plug. We had to be very mindful of that because I knew they were quite capable of doing it."

The 'Internal' initiative appeared to bear fruit when, after protracted and at times testy negotiations a 50/50 black/white Transitional Government was sworn in on 4 March 1978, with Smith becoming joint Prime Minister with Sithole, Muzorewa and Senator Chief Chirau.

PK's co-minister at Information, Immigration and Tourism was Dr. Elliot Gabellah. Those who thought a hard-line 'Rhodesia Fronter' would be unable to adjust would be surprised. PK told close associates he thoroughly enjoyed working with Gabellah and held him in very high regard.

"Muzorewa was a windbag with a certain amount of charisma," remembered PK. "He was helped enormously by the British government, starting with the Pearce Commission. Not much of a leader, easily manipulated by others. He had no idea of government and he was given real power despite what our detractors say about him having been a puppet of the whites. Ultimately, he was easily manipulated by Carrington at Lancaster House."

But the Carter administration quickly announced it had no intention of recognizing the 'Internal Agreement' because the government was illegal. PK called the decision "… staggering in its absurdity—how could the Geneva conference have been staged by the Anglo-Americans if the government were illegal?"

"Meantime," recalls Marge Bassett, "Minister carried on as always; everyday a fresh carnation from a florist in Baker Avenue delivered in the morning. And he always enjoyed his visits to his Indian tailor who worked on Manica Road with Luigi, his valet from Mozambique always in attendance. But he liked to have his shirts laundered in Paris; he said it was the only place where they did it right."

"We ultimately discouraged him from wearing the wretched flower in his buttonhole, but it was not easy," recalls Lin Mehmel. "We made the point that it was not appropriate for him to be seen with a flower in his lapel while people were out in the field fighting and dying, and he agreed."

Says Lotti:

> PK was no follower of fashion, but appearance was incredibly important to him. He was influenced by his parents' sense of style however. They were considered the best-dressed couple in South Africa. Pride in what one wore was something that ran in the family. At the end of the day I think PK was very much like his father in many ways. Like Major Piet, he was very quick-witted; seldom did he stumble over a reply. And like his father he was a sociable person who loved company, particularly the company of people who interested him.
>
> With people who irritated him he became icily polite. He did not judge people on their background. He took people as they came and as long as they were kind or had something to say he would be forthcoming. He did not like people who tried to be what they were not. Then he could be quite nasty; I used to feel like I was sitting on needles wondering what was coming next.
>
> Food and wine he loved and knew a lot about. But he never drank a lot and never after dinner. Mornings he was a little slow; not his best time. Of an evening he would have a whisky then a bath. The bath was where he did a lot of his thinking.

In an interview with Phillippa Berlyn, PK addressed a number of topics. On Rhodesian culture: "I think there is a great deal to be learned [in Rhodesia] about the art of good living ... people do not leave cocktail parties at a reasonable hour … they tend to stay on after dinner to the intense irritation of the host. And too much time is spent drinking before dinner …"

On music: "I am most fond of the opera, particularly the works of Verdi such as 'Don Carlos', 'La Forza del Destino' and 'Othello'; also Puccini and the French composers Meyerbeer and Gounod. Some of the modern dance tunes are diverting but generally speaking I dislike the products of what are known as the 'pop groups'. I'm always very pleased to listen to the martial music of military bands."

"I did not think that music was one of his more memorable talents," remembers Lin Mehmel. "Having said that, unmelodious as the rendition was, he could sing vast chunks of opera, word perfect. He had a passion for military music. He frequently bemoaned the loss of the 'gramophone' and lamented the fact that good music was hard to come by on the 'wireless' these days."

Continuing with Phillippa Berlyn, he discussed literature: "My tastes in literature are very wide, ranging from the Roman and Greek classics through historical works, biographies, good novels and amusing nonsense such as the works of Nancy Mitford, to semi-scientific works on such subjects as Egyptology, zoology, anthropology and archaeology. I dislike intensely Russian authors such as Tolstoy and Dostoevsky."

On poetry: "I am relatively unmoved by poetry other than the robust works of men such as Kipling and Macaulay; but the exception to this is Oscar Wilde whose writing I greatly admire."

On food and wine: "This is dependent on the place and circumstances. In civilization I like the best of haute cuisine in France and Italy, and have the highest regard for the various seafoods of Spain. I also enjoy game, the preparation of which is better understood in England than anywhere else.

"Although I like champagne, I am essentially a red wine drinker and favour claret and burgundy, though I believe it is usually better to drink the wines of the particular country that one happens to be in because they suit the food better."

On the perfect dinner: "There are of course numerous perfect dinners so one can only choose one of many possibilities and permutations. Good

Russian caviar with a glass of vodka can never be wrong to begin with followed by a bouillon, then a Lobster Grenadin and a Chateaubriand, very underdone with green peas, followed with well-matured Brie, finally ending with a mousse of some sort. For a smaller occasion, one could start with a dozen Belon or Colchester oysters, followed by roast grouse or partridge, then crêpes suzettes, ending with a savoury."

On hobbies: "I like and am amused by an enormous diversity of things: Egyptology, anthropology, archaeology, zoology, and palaeontology. I am very interested in farming. Art—I have a few pictures; furniture and so forth. I ride and swim, but the recreations I most enjoy are hunting, shooting and fishing. Nowadays there's little time for that because the job comes first. But that does not matter as my job is probably more interesting and stimulating than any recreation. I shall be eternally grateful that the privilege has fallen to me to play some role in this epic period of Rhodesian history.

"History is fascinating and one of my most vivid memories is of being shown the battlefields where Allan Wilson's men perished by a Matabele warrior who was there. The man, Siacha, was married to Lobengula's daughter, Sidambe, and the battle was his first and last. He recalled everything perfectly and even pointed out the tree under which Wilson stood. I was able to dig bullets out of the trees. The man who commanded the impi was Induna Johaan who forbade looting of the bodies. It was he who said, 'They were men among men and their fathers were men before them.' That was history and history is very important. Without studying it we cannot know how people will react to situations and that is the crux of politics."

Hilary Squires remembers some lighter moments in those gloomy days:

There was an informal cabinet get-together every Monday after 4.30 p.m., with no civil servants present. There were four serious smokers: Lardener-Burke chain-smoked cigarettes, David Smith and Roger Hawkins chain-smoked cheroots and Elly Broomberg smoked a pipe. PK smoked cigarettes occasionally. But on this particular occasion the smokers were having a field day and the air-conditioning was switched off. PK ostentatiously reached inside his coat pocket, withdrew a large cigar, lit it and blew a plume of light blue smoke about ten feet into the already congested room. Ian Smith watched the pantomime then spoke: "Mr. van der Byl', he said, "must you add to this disgusting pollution by smoking that revolting thing?" To which PK responded in that adenoidal drawl of his: "Waaal, Prime Minister, I find that this stops me talking." "Well, that's fine then, carry on smoking it," retorted Smith.

In March, PK introduced Ian Smith to Franz Joseph Strauss, the Minister President of Bavaria, when he visited the country. Strauss told Smith that in his opinion the Soviets were running the OAU and had 'Black Africa' well under control. Smith was greatly impressed with his grasp of the issues.

In April 1978, personal tragedy befell PK with the slaying by ZANLA insurgents of Lord Richard Cecil. PK had encouraged Cecil to visit the land his forefathers had been so instrumental in creating. Working on a documentary on the war, he died when he and his cameraman, Nick Downie, parachuted with the RAR into a contact in northeast Rhodesia. Separated from the others, Lord Richard confronted a combatant who fired into him at close range. He was hit in the chest, stomach and legs and died of his wounds. The Rhodesian Ministry of Defence reported him as being "killed in action". His body was returned to England for burial.

An Etonian, former Grenadier Guards captain and freelance journalist, PK had dissuaded Cecil from joining the Rhodesian Army, arguing he would be more use to the country's cause as a journalist. In return, PK gave him access to events and locations that were off-limits to other journalists. On hearing of his death, PK commented: "Lord Richard was one of the bravest of the brave and one of the finest young men I ever knew, and represented the best of everything that made the Englishman great, and built the British Empire. He has given his life for an idea and an ideal: Rhodesia."

The funeral service was held at the Parish Church of St. Mary and St. Bartholomew, Cranborne, on 27 April. A memorial service was held for him at the Guards Chapel, Wellington Barracks, on 9 May. Both events were attended by the most prominent personalities from the British aristocracy, including Lord Mountbatten, the British Army and the media.

PK said it was fitting that Lord Cecil should be honoured in the Rhodesian Light Infantry Chapel, particularly as the barracks were named after his family. "Indeed, wherever we look, we are reminded of the way in which the Cecil family have supported and helped to sustain Rhodesia, from the capital city named after his great-great-grandfather to Cecil Square and the neighbouring suburb of Hatfield."

PK later remarked, "The singular thing is the fact that he died playing a part in our battle for no material reason whatsoever. He was tough, energetic, intelligent, nice-looking and also one of the most charming people I have ever known. It is extremely tragic that this young man has been killed; he was undoubtedly going to make his mark on British politics."

"My father never really got over the death of Richard," says Valerian. "He held himself responsible for him being where he was and it troubled him for the rest of his life."

With acts of terror increasing, it was reported that two women in their sixties were shot and killed in the dining room of Inyanga's Montclair Hotel. In another incident, a 16-year-old schoolboy, Derick Hattingh, fought off a gang of terrorists at his family home in Glendale. Tragically, his 13-year-old brother was killed. Their father Mike, "a gentle giant of a man", had been killed earlier on active duty with the Police Reserve.

"Of the many tales of heroic acts of this type … this compares with the greatest," PK said. Commenting on events farther north, PK attracted criticism when he called the bloodletting in the Congo's Kolwezi region "a blessing in disguise". He went on to suggest the world should wake up to the realities of life in Africa. "President Carter," he added, "has admitted this was a Cuban and Russian enterprise. So much for Andrew Young's line that the Cubans are a stabilizing influence in Africa. But it is a pity that this sort of ritualistic sacrifice has to be made and these miseries inflicted before anyone wakes up to what we in this country have been warning against for years. Rhodesia," he said, "has to survive the Carter era. Whatever comes after can't be worse."

Later, after a secret trip to France where he met Tiny Rowland, PK briefed Smith that Kaunda was back in the picture. Tired of Nyerere's meddling, he indicated he wanted an exclusive meeting with Smith and Nkomo. Smith was interested. But the terror continued.

Another atrocity occurred on 23 June when eight English missionaries and four children were slaughtered at Elim Mission. Formerly Eagle School, the mission lay in isolated mountainous magnificence in the Eastern Highlands close to the Mozambican border. The killers dragged black students from their beds and harangued them for paying school fees to a "racist government". The terrified whites were removed and butchered elsewhere. The youngest victim was three-week-old Pamela Lynn. She was found wearing her white smock with large sock-shoes, a bayonet rammed through the side of her head. Her left hand was raised, frozen in a fist. Her mother Joyce lay next to her, her head pulped, her arm around her in a protective embrace. Alongside them lay a pretty child stamped to death by heavy boots. Catherine Picken, a survivor of the 1960s' Congo massacres, lay with a long-handled axe imbedded in her head, her blood-stained curlers splayed nearby. Two women and two children, one in pink pyjamas, the other in a floral nightdress, lay in a huddle next to what had been the cricket pavilion. They had all been raped, then bayoneted to death. Reverend Evans, his face split with an axe, lay face down, his hands tied behind his back.

It was subsequently revealed that an army officer had tried to warn the missionaries just days before the massacre, but was rebuffed.

Challenged by Conservative MPs in the Commons to comment on the atrocity, Dr. Owen would only condemn the intransigence of the white Rhodesians. Writing in the London *Sunday Express*, John Junor called Owen "a pompous, prissy little prig". Enraged, PK asked why "David Owen consistently refuses to condemn the murderers of missionaries and their families in Rhodesia when there is overwhelming evidence to show that these dreadful atrocities were committed by the Patriotic Front".

On 15 July, PK visited the fourth village massacre that had taken place in three weeks. Seventeen people, nine of them children, had been burned to death in a hut. Seen as part of a campaign to intimidate the rural populace against support of the Salisbury Internal Agreement, PK described it as "... too appalling to adequately express one's horror. Death at the end of a rope is too good for those who caused such terror and indescribable pain to these people. If this is freedom fighting, the world has come to a sorry pass".

On 11 August, two Conservative MPs were taken to Grand Reef Forward Air Field and shown the bodies of two ZANLA men. In one insurgent's pocket was a diary detailing their involvement in the Elim atrocity, along with a list of looted property. "We killed twelve whites," it read, "including four babies, as remembrance of Nyadzonya, Chimoio, Tembué and in Zimbabwe massacres [sic]."

CHAPTER SEVENTEEN
Vicounts down

On 14 August 1978, pursuing the Lonrho initiative, Ian Smith, Jack Gaylard and Derrick Robinson flew to Lusaka to meet Kaunda, Nkomo and Nigerian Foreign Minister Brigadier Joe Garba. With Tiny Rowland watching in the wings, the talks were positive, with Garba promising to fly to Mozambique to brief Mugabe and bring him on board. The Rhodesians parted company with a feeling of optimism but a few days later Nyerere, the man Ian Smith referred to as "pure evil", had vetoed the budding plan insisting his 'man' Mugabe was being marginalized. Nyerere repeated his "absolute prerequisite" that the Rhodesian Army be disbanded before any further talks.

In Mozambique Samora Machel followed the Nyerere line while finally admitting to holding 20,000 religious dissenters in concentration camps, but refused to bow to pressure and release them.

On 29 August 1978, Texas Governor John Connolly flew in to Harare declaring, "It is fairly difficult to defend the Carter administration's position on Rhodesia."

Hilary Squires remembers a dinner party PK threw for Connolly and his wife Nellie:

> Connolly would go on to serve as Richard Nixon's Secretary of the Treasury, but he was also the man who had been riding in the car with President Kennedy when he was shot. A bullet passed through his chest while the president was hit in the head. I asked Nellie to retell the events, which she must have repeated *ad nauseam* but she was utterly charming and took me through the sequence of events in fascinating style. It was like

living and talking to actual history as it was being made. I had a difficult time explaining our Exchange Control regulations to Governor Connolly. It was almost beyond his comprehension that a government should be in a position to tell a citizen how to spend his or her money. In his view it was your property and yours to do with as you pleased. Unfortunately that was not quite the case with us in Rhodesia.

Late on Sunday afternoon, following Connolly's visit, grand-scale terror came to Rhodesia with the downing of a Viscount passenger aircraft minutes after departing the resort town of Kariba. Packed with weekend holidaymakers returning to Salisbury, the horrific details sent shock waves through the country.

Heroically piloted by Captain John Hood and co-pilot Garth Beaumont the aircraft was struck by a SAM-7 missile. The last transmission from Captain Hood heard by air-traffic controllers was, "I can't ... they're going like f ...", followed by the words, "Mayday. Mayday, Rhodesia 825. I have lost both starboard engines. We are going in." Captain Hood told the passengers to brace themselves and prepare to crash. His final words were to his passengers "to be brave".

With remarkable skill and accuracy he directed the doomed plane into a space in the trees, and but for an unseen ditch all may have survived. The craft ploughed into it and burst into flames, leaving a scalded path in its wake. First out were stewardesses Dulcie Esterhuizen and Brenda Pearson who went immediately to help their Captain and First Officer. Finding the cockpit severed from the fuselage, there was nothing to do. Both Captain and First Officer, blackened by fire, were burned to death; dead at their posts. Then the two went to the aid of the passengers. Most were dead, some were crying out for help and others were silent, in shock. With a fire burning all around them and metal too hot to touch, the stewardesses struggled to drag survivors from the wreckage. Some were shouting to say they were trapped, and needed only a calm voice to tell them to unbuckle their seat-belts and move away.

Dr. MacLaren, a Harare dentist returning from a locum in Kariba, found himself hanging upside down looking at the flames that threatened to engulf the plane. He tried a window but the handle snapped off in his hand. Struggling through the wreckage he reached Sharon Cole and daughter Tracy, and together with the Hargreaves, exited the plane through a hole in the fuselage. Then, along with his friend Tony Hill, he went back and pulled the survivors to a place of relative safety some hundred metres from the burning wreck. A few sat silently while terrified children clung to their parents. Some asked for water and bandages.

Cynthia Tilley, who had recently lost her 15-year-old brother to a terror attack on the family farm, was one of the first to go to the aid of the survivors. Along with Brenda and Dulcie, having exhausted the available dressings, they tore their dresses into makeshift bandages and tried to comfort the wounded. Of the 58 who started the flight, only 18 had survived.

In Salisbury, relatives and friends waiting at the airport were told to go home. Off-duty SAS commander Major Garth Barrett was told to prepare a reaction team for the morning. SAS Darrell Watt recalls: "I'll never forget. We were in our barracks when we were told a plane had gone missing. At first I thought they must be talking about a military aircraft, then discovered it was an Air Rhodesia Viscount with a full complement of passengers and crew. I felt a shudder run through my nervous system. I had no idea what lay ahead, but the events and the images that confronted me that day changed me forever."

From the crash site, Dr. MacLaren led a small party to look for help and water. At an African village they received grudging assistance. Returning with water, Sharon Cole stopped suddenly. "I hear African voices," she whispered. The group stopped and listened carefully as a gruff voice said "*Buya lapa*" [come here], and realized with horror that 12 ZIPRA insurgents had arrived at the scene. An elderly Englishman was heard to shout: "What do you bastards want now?"[70]

Terrified, MacLaren led his small group quietly into hiding in a dry

---

[70] David Caute: *Under the Skin*. Penguin Books, 1983

riverbed. The other survivors were ordered to a place some distance from the wreckage. The crippled pleaded incapacity and asked to be left to lie where they lay. The strong were ordered to move the incapacitated. Those who could stand did so while the maimed lay on the ground. Satisfied all were in place the commander unclipped his 'pig-sticker' bayonet: "You have stolen our land. You are white; now you must die."

With that the firing started. After a while, to save ammunition, bayonets were used. Brenda Pearson was found with five bullet and seventeen bayonet wounds. One girl of four had escaped the firing but was found bayoneted, holding tightly to her dead father's leg.

Hiding in three separate areas were Tony Hill, the Hansens and the MacLaren group. The need for silence had kept everyone isolated. There followed a terrifying search for survivors. One noise from four-year-old Tracy would have brought instant death. MacLaren kept the child close to his chest as the ZIPRA killers stamped within metres of them, shouting for them to show themselves immediately. "It was the longest and most terrifying night of my life," he recalls.

An air force Dakota with the SAS flew grid pattern next morning. "The pilots were trying to plot the search area looking at the aircraft's projected line of flight and the estimated time after take-off when last contact was made," remembers Watt:

> Part of the problem was that no one had any idea how far Captain Hood had kept the aircraft aloft after losing his engines, so there was a lot of guesswork going on. We sat at the doors and windows straining our eyes to see what we didn't want to see—the smouldering wreckage of a downed civilian airliner. I knew that was the reality but it did not stop me hoping for a miracle. There was bad turbulence and headwind that morning. We flew for what seemed like forever. Tracts of the area were unpopulated wilderness but the rest was Tribal Trust Land which was fairly heavily settled. Most of the dwellings were thatch but some were tin and the flash of metal in the

bright sun kept deceiving me. I was feeling very frustrated when suddenly someone shouted and the plane banked sharply. There below were the blue lines on silver of the Air Rhodesia livery and I knew we had found Viscount *Hunyani*. It was hot and I could see the heatwaves distort the light off the mangled fuselage. There was a 40-knot wind blowing outside, making the conditions dangerous for parachuting, but nobody wanted to stay in the plane.

I watched the dispatcher and soon we were in a tight orbit over her. Hooked up, I flung myself out the door and struggled immediately with the wind while I looked anxiously below me for signs of life. I landed very badly near the wreckage and basically broke my leg but I had to keep going. Having dumped my 'chute and checked to see if all the rest of my blokes were on the ground, we started looking. The medics rushed to see who was dead and who was alive.

Then my eyes filled with the worst sight any civilized man could be asked to bear; it made me feel light-headed and slightly queasy. Death was not new to me; I had been involved with it for a long time but nothing I had seen or done prepared me for what was in front of me. I think it was the dead children that destroyed me emotionally.

Then I heard a soft voice and looked into the bush. Out of it appeared a pretty lady covered in blood and dirt but she forced a sort-of smile as our eyes met. "You can't believe how pleased we are to see you," said Mrs. Hansen.

I said, "How can I help you, ma'am?"

She said, "Please come with me."

I followed, amazed at how calm she was, and then I saw her husband. He was shaking and unable to talk. He just shook, wide-eyed, in shock, and one of our guys went to console him.

"Please come with me," the lady said again, and I followed. "After we crashed," she explained, "we went to the toilet and that was when the terrorists arrived. They didn't see us so we lay down and hid. When I saw what they were doing I decided we were about to die but I didn't want them to have my wedding and engagement rings so I dug a hole and buried them. Will you come with me to find the place so I can recover them?"

I helped her uncover the rings and after she'd put them on she smiled at me. "Thank you so much," she said. She was incredibly composed. I would love to meet her again.

I returned to the crash site and all was silent. The dead were grey from all the ash that had settled on them. None of the men were talking. They were hardened SAS operators and they were standing around looking broken. The choppers came in with more troops. I did a check and found the tracks but we were refused permission to follow—another tracker team was to come in and do the follow-up. I was very upset; I know I would have got them, but we were told we had other tasks to attend to.

I'll never stop thinking about that day and will always regret the fact that I never got to go after them. If there is a hell they deserve a place in it.

After being missed by the search aircraft, the MacLaren five were finally found by a police Land Rover, having walked 15 kilometres to the Kariba road.

Back in London, David Owen refused to comment. In a BBC interview, Joshua Nkomo admitted responsibility and burst into laughter. The British press were muted although Max Hastings "felt not the smallest sympathy for the Salisbury regime".

In Salisbury, the Prime Minister, service chiefs and most of the cabinet attended a memorial service at the Anglican Cathedral. Broadcast live to the nation, the Very Reverend John da Costa, the Anglican Dean of

Salisbury, preached his famous 'deafening silence' sermon.[71] While the country mourned and calls for retribution grew louder, the stakes were further raised with another mortar and rocket attack on the eastern border town of Umtali. Meanwhile, it was announced that the Soviet Union was shipping an additional 137 SAMs to Zambia to replenish stocks.

Soon after the Viscount disaster, Smith took a delegation to New York to peddle the internal settlement. He found Secretary of State Cyrus Vance courteous but unhelpful. Vance was importing oil from Nigeria and was unwilling to face down the African lobby.

"So much for all the American talk of democracy and human rights," PK said, but denied calling Vance "a figure of fun—because there was nothing remotely funny about any of his propositions". Also campaigning in New York was disaffected former RF politician Allan Savory. PK was unimpressed: "We know his position ... appeasement and an accommodation with the Patriotic Front. He has proclaimed this loud and clear. We also know that he is conniving with the American State Department and the British Foreign Office to defeat what the bulk of the people want."

During the visit, Smith spoke informally to Kissinger while in New York. Costa Pafitis recalls: "The Americans had us sewn up. At every hotel we stayed in, they told us the switchboard had just broken down. The only photograph that was released to the press was one of Ian Smith standing next to Mickey Mouse. Carter refused to be photographed with Muzorewa. It was very mean-spirited, the whole thing. Carter's people were determined to have Mugabe in power."

Back in South Africa, power shifted when P.W. Botha replaced John Vorster who resigned in the wake of a financial scandal. At the same time, the Rhodesian CIO arrested three CIA agents. Accused of undermining

---

[71] A plaque commemorating the disaster has been removed from the Anglican Cathedral in Harare on the orders of Bishop Kunonga. A fiery supporter of Mugabe and ZANU-PF, he has been accused of a wide variety of crimes against humanity. The Archbishop of Canterbury has refused to intervene.

Muzorewa, alarm bells rang in Washington at the possible exposure of CIA dirty tricks in Africa. A gentleman's agreement was brokered for the release of the agents when the Americans agreed to reverse CIA/Carter policy in Rhodesia. PK was unimpressed, and his protestations were later vindicated when the USA denied any deal had been struck.[72]

Following raids on insurgent camps in Zambia, Britain announced new aid to help Zambia deal with "unprovoked Rhodesian aggression". To quash a rumour that the Zambian Army had fired a British Rapier missile that downed the Viscount, Kaunda forced Nkomo to admit it was Soviet-supplied and his men, ZIPRA, had fired it.

On 29 October 1978, a new weapons consignment arrived in Lusaka from Britain, which included surface-to- air missiles "to protect ZIPRA facilities". Some months later, two Zambian Air Force aircraft were shot down in a friendly-fire incident. Unconfirmed reports indicated the British-supplied missiles had been responsible.

In early November, Conservative MPs Douglas Hurd and John Stanley met PK and Peter Walls. Hurd later described PK as "the most ignorant and offensive person in authority whom I have ever met ... a false Englishman in the manner of von Richthofen ... against elections, against everything except intrigue and condescension".

On 11 November 1978, PK gave an interview to New Zealand's *Evening Post*:

> I can't understand the West except in terms of the old Churchillian remark that if you feed the crocodile enough you will be the last to be devoured. I get the impression that we are expendable and I understand that. But the reprehensible thing is that this is done in the spurious name of human rights and freedom. That's total nonsense ... race relations in Rhodesia are absolutely first class, otherwise 75 per cent of the security forces would not be made up of good, honest black people.

---

[72] Ken Flower: *Serving Secretly*. John Murray, 1987

We're not fighting for white rule; we're fighting for a pitch-black government. I've never had a more constructive colleague than Dr. Gabellah; he's absolutely first class.

The Europeans know there will be big changes; we accept that as long as we're not pushed about. In Africa there is a direct relationship between the liveability of a country and the size of its white population. We will have an all-black government but it's in everyone's interests to leave the white man in peace, his daughters unraped and his sons unmurdered. Phase him away and you'll have the biggest disaster of the century.

In December 1978, former US Democratic presidential candidate George McGovern visited Rhodesia. In a rare slip for such a senior politician, he admitted in a press conference that recently visited Zambia, Tanzania, Kenya and Mozambique were not true democracies. PK responded: "My admiration for the senator's virtuosity grows with every statement he makes."

In January 1979, PK was angered to learn of turmoil in the army when the Selous Scouts discovered a bug on Colonel Ron Reid-Daly's phone. As PK's favourite soldier, he watched Reid-Daly closely. As it turned out, men in the field had been reporting suspicious events for some time. On a number of occasions, OPs (observation posts) had seen vehicles leaving enemy camps minutes before they were hit. Since the formation of ComOps, Reid-Daly had been nervous that his unit had been infiltrated. Suspicion soon fell on CIO boss Ken Flower. A Cornishman, son of a pastor, he had excellent contacts with British Intelligence, with the full knowledge and confidence of Ian Smith. Reid-Daly was not so sure of his real loyalties and took his hunch to General Walls, but he had no proof and the Supreme Commander advised there was little he could do.

With morale already undermined, the Selous Scouts were then engulfed in an investigation for a contravention of the Wildlife Act. Renowned and trusted trackers, the Scouts normally enjoyed freedom to survive any way they chose in parks and wilderness areas. It transpired that a decorated officer, Anthony White, stood accused of operating an illegal taxidermy operation for mounting kudu and impala heads. Shot for the pot, the heads would otherwise have been left to rot. Reid-Daly felt the hand of Ken Flower and called General Walls, who summoned him immediately. After explaining the events, Walls expressed his sincere regrets, assured Reid-Daly of his support and reported to Smith, who ordered him to get to the bottom of it. The investigation fizzled out but a dangerous climate of score-settling and infighting had taken hold. Shortly thereafter, Reid-Daly picked a fight with Army Chief of Staff John Hickman at the RLI officers' mess and was court-martialled.

Thirty years later, Reid-Daly had a visit from a troubled Peter Walls. "I'm truly sorry Ron," he said, "I did not realize it, but it was the Brits behind the whole thing; they took us for a ride." Up to that time Reid-Daly, who had resigned following his court martial, was sceptical of the full extent of British penetration, but is now a little less so. "Maybe it *was* Flower and the CIO who set me up. Who knows what else he was up to? Looking back, perhaps the British did see me as a threat. They were getting the better of the Rhodesian politicians but were wary someone in the forces would stage a coup. I was one they were particularly worried about and they were right. I would have done it in a heartbeat."

The incident affected Hickman, who allowed his personal life to come increasingly under public scrutiny. It was one of the few areas where Hilary Squires took issue with PK's judgement. "When I took over as Minister of Defence I fired Hickman and many said it was about time this sort of 'extramural' activity was stopped. It had been going on for years under PK's watch and was an embarrassment in the eyes of the other services."

With perhaps some ambivalence PK took to the hustings in January 1979 in support of the constitutional amendment that would usher in black rule. Without bitterness he warned that rejection would spell "disaster", rendering the country "uninhabitable".

"I think you must admit that this is as good as we could get and infinitely better than the majority of people ever anticipated. And with each passing day," PK added, "indications were [that] things would get worse, not better.

We must join to make it work because there is no alternative." He wrongly believed the USA supported the plan. In the referendum of 30 January, 85 per cent of the white electorate approved the new constitution.

Also on this day Lotti arrived for a visit. "PK phoned in November and asked me and my cousin Walburga to come to Rhodesia and we happily accepted. I was studying at the time; not very successfully I must add. January the following year we arrived. It was an eventful time. January the 30th was the day of the referendum which would decide the future of the country. Marge Bassett, PK's secretary, collected us at the airport."

Rita McChlery remembers Lotti's arrival in Salisbury: "Will any of us in the office forget the day he brought his beautiful Lotti to meet us? He was so proud and happy to have won her heart, and we were all so delighted to see him so happy."

Lotti recalls: "PK was naturally very busy, and then the following day King Leka of Albania arrived and there was more drama."

Recalled PK:

Leka had become *persona non grata* in Spain and phoned me in the middle of the night asking for asylum. I said absolutely. I didn't discuss it with anyone or tell anyone else. King Juan Carlos was sending his plane to Libreville and [Jack Malloch] was going to bring him back on one of the 'meat planes'. Little did we realize what a hornet's nest we were stirring up.

My Christ! What a ghastly day that was. A day of unimaginable complications. That's why I got the Knight Grand Cross of Scanderberg. I was on the radio all day to Jack Malloch. Called out of a cabinet meeting 16 times. Poor Ian Smith had no idea what the hell was going on.

All would have been well, but on arrival in Libreville the Gabonese authorities took strong exception to all the weaponry King Leka was carrying. His father King Zog had survived something like 60 assassination attempts, so not surprisingly, he was a little paranoid. Bongo wanted to have the lot thrown into jail. It might have been alright if it had been just the King but he had his 'bandits' with him and Jean-Pierre from French Intelligence was upset. He felt the President had to be informed otherwise heads would roll. They were carrying some quite sophisticated weaponry. Then the French, the Spanish, the Soviets all arrived at the airport to complicate matters.

I had to pull something out the bag and remembered Bongo had renounced Christianity and converted to Islam. Not a lot to do with his spiritual convictions I suspect, but a lot to do with getting on the right side of the Arabs. I took a gamble and sent a message to Bongo, upbraiding him for flagrant violation of the Holy Koran by virtue of holding Leka, a Muslim king, to ransom. That threw Bongo and he let him go … worst day of my entire life. Funnily enough, Bongo decorated me later; awarded me the Etoile Equatoriale.

The end of February 1979 was a big occasion for Marge Bassett. "My Meritorious Service Medal was the highlight of my life," she says. "I had been personal secretary to Mr. van der Byl for 15 years and received the award at an informal ceremony at Milton Buildings."

In February the Conservatives promised to recognize the upcoming April elections if they were transparently free and fair. Conversely, Labour's attitude was best reflected by Lord Hatch's remarks at the Ridgeway Hotel in Lusaka: "It is time we brought this chap Smith to heel. We should shoot down another of his Viscounts."

PK deplored the remarks, suggesting it might have been better if Baron Hatch's mother had been "barren". Days later Hatch's wishes were realized when Viscount *Umniati* was hit by a projectile and exploded minutes out of Kariba airport. This time, all 59 crew and passengers were killed outright.

It transpired that a warning had been given to Danish Airlines in Lusaka on 12 February to "stay on the ground", but no one had seen fit to warn Salisbury. Since the first Viscount tragedy, basic precautionary tactics had been implemented—varying the routes, climbing quicker to exit the range of shoulder-fired missiles and painting the aircraft dull matt-grey. Two flights left that day and the passengers' fate was decided by an arbitrary distribution of red and green boarding cards. Red cardholders would die on the first flight, greens survived, including an off-duty General Walls. In a savage irony, the Boyd family of six—dear friends of *Hunyani* hero Dr. MacLaren—drew red cards.

Lotti and Walburga nearly boarded the fateful inbound red flight. "At that point I was sure PK was keener on my cousin than me," Lotti recalls. "We went to the Victoria Falls with MP Ron Goldin. It was Sunday morning and I was having so much fun I decided I did not want to leave the Falls as planned, and decided to have another day there. We were staying at the Casino Hotel and that evening there was a very strange atmosphere. Only later did we find out that the Viscount on which we were booked had been shot down. This explained the sombre mood. Unfortunately Ron Goldin was on it. Next morning we left the Falls. Air Rhodesia managed to get an Air Malawi flight to take us out. We flew very low and zigzagged; it was a very strange experience. Three weeks later I realized things between PK and I were quite different and we decided to get married—it all happened rather quickly."

PK remained evasive about Princess Charlotte: "There is no substance in this at all," he told *The Herald*. "No engagement exists between me and the Princess. I find this unfounded newspaper speculation extremely irresponsible." But it was noted his composure slipped at a subsequent political gathering when he "visibly blushed" when questioned about the lady.

The lady in question recalls:

> I then went back to Europe to report to parents and to go back to university. PK couldn't travel for a while because he was very busy. The reaction to the news was mixed. My mother asked if he was Catholic and I answered no. Asked his age, I said I didn't know. She asked if he would allow the children to be raised as Catholics and I said yes. Then she asked me who I

was going to marry. PK then came to Austria, which he was not supposed to do, to meet my parents. Within ten minutes of meeting him they adored him. Two weeks later I flew from Europe with my mother and we spent some time at Fairfield with my in-laws whom I liked enormously; then we flew to Salisbury. My mother liked all the people she met and both of us loved Salisbury.

CHAPTER EIGHTEEN
Black rule

While Joshua Nkomo triumphantly accepted responsibility for the second Viscount at a press conference in Ethiopia and the Rhodesian public fumed, the country's forces prepared retaliatory strikes.

On 26 February 1979, Hawker Hunters of No. 1 Squadron attacked ZIPRA bases near Livingstone, north of Victoria Falls. An audacious bombing raid deep into Angola was planned next. In a press statement, PK said: "Terrorist training camps beyond our borders, far from holding refugees, are military training establishments turning out an even greater number of murderous terrorists. Those countries which harbour and give comfort and assist, and indeed encourage the inhuman and criminal activities of these forerunners of Soviet imperialism must accept the consequences of their reckless policy."

Borrowing a page from the Israeli war manual, four Canberra bombers took off on 26 February from a runway on the edge of Wankie National Park. Crossing Zambia on a 4,000-kilometre round trip to Angola, they had just two Hawker Hunters flying top-cover. Twelve SAS men and a Dakota waited in Wankie in case anyone needed rescuing. Vulnerable to Cuban-piloted MiG-21s and flying low to avoid Soviet radar, bad weather ensured navigation was only possible by instrumentation. Despite this, the leading navigator was inch-perfect, taking the four bombers to 300 feet five minutes out. Sudden bright sunshine allowed a perfect run-in. Flying four-abreast, the bombers hit the garrison simultaneously. Radio intercepts revealed an enemy in utter shock. Also on the intercepts was the bonus news that jittery ZIPRA forces had earlier downed a Zambian Air Force Macchi jet-fighter during the overfly confusion.

Adding insult, on 12 April 1979, the Rhodesian SAS drove brazenly into the city of Lusaka and attacked Joshua Nkomo's house. Nkomo, apparently tipped off by British Intelligence, was not home but the raid caused considerable embarrassment to Kaunda who was hosting an OAU conference at the time.

"Poor old Kaunda," wrote Smith. "I felt a certain sympathy for him having to put up with all these humiliations. The news of the SAS exploits reverberated throughout the world—our friends were thrilled and our opponents mad. The fact that there were so many OAU leaders in Lusaka was cause for considerable alarm—what if we had killed them? It would have been easy enough but that kind of action was never part of Rhodesia's code of conduct. We despised terrorists but never believed their despicable acts gave us licence to reciprocate."[73]

But for Ian Smith, the end of the line had, in a sense been reached. Soon after the SAS raid Muzorewa was elected in a 70-per cent turnout, the fairness of which even the country's harshest critics were forced to compliment. Predictably, no one other than South Africa recognized the new government. President Carter explained the country's new constitution under the Muzorewa administration was unacceptable because it was "the work of white people".

PK wrongly assumed Thatcher would honour her pre-election pledge to support the Muzorewa election but there were other dynamics at play. Nigerian hard-man General Obasanjo ordered the seizure of BP's Nigerian assets if they recognized the election. This helped to clarify the Conservatives' Rhodesia policy. British commercial interests would always trump British morals.

Professor Richard Wood writes: "Thatcher promised to recognize Muzorewa. Nkomo and Mugabe had refused to participate in the election. The gooks [ZANLA operatives] of all stripes attempted to cow the people into not voting but they did anyway. Everything was undone, however, by Jimmy Carter failing to recognize Muzorewa. Carter of course owed his election to the Afro-American caucus. Then Carrington persuaded

---

[73] Ian Smith: *The Great Betrayal: The Memoirs of Ian Douglas Smith.* Blake Publishing, 1997

Thatcher to follow Carter's lead." In recently released files, Katherine Haddon reports Mrs. Thatcher initially banned contact with Robert Mugabe, refusing to talk "with terrorists until they become prime ministers". "The people of Rhodesia have the right to decide themselves who shall be their government and whether they approve the internal settlement," Thatcher wrote on a letter she received from Australian premier Malcolm Fraser that month. Soon she sent Lord Harlech on an African tour to assess positions, but was vehemently opposed to Carrington on the issue of him meeting either Nkomo or Mugabe.

"Carrington," says Richard Wood, "was hostile to Rhodesia even when he was Secretary of Defence in the Heath Government. In addition, the Foreign and Commonwealth Office loathed Rhodesia to a man. One reason was because Smith so often failed to fall for their tricks at the almost continuous Anglo-Rhodesian negotiations. They hated him. Jonathan Clark, one of the members of the British High Commission in Harare, whose father was a friend of my family, told me that Carrington ordered the High Commission to 'make it [newly independent Zimbabwe] look good for three years'. Hence the blind eye turned to the Fifth Brigade massacres, and so on, in the early 1980s." PK recalled in a 1995 interview: "I tried to get Mobutu to support the Muzorewa election and he seemed happy to come on board, but would not come out in public. Then, just before the elections, I got my old friend Bulla Nyati down from Zaire. He went and saw Muzorewa and told him not to make the same mistake they had made in the Congo and chase out the whites. 'You will regret it if you do,' he said. I took him to see Ian Smith too. As it turned out it didn't make much difference."

On 31 May, Ian Smith finished his last day in office. He and his wife Janet took one last walk through Independence, the house that had been their own for the last 15 years and which they had grown to love. "We didn't talk, we just felt," Smith recalls.[74] They bade their small staff farewell and left for their new house not far away in the suburb of Belgravia.

---

[74] Ian Smith: *The Great Betrayal: The Memoirs of Ian Douglas Smith.* Blake Publishing, 1997

A surprising first act as Prime Minister, Abel Muzorewa next day appointed PK Minister of Foreign Affairs and of Transport and Power, and of Posts.

Renewing his war with Andrew Young, PK said: "It is difficult to believe that anyone in their right senses could claim the forces of the PF were non-violent … For sheer mindless brutality there is nothing to beat the maiming and torturing the PF have inflicted on the civilian population of this country. If there has not been a blood-thirsting against the whites, what of the attacks on the farms, homes schools and missions—all aimed specifically at innocent white people?"

Commenting on Young's remark that he was "fascinated" by Mugabe's intelligence, PK said "… maybe, but Count Dracula was also considered to be extremely intelligent, so was Ivan the Terrible, Himmler and Hitler. It is an appalling reflection of the times that somebody holding the important position held by Mr. Young should be so determined to twist the truth. He has said some ridiculous things in the past but nothing quite as vicious. I did notice a change in his attitude from the first time he came here [last August] when he seemed rather agreeable. It seems there is more resentment to this country than ever before, now that we have accepted everything that has been demanded of us."

On 8 June 1979, the press reported PK had flown to Liechtenstein to marry Princess Charlotte. Asked if he was settling in Zimbabwe-Rhodesia, he said, "If you're asking if I'm taking the gap, the answer is no." At the time, Charlotte was studying at the University of Innsbruck and unavailable to the press.

Shortly after the announcement he left for Durban to visit Victor Dwyer, his old friend and personal tailor. There it was reported he was "thrilled" and "very talkative" about his prospective union. Dwyer said he had not seen him "in such good spirits for a long time" and that he "would be very upset if he was not asked to make his suit for the wedding". When Lotti arrived at Fairfield a few days later, they lunched with Harold Hawkins and the Biebers before flying to Salisbury on the 13th. The *Financial Gazette*, traditionally critical of the Rhodesia Front and no friend of PK's, wished him well before suggesting he put marital bliss before public life and retire from politics.

Giving little away Lotti told the press that she was Catholic and PK Anglican, and she would wear a long wedding dress. "I'm not very domesticated but can cook and sew and do all those things. But I enjoy reading much more—particularly international politics—and fishing, shooting or riding." PK confirmed that "she bagged three animals with three shots".

"I love it here. I loved this country when I first saw it in February and I like it even better now ... the land, the people and their great courage," Lotti said. On 16 June, she flew back to Austria with her mother, Archduchess Elizabeth of Austria.

"PK could not have chosen better," says Lin Mehmel. "Lotti proved the perfect spouse and mother to three sons. It was amazing how well she coped in a foreign environment at a time of enormous difficulty. She made it all look so easy and I know it wasn't. She was quite remarkable. I consider myself fortunate to count her among my close friends."

On 2 July, *Newsweek* ran an article critical of the Muzorewa regime. It suggested real power remained in white hands and that Muzorewa and his colleagues were irked by the whites in government, particularly "notorious hard-liner PK van der Byl, who rolls his eyes every time a black person speaks, and when quizzed about blacks wishing to wear official wigs in parliament was reported to have said, 'What do they want wigs for? They can just sprinkle a little powder on their heads.'"

On 6 August, Margaret Thatcher confirmed Britain would not recognize Zimbabwe-Rhodesia. Australia's conservative premier, Malcolm Fraser, concurred and was later to play an important support role in Mugabe's ascent to power. Fraser's biographer Philip Ayres wrote: "The centrality of Fraser's part in the process leading to Zimbabwe's independence is indisputable. All the major African figures involved affirm it." An enigmatic character famous for 'losing his pants' in a seedy Memphis hotel, Australian Young Liberals called for his party membership to be cancelled in 2004 after his comprehensive slide to the left.

A new all-party conference was called for mid-September 1979 at Lancaster House, London, under the chairmanship of Carrington.

PK recalled the events: "Then 'Frau' Thatcher got in and started the whole Lancaster House business. We gave it the 'shotgun treatment' ... we tried everywhere to get some support but we were totally undermined by the Brits. Frau Thatcher did a complete reversal. She was on record saying she saw no reason why Muzorewa should not be recognized and even less reason why sanctions should be maintained. Twenty million dollars was raised to pay Bongo to recognize the Muzorewa government. I don't know where it came from. May have been the Saudis but I think not. More likely the Omanis and that would have been thanks to Tim Landon. We hoped if Bongo came on board the Arabs would follow. Unfortunately it didn't work."

On 31 August, PK, and Lotti were married at Schloss Waldstein, the Liechtenstein family castle near Graz. Fifty-five years of a busy bachelorhood were over. Arriving late, Lotti wore a dress of white silk and a 250-year-old lace veil inherited from her grandfather, Kaiser Karl, the last reigning Austrian monarch.

"It was a little nerve-wracking," remembers Lotti, "because until three weeks before I did not know if he was going to be allowed into the country. The Austrian Foreign Ministry eventually relented on compassionate grounds. Soon after the wedding we returned to Rhodesia and this was the period leading up to the Lancaster House negotiations."

On 12 September, PK and Lotti arrived back in Salisbury to attend a final tribute to the pioneers who arrived on the Salisbury plain on that day in 1890 under the command of Lieutenant-Colonel Graham Pennefather. The remembrance was followed by a memorial service at the RLI chapel for nine of the 15 men killed in the recent Rhodesian raid on Mapai.

"A special request was sent by Lord Carrington, who would chair the Lancaster talks, asking that PK not attend. I think Carrington knew that PK knew too much about him and his trickery. This was good news for my honeymoon but bad news for Rhodesia," recalls Lotti.

"Our honeymoon was a hunting safari. We were camped at Paradise

Island on Lake Kariba and far from alone. We went with Piet and Veronica Bosch, my brother Michael and some other friends, plus we had a large contingent of trackers, cooks, skinners and other staff. I managed to shoot a buffalo. After that I hunted on two more occasions with PK courtesy of Rupert van der Riet at his camp on the Sengwa River. We also did some hunting on ranches belonging to Piet Bosch and 'Boss' Lilford. I did some big-game hunting; shot some elephant and buffalo and quite a few different types of antelope."

"There was nearly a mishap when the van der Byls came to our Sengwa camp," recalls Verity van der Riet. "We were in the process of rehabilitating Elza, the pet lioness. She was about a year old when we got her. We had taken her to a peninsula across a small bay from our camp and used to go across to feed her, hoping she would become independent and kill her own food. The only problem was that Mike Gunn had trained her to come to him for food by firing a shot. Rupert was out in the field with PK and Lotti when PK shot something and next thing, out of the bush, Elza came bounding across looking for her food. Fortunately PK did not take fright. He realized it was Elza so luckily she lived to hunt another day."

While the van der Byls honeymooned, the British successfully outmanoeuvred the Muzorewa delegation at Lancaster House. A beneficiary of sustained schmoozing was General Walls. Flattered and plied with everything from test rugby tickets to private audiences with the Queen Mother and Margaret Thatcher his independence and judgement were compromised.[75]

Smith distrusted Carrington from the start. "I'd been dealing with dishonest British politicians since 1963, when R.A.B. Butler lied to us about granting us our independence. I could see right through Carrington and I think he knew it."

In a comical 'spy versus spy' game Carrington secretly telexed plenary session details to Nyerere in Dar es Salaam, who sent instructions back to Mugabe. Rhodesian signals interceptors in Salisbury had meanwhile

---

[75] David Caute: *Under the Skin*. Penguin Books, 1983

cracked the code and were forwarding the counter-intelligence back to the Muzorewa delegation. One message from Carrington to Nyerere read: "Keep your man [Mugabe] talking and all will be his"; clear proof of British bias, but it remains unclear who received the counter-intelligence in the Muzorewa camp. Smith's instincts soon told him all he needed to know. Treachery was afoot and he decided to return to Salisbury

Before leaving Smith confronted Carrington and accused him of steamrolling Mugabe's agenda. Carrington's blustered denial did not impress Smith. "Clever people at the Foreign Office," Smith conceded ruefully. "The British plan worked and they had no real problem with Walls after his time with the Queen Mother."[76] "One of my great regrets was that I didn't insist on the job of military supremo going to Air Marshal McLaren rather than Walls," he later told the author.

Robert Salisbury says, "I think it's quite likely General Walls received some consideration from the British government during the Lancaster House process in return for his help. It was a perfectly sensible thing to do at the time. There was huge relief in government when they offloaded the Rhodesia problem. Soames was thrilled. I warned them it would come back and bite them. Unfortunately I was right."

Smith's observations were later confirmed by Ian Gilmour.[77] "Yes," he admitted with a chuckle, "we were up to our old Foreign Office tricks. That's how negotiations succeed … his [General Walls's] visit there [to Balmoral to meet the Queen Mother] affected him greatly."[78]

Meanwhile, in Bulawayo, PK and Lotti opened the Rhodesia Front fete:

> Ian Smith is fighting a rather lonely battle [at Lancaster House]
> on our behalf and deserves every support we can give him in
> the days ahead. What we held and believed in at UDI appears

---

[76] David Dimbleby documentary: 'Rebellion'

[77] General Walls denies he was swayed, insisting he refused an offer to meet the Queen and the visit to the Queen Mother was at his request.

[78] Ibid

to be largely lost. But I say to you: never regret that we took this brave and bold step. It was not a mistake as our enemies make out. As a result we have achieved an identity as a country. We have built the second most extensive industrial complex in Africa and have made a tremendous success of it. We have had some wonderful years, so look back with pride and look forward with courage. We have to adapt and we must continue to do everything we can to guide events as far as possible. We cannot give in and let down those who have made such tremendous sacrifices for us.

In London, controversy raged over the suspicious suicide of Muzorewa's constitutional lawyer, John Giles. Known to be aware and on top of Carrington's shenanigans, many believed he was pushed off his hotel balcony. Ian Smith disagreed with the official verdict. "I have never believed Giles's death was suicide and never will."[79]

For Ian Smith, it was clear he had no further role to play. Speaking to the press he admitted, "We have now reached a point where it is clear that we are not able to gain any more ground, other than in tying up the details. Accordingly, the time has come to tell our people back home that to continue the fight would be sterile, even counterproductive."

11 November passed quietly, with PK laying the first wreath to the dead of the World Wars. A week later, opening a memorial centre for the disabled at Lake McIlwaine outside Salisbury, PK was angry: "We have been totally and utterly betrayed by the British. Compelled to accept an election in which our enemies—who murdered, raped and pillaged—will be free to compete." But he exhorted his countrymen to fight on for "nothing less than survival. Maybe we have lost a round or even a major battle, but we have not lost the struggle unless we finally surrender". In an interview with David Dimbleby, PK agreed that in a sense the "game was up" because

---

[79] Justice George Smith who was at Lancaster House in the role of Cabinet Secretary maintains Giles was depressed and may have taken his own life.

I was, and remain, absolutely convinced that the British Foreign Office was [engaged] in a deliberate act of policy to bring into power in Rhodesia the most radical government that it possibly could, and the reason for this was it made Britain a hero in the UN and the OAU and top of the pops in the Commonwealth ... for the Foreign Office it was seen as a brilliant coup ... The outcome was deliberate and intentional. Carrington's talk of seeking moderate government was pure bluff. We [the former white Rhodesian political leaders] tried to convince that snivelling idiot Muzorewa not to fall for the British trap. Of course he was crucified for his pains, which he richly deserved.

David Smith and Ken Flower came back to Salisbury during the conference and tried to recruit me to be part of a cabal to get rid of Ian Smith and replace him with David ... this was very foolish because it was something I would never ever have done under any circumstances and gave me the opportunity of warning Ian Smith as to what was going on ... that he was being stabbed in the back. Their argument was that Ian Smith was not being very cooperative in helping Carrington bring about peaceful change ... he was being obstructionist in their view. They felt it would be so much better if he was not there at all.

On 12 December, Carrington installed Lord Christopher Soames as Governor of what was once again technically the colony of Southern Rhodesia, but British efforts to impose a ceasefire were bedevilled by grandstanding by all parties. A war-weary Samora Machel was used to force Mugabe to sign up, but notwithstanding his signature, there was overwhelming evidence that his forces continued to intimidate and terrorize rural populations until voting day. All combatants were supposed to retire to barracks and assembly points, but Mugabe sent young collaborators as stooges which allowed him to keep fighters at large. The message was simple: vote Mugabe or die.

"In late 1979, Tiny Rowland dined with us at our house in Bath Road," remembers Lotti. "It was a fascinating evening, listening to him and PK talk. Although they had gone in different directions most of their lives, they had known each other for a long time, and there was a great deal of mutual respect. They joked about the fact that so recently they were, in a sense, enemies. Soon after that we heard that Josiah Tongogara had been killed in Mozambique and PK immediately smelled a rat."

The cause of death was given as a car accident but speculation persists that Mugabe arranged a Stalinist solution for his charismatic and moderate general. Having grown up on the Smith family farm in Selukwe, Tongogara told reporters at Lancaster House how kind Ian Smith's mother had been to him as a boy. Spotting Smith at an informal gathering at the opening of the Lancaster House conference, Tongogara introduced himself and told Smith Zimbabwe needed the whites to stay on after independence. He had on at least one occasion made it known in public that he and Peter Walls could sort the problem out alone and would do so without the politicians. Tongogara's outspoken reasonableness angered Mugabe and soon he was dead. Rumours as to the nature of his demise persist to this day.

CHAPTER NINETEEN
Mugabe takes power

In the New Year of 1980, there were multiple reports of ceasefire violations by the Patriotic Front.

Both Walls and Joshua Nkomo complained to Lord Soames, who reportedly said, "This isn't Puddleton-on-the-Marsh. This is Africa and they behave differently … they think nothing of sticking tent poles up each others whatnots and doing filthy, beastly things to each other."[80]

On 27 January, Mugabe made a triumphant return. He met Jim Buckley, Soames's secretary, to confirm his forces were in place to enforce electoral victory and later met Soames, who merely told him not to overdo the intimidation. For his part Soames promised to maintain the deception that Britain sought an Nkomo/Muzorewa/RF coalition and would never accept a Mugabe victory. Walls persisted with the "intelligence-driven" view that the anti-Mugabe forces would prevail, and refused to invoke operations *Hectic* and *Quartz*, which would have signalled the Rhodesian forces to intervene.

Antony Duff, Deputy Governor to Soames, later explained to David Dimbleby: "In a way, we were playing a confidence trick on the white population … representing to them that the level of intimidation was not high so as to distort the results." Duff insisted British motives were honourable because "they knew so much better what was good for the white Rhodesians than they, the white Rhodesians, did themselves".

"PK was very busy in the days leading up to the election," remembers Lotti. "The day before, there was another meeting at the house with Ian

---

[80] David Dimbleby documentary: 'Rebellion'. As it turned out, Soames had his mind in other places. Transcripts of nightly conversations where he discussed the daily events with his mistress in Paris were being delivered to Ian Smith every morning by the 'special' department of the Rhodesian Post and Telecommunications Office.

Smith, PK, Peter Walls, Flower and McLaren. The security people were of the view that the combined vote against Mugabe would be enough to win but PK did not agree. He had a very good idea of what was going to happen and, unlike many, did not believe Muzorewa would win. PK never trusted Flower. He always regretted never having asked de Marenches if he was indeed a British spy."

On 17 February, PK said "… amid the chaos and uncertainty we must realize there is no outside agency to which we can turn to for succour. Our salvation lies entirely in our own hands. If we are divided we become mere expatriates in our own land. United we will be a strong force which will play a positive role in shaping our future."

Remembering Soames, PK said:

If I were to write a book on despicable contemporaries, I'm afraid I think Soames would head the list. I went to see him with my co-minister, the very decent and agreeable Elliot Gabellah, and we were treated like dirt from the start. We were fobbed off and given no indication we would be able to see him again. My parting shot to him was I now know what it must have been like to have been a German in 1945.

The most despicable aspect was the shameless way in which he carried out the British government's plan to bring in the worst, most radical government possible … The degree of intimidation was such that he had every possible reason to ban the perpetrators or call the whole thing off … he did neither … went on television and made some flippant remarks. He was there to usher in the worst possible solution regardless.

Walls, was a nice, agreeable sort of man … disliked me … first-rate regimental officer. But as Commander in Chief he was absolutely the wrong man … not only did he get it all wrong in the period running up to the election but subsequently let the whole show down when he was the only one who had the power to put it right … he was brilliantly worked on by the

Foreign Office. He believed he was virtually infallible. In the run-up to elections I and a colleague went to ComOps and told them there that in our opinion the tide was shifting in favour of the Patriotic Front and the contemplated coalition of Muzorewa and Nkomo was unlikely to materialize. We were told we were talking nonsense and that the whole exercise was on course [to a moderate coalition]. We pleaded with Walls to make urgent representations to Soames for remedial action. This happened several times.

With electioneering in full swing, covert operators tried to assassinate Mugabe. A bomb was placed under a small bridge near Fort Victoria (now Masvingo). The plan was to detonate it as his car passed over, following his address at a nearby rally. However, word was leaked and the explosion narrowly avoided.[81]

In another effort to kill the future leader, a black Selous Scout, masquerading as a reporter for *Drum* magazine, gained accreditation to a press conference to be addressed by Mugabe. Having stuffed one of the microphones with explosives, he waited for the conference with an electric detonator to blow his head off in full view of the cameras. But again word was leaked and Mugabe never appeared.

On 24 February, Walls and Flower briefly visited Maputo and reassured the Frelimo leadership that Rhodesia was no longer supporting the Renamo

---

[81] The following report by Trevor Grundy appeared in *Scotland on Sunday* (2 February 2003): "In February 1980, Stannard was driving Mugabe toward the Midland town, Masvingo. Suddenly, he swerved off the road. Moments later the highway on which they would have been driving exploded into a sheet of flames. Stannard's actions not only guaranteed him rapid advancement through the ranks of the CIO but, more importantly, earned Mugabe's trust. While Ken Flower was almost certainly working for British Intelligence for a considerable period of time, Dan Stannard appears to have switched later. He received the Gold Cross of Valour from Mugabe after independence for, among other actions, passing on a warning to Emmerson Mnangagwa of another plot to kill his principal through the detonation of at least five roadside bombs. Disguised as electrical sub-stations and traffic light control boxes, they were placed along the route Mr. Mugabe was due to follow in April 1980. Stannard continued to serve Mugabe at a very high level in the Zimbabwe CIO for many years after independence, enjoying a comfortable and close relationship with Mnangagwa. Whether Stannard was also the source of the other leaks remains uncertain."

rebels.[82] At the next day's debrief in Salisbury with Smith, McLaren and PK, Walls's ambivalence about both Maputo and the Mugabe-surge was worrying to the others.[83]

On 27 February, voting commenced. "Every day we heard that the order to attack would come in the morning, but it never came," recalls a former officer. "By this time, even the British monitors were reporting to Soames that the intimidation was at an unacceptable level, but there was no response from him or Walls. It is a credit to the discipline that prevailed in the Rhodesian armed forces that no one did anything untoward because there were a lot of fingers tight on a lot of triggers and the air of expectancy was unbearable. One shot could have set the whole country alight. No one could begin to contemplate a victory for Mugabe and be asked to stand back and watch it happen."

When the results rolled in it became clear PK was right and Walls was wrong. Seemingly bewildered by Mugabe's victory, Walls's next move confirmed his misunderstanding of events. Calling Margaret Thatcher, he asked her to annul the election because of rampant intimidation. Mrs. Thatcher replied through a Downing Street intermediary that she did not consider the situation in Rhodesia sufficiently serious to warrant her intervention and ignored him. As far as the British premier was concerned, he had served his purpose.

"After the election, but before the counting, we had another meeting at Ian Smith's house with Walls, Flower, McLean, Mussell, Connolly, McLaren and myself," recalled PK. "I urged the commanders to go out and simply destroy the ballot boxes before demanding the governor order another election after a period of tranquillity. No decision was taken but Walls's parting shot was, 'I will never hand this government over to a Marxist or Mugabe government!'"

"PK tried really hard with Walls," remembers Lotti. "To no avail, unfortunately. He was out of his depth. PK never believed he had the

---

[82] Ken Flower: *Serving Secretly*. John Murray, 1987

[83] Ian Smith: *The Great Betrayal: The Memoirs of Ian Douglas Smith*. Blake Publishing, 1997

intellect for the job. PK always said a terrible day for Rhodesia was the helicopter crash in which Colonel Dave Parker, General Shaw and others were killed. He wanted Parker rapidly promoted and he always felt Parker might have been a very positive influence on the course of the war. PK was also very wary of Ken Flower and told me to be careful what I said in his company."

On 4 March, Mugabe was officially declared the winner. One of his first acts was to invite Walls to stay on. Stunned, Walls said he could not possibly serve a Marxist but then accepted after Mugabe assured him Marxism and Christianity were not in conflict.

"I talked to him and gave him the impression I had faith in him," recalls Mugabe. Asked why he had tried to kill him, Walls incredibly denied the charge. "I never trusted Walls," says Mugabe. "We decided to bide our time, then get rid of him."

On 17 April 1980, Zimbabwe became independent with Robert Mugabe as Prime Minister and Canaan Banana as President.

Dr. Peter Hammond of Frontline Fellowship wrote:

> In standing firm against Communist aggression for 15 years, Rhodesia indeed won valuable breathing space for the free world. In much the same way as the 300 Spartans held up the enormous invading force of Persians at Thermopylae, and as the courageous knights resisted the Islamic invasion of the small island of Malta, I believe that, in time, history will recognize that the sacrifices and courage of Rhodesians in resisting Communist terrorism contributed to the ultimate collapse of Communism in Eastern Europe in 1989. Had Rhodesia not resisted, the consequences for South Africa could have been absolutely disastrous. Had South Africa fallen to Communism during the Cold War, the strategic Cape sea route and vital minerals essential for Western industry and defence would have fallen into the hands of the Soviet Union, with catastrophic consequences.

With whites fleeing in large numbers, Mugabe gave an unexpectedly conciliatory speech, talking of the need "to join together. Let us show respect for the winners and the losers. There is no intention on our part to victimize the minority. We will ensure there is a place for everyone in this country". To the South Africans he said, "We offer peaceful co-existence. Let us forgive and forget. Let us join hands in a new amity."[84]

But ominous signs that this talk was an exercise in deception soon emerged with the murder of Gerry Adams, a defenceless 68-year-old Arcturus farmer. Shot on his front veranda by Minister Edgar Tekere in front of a truckload of ex-combatants, Tekere was arrested and charged with murder. Arraigned before Judge John Pitman, Mugabe assigned two friendly assessors to co-hear the case. Pitman was overruled and Tekere walked out of court laughing.

"When Mugabe was elected it obviously came as no surprise to PK," recalls Lotti. "He knew exactly what was going to happen. When it became a *fait accompli*, he was desperate. He always considered Mugabe highly intelligent and did not underestimate him in any way. He obviously did not know how badly it would all turn out, but he knew it would be bad. He very much wanted to get out of politics at this point but he was tremendously loyal to Ian Smith who wanted him to help him salvage something for the good of the country. He felt he started it all with Ian Smith and owed it to him to see it through, but he was intensely frustrated because there was so little he could do in reality. So he took his seat in the new parliament and did what he could.

During this period, about eight months of the year was spent in Zimbabwe and the rest of the time between Fairfield and Europe. He saw as much as he could of people he liked, like Lin Mehmel, Ian Smith, Mark Partridge and Hilary Squires. Initially he had been quite fond of André Holland but changed his mind about him."

"PK's skill was as a debater," recalls Squires:

---

[84] Ken Flower: *Serving Secretly.* John Murray, 1987

He had an unusually sharp repartee, although this was mostly wasted on the Zimbabwe parliament. On one occasion he addressed the assembly using some long and complicated Shona words. With his accent he was making a hash of it and incurred a frenzy of abuse from the black members. In his masterfully high-handed way he then paused and when there was silence, he said "What?" There was a chorus of shouted advice, to which he announced in that arrogant tone, "But that is *precisely* what I said," and brought the house down. Even those abusing him were falling about laughing.

He had one of the reserved white seats in Zimbabwe's parliament and showed an extraordinary flair for diplomacy. Despite having no serious political credentials he managed to travel to Washington and gain access to both General Alexander Haig, President Reagan's Secretary of State, and Jeane Kirkpatrick, then the US Ambassador to the UN and a formidable figure in the Republican Party. To this end I think he was helped by the Conservative Catholic Alliance in Europe, which was chaired by Uncle Otto. It says a great deal for PK's ongoing resolve to do what he could for Zimbabwe and the white Rhodesians. Unfortunately, by this time I don't think anyone was too interested, but PK kept trying.

In an interview with Julie Frederikse in 1980, PK was asked why so many journalists had been deported during the war. He was unrepentant:

You should have asked why *more* journalists were not deported. I don't believe you can defend Western Christian civilization against Soviet expansionism with liberal laissez-faire policies. We were far too tolerant and acquiescent about the whole thing. South Africa's going to be a very hard nut to crack and the South Africans will not—hopefully—be inhibited by the ridiculous considerations that we were, of being over-considerate about the enemy. There was far too much influence of Sandhurst and the Metropolitan Police here. The lesson of the Rhodesian War … is that you can't fight by the Queensbury Rules.

Tiring of state media's saturation *chimurenga* (liberation war) propaganda, he bluntly asked the ZBC (Zimbabwe Broadcasting Corporation) if another revolution was being planned,but received no reply. Similarly, he criticized the government for its "repeated denunciations of colonial exploitation, capitalism, and the suppression of the masses. But this is now past—the honeymoon is over. Face reality, halt provocative statements and accept that free enterprise is the only way to realize hopes of economic growth. The system you are denouncing is the only means by which you will acquire the money you need for your programmes".

On a visit to Strasbourg in July 1980, he told reporters that whites were becoming very nervous listening to the invective on the airwaves. "Who," he asked, "is going to invest in a country that proclaims its goal is a socialist state?" Asked if he intended to leave, he said he would not. He had a responsibility toward his constituents and his black and white soldiers. He hit out at Britain: "The British government … brought about exactly what we warned would happen: a Marxist government. I am staying to try and influence them toward moderation. I'm afraid I have not been very successful thus far."

Despite the bitterness, entertaining exchanges continued in the Zimbabwean parliament between ZANU MPs and their white counterparts. To shouts of "Racist!" and "Fascist!", Donald 'Strippy' Goddard, MP for Lundi, criticized the "bloody peasants" for mismanaging donated farmland. He accused the shouters of "a peasant mentality" and when one of them called *him* a peasant he replied, "At least I don't smell like one."

On one occasion, PK was accused of disrespecting the house for slouching with feet on the table. Coming quickly to his feet he explained derisively that "putting one's feet on the table is a privilege of the front bench honoured by time and hallowed by precedent over the centuries".

Happier developments took place within the family. A first child, Pieter Vincenz, was born to the van der Byls on 31 December 1980 at the Kingsbury Maternity Home, Cape Town. Asked if he was happy with a son rather than a daughter, PK said the situation was "very satisfactory". Lotti remembers: "Many were sceptical about PK becoming a father at the age of 57, but he adored fatherhood and was an excellent father. Never too busy to play with the children or attend to them and he took a lot of time out to read to them and encourage discussion and airing of views."

Back in parliament, debates grew stormier in 1981 with Esmond Micklem accusing the government of "reckless expenditure verging on disaster". Goddard called the government's economic record "disgusting", saying the country's financial situation, despite massive aid inflows, was worse than it had been during war and sanctions. To stifle debate ZANU-PF members quit the chamber, ensuring there was no quorum. PK slammed the instigator, Deputy Prime Minister Simon Muzenda, for "a ridiculous childish device which was a travesty and a mockery". He went on to accuse Health Minister Herbert Ushewokunze of "criminal irresponsibility" for ruining the second-best health service in Africa.

Ushewokunze snarled that he (PK) "should quit belching out nonsensical garbage". To which PK replied:

Man proud man drest in a little brief authority
Most ignorant of what he is most assured
His glassy essence, like an angry ape
Plays such fantastic tricks before high heaven
As make the angels weep.

Ironically, despite constant white-bashing, Mugabe was quick to deploy white-led RAR battalions to crush a ZIPRA armoured column loyal to Joshua Nkomo which was threatening Bulawayo. Civil war was narrowly averted, but Mugabe's gratitude was temporary. By the end of the year Peter Walls had been fired, deported and replaced by Rex Nhongo (aka Solomon Majuru).

With tensions rising, Smith solicited an urgent audience with the Prime Minister and urged him to change his extreme policies, but to no avail. Up to that time Mugabe had listened to Smith but, in a sad sign of what was to come, the two never met again.

Later that year Wally Stuttaford, an elder statesman of Smith's newly named Conservative Alliance party, was arrested on charges of "organizing a coup". Tortured in custody, he was released months later, physically and mentally broken. Suing successfully for damages, Mugabe dismissed the court-awarded sum as "a waste of the country's money".

By 1982, Marge Bassett had had enough of the new government's shenanigans: "Through the war we had no security to speak of. Nobody came near our offices with a weapon, but then people started appearing in the ministry with AKs and I knew I did not want any further part of Mugabe's lot. They wanted to position an armed guard in my office. We decided to leave and went to South Africa the next year."

Despite local gloom, Lord Carrington paid a happy visit to Harare in early 1982, rewarding his protégé with a £200-million aid package. All in all, £900 million was pledged by the West. Ian Smith's attempts to have an audience with Carrington were rebuffed. Later that year, Smith and his wife Janet were arrested during a police raid on their house.

"In 1982 ,we travelled to the UK together," remembers Lotti. "He [PK] really enjoyed being able to move around freely again. It was the first time in a long time that he had not felt like a fugitive. I must say, despite all the problems, I was thoroughly enjoying life in Harare. Ron Goldin's widow, Tania, was very kind to me. We continued to mix socially in mainly political circles. Through this time, back in Zimbabwe, PK thoroughly enjoyed his time at the Harare Club and the poker games with the judges, Brigadier Passaportis and others."

Valerian remembers, "I sat outside the Harare Club while Dad gambled. I think he only won once in all that time and when he did he gave Pieter and me $100."

"In 1982, PK sold the ranch in Matabeleland to a Mugabe minister with a chain of supermarkets," recalls Lotti.

PK was still very involved politically, but increasingly despondent about the country's prospects and this caused him to get very depressed. There are those who like to think PK was in politics for the fun of it. Little did they know how wrong they were. He loved Rhodesia and there was nothing he wouldn't have done to save it from tragedy.

Around this time he had a little fun with Mugabe. Mugabe announced in parliament he was changing the national anthem. Mugabe must have known the existing one was chosen by PK. Mugabe explained that while searching for a definitive tune, 'Nkosi Sikelele Africa' would be sung. PK was pleased to tell Mugabe how thrilled he was because 'Nkosi Sikelele' had been chosen by his father for the coronation of King Goodwill. Mr. Mugabe was quite taken aback.

Pieter Vincenz was about two when we had a fright. He was devoted to Janet Smith who had quite a library. Unbeknown to us he had commanded Farnabeck to take him to the Smiths' house to get some more books. We awoke from an afternoon siesta to find him missing and there was consternation until we found out what had transpired and that he was safe with Janet. Janet Smith was a wonderful woman … kind, gentle and very intelligent.

In March 1982, PK was devastated to hear his old friend and stalwart Rhodesian Jack Malloch had died at the controls of his Spitfire. "Lotti and I were in Schipol, just about to board one of Jack's aircraft when we heard he had been killed," recalled PK. "We arrived in Johannesburg and I called Dan Hamman from SA Intelligence, who confirmed the report. He was absolutely shocked; speechless. Bloody shame. Jack was finally on top of things and then he gets killed. I'm certain he had a bloody heart attack at the wheel because he would never have flown that thing into the storm he went into. I don't think it was any more sinister than that. I don't think he was knocked off. Silly old arse flew the thing making some bloody film or something. That's the problem with aviators; they always seem to knock themselves off in the end. Terrible tragedy."

In July 1982, South African Special Forces raided Thornhill Air Force Base in Gweru. Thirty white officers were immediately arrested on suspicion of complicity. All were brutally treated in detention, while seven were eventually charged. They were handed to Rogers Matongo, the ZANLA ex-combatant who had slaughtered the nuns and missionaries at Musami Mission five years earlier. The airmen were brutalized for weeks. Finally brought to trial, the men were acquitted ten months later by Justice Enoch Dumbutshena, the country's first black judge. Immediately redetained outside the courtroom, they were eventually released and deported in December 1983 after belated intervention by Margaret Thatcher.

In December 1982, Mugabe formally presented Colonel Perence Shiri with the colours of the North Korean-trained 5th Brigade. Shiri, 'the Black Jesus', would be tasked with resolving the 'Ndebele problem', which meant liquidating over 20,000 tribespeople in rural Matabeleland. Moving from village to village, they spread a reign of terror, raping, murdering and pillaging. Gruesome details eventually emerged.

"They hit me in the stomach with the butt of a gun," one woman who had been pregnant, recalls. "The unborn child broke into pieces in my stomach. The child was born afterwards, piece by piece. A head alone, then a leg, an arm, the body … piece by piece." A young girl remembers: "We were lined up … there were 62 people. They took us one by one and beat us. We were beaten until about 3.00 a.m. The 5th Brigade marched us to the Cewale River. All 62 of us were lined up and shot … one of my brothers was killed instantly from a bullet through his stomach. By some chance seven of us survived with gunshot wounds. I was shot in the left thigh."[85]

Donald Trelford, editor of *The Observer*, finally ran a story based on journalist Peter Godwin's investigations. His proprietor, none other than Tiny Rowland, was incensed and apologized to Mugabe. The Conservative

---

[85] Peter Stiff: *Cry Zimbabwe*. Galago Publishing, 2000

government reacted calmly. The Zimbabwean authorities were, in their considered view, only responding to a "legitimate national security concern".

Mrs. Thatcher confessed that, unlike her husband Dennis, she had changed her views on Mugabe and grown to "rather like the man". Joshua Nkomo fled the country. Dumiso Dabengwa and Lookout Masuku, the former ZIPRA generals, were both arrested and detained without trial.[86]

"PK was incredibly upset about this," Lotti remembers. "He was very depressed by the world's inaction. He kept asking where all the journalists were who had hounded him during the war. He tried to get people to respond, but with little success. In a sense his worst fears about majority rule were becoming a reality."

---

[86] In March 1986, Lookout Masuku was released from prison. He died a month later. Dumiso Dabengwa was released in December of that year.

CHAPTER TWENTY
The end

Years later, Sir Martin Ewans, the British High Commissioner in Harare at the time of the massacres, was quizzed by Fergal Keane:

Keane: Did you protest personally to Mugabe about what was happening?
Ewans: No, I didn't. I think this business has really perhaps been rather blown up. It wasn't pleasant and people were being killed but, as I said, I don't think anything was to be gained by protesting to Mugabe about it.
Keane: What was the advice from London about how one dealt with Mugabe, particularly around something like Matabeleland?
Ewans: I think the advice was to steer clear of it in the interests of doing our best positively to help Zimbabwe build itself up as a nation.

While the Matabeleland massacres continued, Mugabe received a hero's welcome at the UN General Assembly. One-time Mugabe supporter, journalist Geoff Nyarota, remembers the trip:

> I covered the visit of Robert Mugabe to New York in 1983 where he addressed the United Nations General Assembly. The delegation was huge by any standards. Numbering around 30, it included the usual coterie of foreign affairs officials, officers from the Prime Minister's department, the press corps, secretaries, medical staff, a culinary technician and other domestic staff. The entire delegation was booked, quite extraordinarily, into the Waldorf Astoria on Park Avenue, then the world's most expensive hotel. During our own stay, management never got wise to the fact that their

important guests from the newly independent Republic of Zimbabwe gave the culinary delights of the hotel's world-famous restaurants a wide berth while smuggling into their plush rooms hamburgers from the nearest McDonald's outlet. Meanwhile, junior staff at the UN mission was kept on their toes buying colour television sets, a novelty then, for delegates, using their generous allowances. The Mugabe government launched its campaign of mismanagement of the economy as soon as it entrenched itself in power. Let's call a spade a spade here. While Smith's Rhodesia was buffeted by international sanctions and civil war for more than a decade, the economy was robust when the new government took over. So was the infrastructure. The Zimbabwe dollar was stronger than the US dollar in 1980. While our ruling and wealthy elite wallow in the lap of luxury, the masses responsible for their empowerment or their enrichment wallow in abject poverty.

To keep the masses fooled, a Leadership Code was introduced in 1984 which promised to punish rapacious politicians. Subsequently, little attention was paid it and no one was prosecuted, although it was believed Emmerson Mnangwagwa's net worth had grown to US$100 million by 1990 and army commander Rex Nhongo (now Solomon Majuru) made himself one of the richest men in Africa.

On 20 July 1984, Mugabe received an honorary degree from the University of Edinburgh. Recommending him to Principal Dr. John Burnett in 1982, Lord Carrington lauded Mugabe's "scholarship, respect for British institutions and stature as a leader".[87]

While Mugabe drew accolades around the world, PK's political fortunes suffered a reversal when he was beaten by former Smith minister Chris Andersen in the 1985 elections. Following this, PK accepted an invitation from Smith to become one of his ten given senators.

---

[87] *The Scotsman*, 3 June 2007

The actual election, conducted in an atmosphere of brazen intimidation, was a miserable charade. Parliamentary seats reserved for whites were abolished in 1987. In his last speech to parliament PK denounced the political "turncoats" such as John Landau and Denis Divaris who had joined ZANU-PF as "dreadful souls screaming in agony". As sole survivor of the 1965 parliament, he said he hoped "I would have been cherished as a national monument and not flung into the political wilderness".

On Saturday, 6 September 1986, PK was guest of honour at the Rhodesian SAS Association Annual Reunion and Memorial Service at Durban Collegians Club. Former commander Brian Robinson remembers the night: "This was without doubt the funniest speech I have ever heard. Told almost entirely at his own expense, he absolutely brought the house down, so much so that the evening's entertainment included a professional comedian, but after PK this poor bloke had an impossible act to follow. He did his best but it all fell flat and I actually told him to call the performance off to spare him any more embarrassment."

Lotti recalls:

In 1986, when Pieter Vincenz went to school we started spending more time in the Cape and PK became a little more involved with the farm, but farming was never in his blood. He loved politics and missed the cut and thrust of debate. It was hugely stimulating for him. He enjoyed writing his speeches too. Very often much of his speech preparation was done in the bath. There is a misconception that he did not like South Africa. He loved the country of his birth but he did have a problem with the Afrikaner Nationalists, most of whom he did not like at all ... nor did he like their policies. The fact that he was Major Piet's son and Piet had been in Smuts's cabinet did not endear him to John Vorster who hated PK, and I think the feeling was fairly mutual. What was not well known was that Smuts did not really warm to PK's dad. He used him politically but withheld real power, only making him Minister without

Portfolio. He was also Minister of Native Affairs which he thoroughly enjoyed. Despite this Piet was full of praise for Smuts as an intellect and a leader.

In 1987, Joshua Nkomo, following a *rapprochement* with Mugabe, was appointed Vice-President, rendering Zimbabwe effectively a one-party state. Dumiso Dabengwa became Minister of Home Affairs and a feeding frenzy of perks and acquisitions followed. Mugabe had shrewdly purchased indefinite support. One of Nkomo's first acts as a million-acre farm owner was to board a helicopter and forcibly evict scores of peasants eking out a livelihood on the land.

On 18 January 1989, F.W. de Klerk became President of South Africa and, with his release of Nelson Mandela early in 1990, began the unthinkable journey to majority rule. At the same time, PK travelled to Oman to join Sultan Qaboos Bin Said, Norman Schwarzkopf and others for an informal get-together.

Writing to the South African Embassy in Vienna about the new Russia, PK warned it would "continue to be a very dangerous menace". On the changing face of South African politics, he called for the formation of a federal state, warning the ANC would win because it was "free to intimidate and terrorize the townships in the best traditions of African nationalism".

By 1990, Mugabe was no longer worried about world opinion. Open use of thuggish state propaganda ("Don't commit suicide, vote ZANU-PF and live") was the sort of stuff used to win elections. After CIO officers had been pardoned for shooting ex-Gweru Mayor Patrick Kombayi, former Chief Justice Enoch Dumbutshena lamented, "We have a president who does not believe in the rule of law ... The President has given a licence to kill ... those who are not members of their party ..."[88]

But for Mugabe the real fly in the ointment was the few remaining whites whose success tormented him. Always suspicious they were fomenting

---

[88] Martin Meredith: *Power Plunder and Tyranny in Zimbabwe.* Jonathan Ball, 2002

opposition he called them "recalcitrant racists who ignore the blacks from the confines of their white clubs".

Still the darling of the West, Mugabe spent his way to glory, hosting conferences, building monstrosities and courting the politically credulous. One such status symbol was the new Harare airport. Bringing in Kofi Annan's son, Tojo, as consultant, billions of dollars disappeared on a building which today hosts less than six flights a day.

On 27 July 1990, Casimir was born. Lotti remembers: "Soon after Casimir arrived I met up with a mutual friend, a Swiss banker. Like many Swiss, he did not have a great sense of humour and looked quite bewildered. Very politely he asked me to explain PK's recent comment to him when he had remarked upon PK's fecundity at an advanced age. PK had dismissed his question by telling our friend that: 'There was nothing to it old chap. You have no idea what can be achieved when the wind is blowing in the right direction'."

In 1993, the dreaded process of eviction of white farmers began at the same time a parliamentary report indicated that "corruption was so pervasive and civil servants so venal" that virtually no service was now provided without a bribe.[89] No meaningful business for any individual occurred without a party card.

When Roger Boka, a ZANU-PF-sponsored 'tycoon' requested assistance to wrest control of the tobacco industry from the "white racist Selous Scouts", he was loaned billions in public money to build rival tobacco floors. Setting off on an unprecedented trail of theft, fraud and bankruptcy Boka was eventually packed off to comfortable exile in the United States by his embarassed patrons. At the same time, PK was asked to speak at Stellenbosch University, which he agreed to do with some apprehension:

> I am particularly conscious of the fact that Stellenbosch is, in a sense, the country's cultural and linguistic centre. We must now contemplate a black government in a unitary state which

---

[89] Ibid

will seek to impose its own culture, language and traditions, which is of great concern to us in the Western Cape because our indigenous compatriots, the coloured people, share the same language, culture and religious beliefs as we whites do. As a result, the Afrikaans language is going to be under considerable threat because the opposition of black people to Afrikaans is manifest and this will affect us all in this part of the country. The Afrikaans language is as much part of South Africa as is Table Mountain and Groot Constantia, and I would hate to see it interfered with because it binds us as a people in this part of South Africa. I regret to say it but I fear a unitary polity will be a massive threat to us here and urge you all to press for a high degree of local autonomy in any future dispensation if we are to preserve more than three centuries of cultural development for the benefit of our children. We must defend what we have and be willing to share.

In Britain Foreign Secretary Douglas Hurd, long a Mugabe fan, recommended the Zimbabwean president for a knighthood. Warned that Mugabe was a hard-liner at heart, Hurd laughed: "His heart? Who cares what's in a politician's heart?"

He had his wish. On 17 May 1994, Mugabe was made Knight Commander of the Order of the Bath by the Queen at a ceremony in Buckingham Palace.

David Dimbleby asked Hurd on TV 14 years later about his involvement: "Weren't you Foreign Secretary when he was given the knighthood?" the interviewer asked.

"I think not," said Hurd.

"1994 ... what were you in 1994?"

"Foreign Secretary," mumbled Hurd with head down, much to the mirth of the audience. "It was not by me," he blustered. "I must plead total amnesia ... not by me and not by the British government!"

"If not the British government, then by whom?" asked Dimbleby.

"... I do not know ... I simply do not know the answer to that question."

Asked to explain how *any* government (if it was not the British government) could honour Mugabe for massacring people, Hurd replied lamely, "It was because he hosted the Commonwealth Conference."

Hurd then argued that the British Foreign Secretary can't pass judgement on "disagreeable people", but did not explain why this rule did not apply to white Rhodesians. An equally amnesic David Milliband, appearing on the same programme, also claimed no knowledge of Britain's role or the fact that Mugabe had been the recipient of a knighthood.

Also in 1994, a leaked report indicated all 'designated' [confiscated] farms had been grabbed by ruling party chiefs using funding supplied by the British government to the sum of £44 million. British subsidies effectively helped legitimize the 15 years of brutish evictions that would follow for 4,000 white farmers. Mugabe fumed the "Breeteesh" had originally stolen the land. He conveniently failed to acknowledge that 80 per cent of farms seized were bought *after* independence, following receipt of 'Certificates of No Interest' from the Zimbabwean government.

Amidst the unfolding genocide in Rwanda, Nelson Mandela became President of South Africa on 10 May 1994. While the world applauded PK, far less joyful, commented:

> In a way, de Klerk did to South Africa what Muzorewa did to Rhodesia. He sold the pass, which he didn't need to do. We could have carried on in Rhodesia and so could South Africa. Muzorewa was screwed by the Brits. The Afrikaner Nationalists screwed themselves. Roelf Meyer and the rest of them have destroyed South Africa.
>
> We whites are useless, effete. What spearheaded the run into degeneracy and degradation is the Afrikaner Nationalist; he epitomizes it; what's happened to him—and it's everywhere that is our Western, Christian civilization has no future. It's finished and it's very sad. Rhodesia was the last really admirable society of the old Empire. Just wonderful people the Rhodesians; every single thing they should be: very brave, compassionate,

enterprising, good-natured and good-humoured, totally without prejudice and hang-ups. They put on a wonderful show. Unfortunately all for nothing in the end. They set a shining example for the degenerate post-war Europeans.

The tragedy is how well white and black got along. Perfect examples were the army and police, which were mostly black. The races got on in almost total harmony. We never had any major defections. It was bad luck Reagan did not come to power sooner. In the end Mrs. Thatcher cut our throats. It was a gross misfortune that that Commonwealth Conference came up when it did just after she assumed office. Bloody bastards in the Foreign Office got busy then. Carrington seemed to enjoy doing the dirty on us. And don't forget the Soviet Ambassador—Solodnikov—he was also fiddling behind the scenes in Lusaka.

People like Terreblanche [the Afrikaner extremist leader] and that lot are like a musical bad joke. In the end they didn't have the balls to do anything. Absolutely useless.

The Afrikaner is the biggest bloody fake. Individually outstanding, collectively they are useless. They've been ruined and vitiated by apartheid. They engineered the destruction of Rhodesia in order to buy themselves time because they were too wet and frightened.

The tragedy of Rhodesia, in the final analysis, is that it wasn't the Soviets, or the terrorists, or the British who destroyed the country; it was South Africa. And they thereby sealed their own fate. Unfortunately Zimbabwe has given a clear indication of what is to come.

In mid-1995, Mugabe earned the lifelong antipathy of British gay rights leader Peter Tatchell for declaring male homosexuals "worse than dogs and pigs ... beasts ... guilty of subhuman behaviour". A fearless campaigner, Tatchell subsequently attempted two citizen's arrests on Mugabe, the second in Brussels leading to a severe beating from Mugabe's guards, which caused permanent eye injury.

In 1996, a publisher and two journalists were summarily arrested when a report appeared confirming Mugabe had fathered two children in an adulterous relationship with a secretary. The three were vindicated when Mugabe later married Grace Marufu, his divorced secretary, in a lavish 12,000-guest jamboree using money allegedly pilfered from USAID funds. They were married in Harare's Catholic Cathedral, following a hasty annulment of Grace's previous marriage, by Bishop Chakaipa as head of the Diocese.

The new First Lady immediately set about building herself a mansion in an exclusive Harare suburb in a scheme later condemned by the High Court as corrupt and illegal. Known as 'Gucci Grace' or 'Dis Grace', she spent $150,000 on one trip to Paris and by 2002 had withdrawn $20 million from the Reserve Bank of Zimbabwe for her personal needs.

But she was merely a symptom of the disease and State profligacy, which, along with the destruction of the farming sector, has led to unprecedented economic hardship. In 1997 'war veterans', feeling left out of the State-sponsored plunder, marched on State House to demand financial redress. A fearful Mugabe immediately authorized massive payouts, staggering the already collapsing bourse and causing a currency collapse. The same year, PK, Tim and Chris Landon met for the last time in Zimbabwe at the Landon family ranch in KweKwe. Chris's son, Jaime, remembers: "The manager organized a gathering of local farmers and of course, the usual ZANU-PF lot turned up. The latter were treated with due hospitality and spent most of the afternoon listening spellbound to none other than PK, who regaled them with tales of Midlands folklore in the local dialect, which, by their own admission, he spoke better than them!"

Looking for new plunder, in August 1998, Mugabe sent troops to fight an unpopular war in the Congo in support of his old friend Laurent Kabila. Using EU and World Bank funds initially, Kabila later rewarded him and his henchmen with diamond, cobalt and timber concessions.

Harping on a familiar theme, a month later Mugabe spoke of "rich farm lands in former white colonial hands" and argued that expropriation would "cure the economic and social ills bedevilling the nation".

"PK was treated for bladder cancer in 1995," says Lotti, "and suffered from haemocremathosis most of his life. It is not commonly known that he had to be bled every three weeks because he got it done very quietly and never complained."

Hilary Squires remembered one of their last chats:

> PK being multilingual and now the father of three boys, I asked him what languages the children spoke. He said they spoke German to their mother, French to the nanny, Afrikaans to the servants and English to the horses.
>
> I miss him very much. If there is any substance in the view that there is a life in the hereinafter, he is one of the first people I shall be looking up. Politics was not a lark for him as some have suggested; it was his abiding interest and passion particularly at the international level of cause and effect. He was a *bon viveur*, which caused many to believe he was something of a political dandy; that was the caricature bestowed on his father by the editors of the Nationale Pers Newspapers. He may not have been the greatest commanding officer but nobody would have led a cavalry charge with greater gusto or verve. He had enormous courage and a fine brain and Ian Smith knew that. He directed those energies into the areas where he felt he could do the most good for Rhodesia.

Lotti remembers:

> During the last four years of his life, he really struggled with his health. He did a lot of reading and corresponding but he was not well at all. He enjoyed seeing people like Peter Bieber and Ron Reid-Daly. Overseas he saw quite a lot of Tim Landon whom he liked and respected enormously.

On 27 May 1998, PK left Zimbabwe for the last time, and in early 1999 his heart problems worsened considerably. He had a bypass which seemed to work but a few months later, just before we were due to travel to Europe, his blood pressure rose and we were unable to fly. On 15 November 1999, four days after his 76th birthday, he died at Fairfield. The last years were not easy for him but he was able to do most of the things he wanted to do and right to the end he retained his wonderful sense of humour.

He was buried on a hill overlooking Fairfield Farm.

Months after PK's passing Mugabe lost a referendum that would have given him dictatorial powers. Furious, he played his political trump card and commenced the seizure of over 4,000 commercial farms owned by whites that still provided the economic mainstay of the country. In a brutally orchestrated campaign of violence and mayhem he interfered with the commercial enterprise of .03% of his countrymen and smashed what was left of a sustainable economy. Outside of war the Zimbabwe economy became the fastest collapsing in history. At least four million citizens have fled. Those that remain seem destined to a life of abject poverty. The country is effectively a failed state.

The world has had its woeful way. The small band that fought to stave off this catastrophe has lost much, but not their pride, and history will be kind to them. It would have brought him no cheer, but Robert Mugabe has proved PK van der Byl was right and the rest of the world was wrong.

જ જ જ

PK kept close to him a poem, written by R. Drysdale:

Ten years old and four feet high
History and UDI
Today we've struck a blow, said he
For Justice and Christianity
For principle we've made a stand
Courageous people, splendid land
Civilized we stand or fall
God save the Queen, God bless you all
And like the years good friends have gone
David and Richard, Mike and John
Crash and ambush, mine and mortar
Cold and heat, dust and water
Freckled Dave, laughing Paul,
And Pete my bravest friend of all
Write their names on Rolls of Honour
Scripted bold in golden splendour
For us there'll be no Victory Day
The dogs of war have gone astray
Now principle becomes surrender
Expediancy the legal tender
Is justice just for those who shout?
Is this what Christ is all about?
Will someone tell us why we fight?
What once was wrong is now what's right
Where am I going? Where have I been?
Somewhere … Nowhere … in-between
Years of waste … and so I cried
The day my good friend Johnny died.

જ જ જ

Index

Hannes Wessels was born in 1956 in Salisbury, Southern Rhodesia (now Harare, Zimbabwe) but grew up in Umtali on the Mozambican border. As a boy, holidays were spent with Game Department rangers; time on safari in Mozambique with the late Wally Johnson was a big influence on him. Wessels also grew to know Robert Ruark whose love of Africa, its people, politics and the written word left a lasting impression. He saw action in the Rhodesian bush war before acquiring a law degree which he chose not to use. He has hunted big game in Mozambique, Zimbabwe, Zambia and Tanzania in a 20-year career. In 1994 he was severely gored by a wounded buffalo which almost cost him his life. While no longer directly involved in hunting, he is part-owner of a lodge and game ranch in Zambia on the Lower Zambezi and remains keenly interested in all matters relating to African wildlife and conservation. He has published *Strange Tales from Africa* in the USA, a collection of anecdotes from his hunting days. He is also a syndicated writer for *Outdoor Life* in the United States and is currently writing a history on the Rhodesian SAS. He is married to Mandy and has two daughters, Hope and Jana, and lives in Darling in the Western Cape province of South Africa.